JOHN S. KNOX Liberty University

MATTERS
OF THE
DARK

Kendall Hunt
publishing company

Kendall Hunt
publishing company

www.kendallhunt.com
Send all inquiries to:
4050 Westmark Drive
Dubuque, IA 52004-1840

For Uncle Richard, who always challenges me to think better, react slower, and love deeper.

CONTENTS

PREFACE

I had never even thought about writing a textbook focused on social problems as an academic. Yet, after years of teaching sociology at the university level, I noticed a disturbing trend in the sociology textbooks offered by publishers. Every book that the students were required to read in my classes addressed the issue of social problems solely from the conflict theorist approach. For these authors, social problems apparently occur because people in all societies, historically, are battling for resources, with certain people groups typically being vilified for being oppressive, exploitative, and not Marxist enough.

I pride myself on being a balanced social scientist, so I appreciate that conflict theory is certainly a facet of many social problems, but ala Durkheim, I strive to eschew reductionism in my classes and try to find a more balanced approach to understanding and offering learned advice on social problems. Thus, social problems are a combination of conflict theory and symbolic interaction and functionalist theory. In explanation, a quick understanding of these three approaches goes as follows: (1) Conflict theory is basically, "Give me that!"; (2) symbolic interaction is basically, "What is that?"; and (3) functionalist theory is "We can do this!" By the way, I am a functionalist.

Ostensibly, when social problems occur, they are typically the result of a breakdown or dysfunction in one of these areas. For instance, a social problem regarding conflict theory could occur because someone deserves access to a resource that someone else selfishly hoards. A social problem regarding symbolic interaction could occur because people cannot agree upon a mutual definition or prioritization. Finally, a social problem regarding functionalist theory could occur because people become cold-heartedly rigid regarding social stratification or social roles, and so on.

After teaching my first term of social problems classes, though, I recognized that most of what the students were to read and what they were to hear from me focused mainly upon the "What is it?" and "Who did it?" questions surrounding social problems. What was missing was a clear, scientifically-sound, biblically evident perspective on how to solve the social problems discussed in class. So, I came up with a new assignment in class years ago which I called, "A Social Problems Solutions Journal."

While it is important for students to understand the what and how big aspects of social problems, they also desperately need to learn the "What can we do about it?" answers. Therefore, each week I set aside some "lab time" in class for the students to work together to find, compile, and share solutions regarding the aforementioned three questions on social problems. It was amazing. It transformed the class from just a depressing journey through contentious, malevolent, destructive social interactions to a more hopeful, beneficial time where we worked together in understanding just why social problems happen and how to effectively and productively address them—and from a scientifically sound, Christian worldview too.

The atmosphere of my sociology classes changed for the better, and the students ended each week not just being programmed with theories and statistics—but empowered with practical knowledge and tools to affect real change in their own cities, states, country, and the world. Even more so, I felt inspired to create a textbook that mirrored the Social Problems Solutions Journal's fundamental goals. Hence, each chapter that discusses a social problem first defines it, then discusses its parameters, and finally offers potential solutions to the problem itself.

Of course, most social problems cannot be solved quickly, but this book provides at least some insights toward a remedy. Speaking of which, I have also included contributions from experts in various capacities in society—deans, chairs, and directors but also missionaries, retirees, and graduate business majors. Like my Social Problems Solutions Journal, I want this book to be informative and productive regarding real society with its real social problems.

Even more so, I want to create an applied sociology resource for students that is based on more than just political agenda and private matters pretending to be public matters. By the end of this textbook, hopefully students will have a better understanding of the sociological forces embedded in social problems, but more than that, I hope that they use this information in productive, beneficial, practical ways to help people suffering and needful in greater society. Social problems shroud the world with sorrow and suffering. People's knowledge, wisdom, shrewdness, imagination, praxis, and compassion—especially founded on the goodness of God—can light up the world like a brilliant candle in the darkest of caves.

ACKNOWLEDGMENTS

First and foremost, I again offer my sincerest gratitude to my old schoolmate and friend, Daniel Schallau, for sharing (yet one more time) his amazing artistic talents to help me visually reach and teach my readers about the ways and "whos" of Sociology. I love our conversations, and I love how I can describe a sociological idea or concept to you and somehow you read my mind. You always put it into your art perfectly. Your imagination is only outmatched by your talent, bro. Thank you, sincerely.

Second, I appreciate the estimable talents of Grant Knaus, my work study assistant at Liberty and the only videographer for my books (this is book two for him). Thank you for your keen video perspectives and for your willingness to help create more beautiful videos for yet another one of my books.

Third, I appreciate the editorial and proofing assistance of my brother-in-Christ, former racquet-ball partner, and local Nampa pastor, Keith Freedman. This is book seven or eight for him (I have lost track). Thank you again for your savvy editorial suggestions, and for your willingness to read over yet another of my books.

Fourth, I appreciate the editorial and proofing assistance of my new graduate student assistant (and friend) Quinn Weinzapfel (who also penned several of the case studies contained therein), and my old Liberty buddy, co-author, and work office neighbor, Kenny Warren. I am grateful for your keen eyes, scholarly reflections, honest remarks, and philanthropic intentions. You two are a blessing in my life, sincerely.

Of course, once again, I could not have completed this book without the ongoing support and love of my wife, Brenda, and my very patient sons, Jacob and Joe. This is my ninth book in my academic career, so you three have come to understand that writing a book takes time, and you graciously allow me that time. Your ongoing kindness inspires me—to the core—to not give up and to write the best book I can that will honor your sacrifice and faith in me. I love you all so very much.

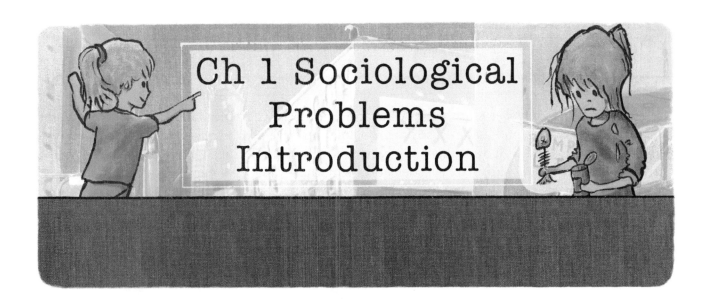

Ch 1 Sociological Problems Introduction

It can be truthfully said that social problems have existed since the dawn of recorded human history. Across the globe, no people group has ever lived in an idyllic, peaceful, Utopian society for a long time without social blemish or conflict. In truth, when human beings live together in communities, troubles (public and private) are bound to follow.

To a greater or lesser degree, everyone who has lived on Earth (including those reading this right now) has observed or personally experienced a social problem that has impacted them, their family members, their friends, their city, and so on. Social problems are seemingly inescapable, which is troubling to most people. Social problems feel wrong. They frustrate and challenge our sense of how life should be (Tastet, 2018). They put the innocent in danger and cause unnecessary harm and destruction. They exist in direct opposition to most people's worldviews, values, and perspectives of society.

American sociologist C. Wright Mills once wrote,

> The more we understand what is happening in the world, the more frustrated we often become, for our knowledge leads to feelings of powerlessness. We feel that we are living in a world in which the citizen has become a mere spectator or forced actor, and that our personal experience is politically useless and our political will a minor illusion. (Mills & Mills, 2000, p. 184)

Social problems are a negative force to contend with, both socially and personally.

© Jacob_09/Shutterstock.com

WHAT IS A SOCIAL PROBLEM?

Not surprisingly, *social problems* are intrinsically and extrinsically complex, and their sources/causes difficult to ascertain. Simultaneously, social problems can have an objective and subjective reality—being measurable (what is it, how much is it, where is it, how often is it) and yet driven by arbitrary, partisan beliefs (why is it bad). To be a social problem, there must be a negative public impact, and yet, people often mistakenly believe their personal opinions or private matters to be a community or global issue (Shaw & Lorenz, 2016). This is especially true in *postmodernity*, where radical individualism reigns and *experientialism*—not *evidentialism*—is the cultural norm, which can lead to even more social problems.

As mentioned earlier, people are well aware of the social problems surrounding them. It is impossible to watch the news, surf the internet, skim through Facebook or Twitter without seeing a social problem being inflicted upon a society or community around the world. One's awareness can be even closer with personal trauma or seeing a family member or friend suffering in society experiencing a social problem. At work, at play, or at church, social problems are often the center of human concern and discussion.

Defining social problems typically starts by determining the cause(s), which can be man-made or biological. In nature, social strife can occur with grand global manifestations such as plagues, pestilence, or disease. Regarding human society, social problems can be either purposefully created or mistakenly identified by people as a deviation from group values, a decline in the effectiveness of social institutions, or an abuse of political power.

THE SOCIOLOGICAL APPROACH

Sociology is perhaps the best place to start in dealing productively with social problems. *Sociology* is the study of human relationships, choices, and actions. It investigates and theorizes on how human interaction impacts society—both locally and globally—and seeks to understand the *consequences of difference*, deviance, equity, and culture. Moreover, it can help people to be proactive and not reactive as it is philosophically based upon *scientific methodology* and not just a political or personal agenda (something that will be addressed in future chapters).

This is when and where sociologists can help to scientifically pinpoint and hopefully alleviate avoidable suffering stemming from the social problem(s). Social conditions are carefully measured, providing relevant and crucial data, and public opinion is then probed to determine general attitudes about the social problem. The social imagination is scientifically applied, putting the social problem in context and into proper consideration (and will be discussed more fully in Chapter 2). Possible social theories and policies are then formulated, suggesting public and private courses of action. Finally, these approaches are scientifically evaluated, with an estimation of social effects accompanying the proposed solutions (Angelstam et al., 2013).

Of course, although sociology can help people better understand the world around them and many social problems that they may encounter, it is not a balm nor remedy for all social ills. Sociology is an academic discipline that was founded, developed, and furthered mostly in Western civilization; thus, it is based upon Western social values and principles that have not always been embraced or affirmed in other non-Western cultures.

For instance, while someone in Oregon might consider *women's suffrage* (the right of women to vote) to be a historical landmark, in Pakistan that social freedom may be considered an abomination to the social order established by God. Likewise, the legal precedent for universal, egalitarian socioeconomic opportunities may be lauded in France but is shunned in India, where the *caste system* (a rigid social stratification system) still restricts social mobility and opportunities.

Adding to the challenge of dealing with social problems, many people confuse *common sense* with sociological thought. Most people make assumptions about reality. Part of this helps people survive, but sometimes it can have negative effects. Understanding the "reality" of common sense puts some assertions into perspective as well as the ones making the commonsense assumptions.

Authority should come from confirmation of facts—not from an assumed authoritative voice. Witt (2009) states, "Commonsense knowledge, while sometimes accurate, is not always reliable, because it rests on commonly held beliefs rather than on systematic analysis of facts" (p. 8). Thus, it may be popular, but it is not scientific at all and can lead to even more dangerous, destructive social problems.

For example, the "Woke Movement" makes key assertions about latent racism (Kynard, 2018), and the "Me Too Movement" (Lee, 2018) makes key assertions about the latent sexism of most men in American society. Are the presuppositions and conclusions of these movements based on scientific fact or something else? Clearly, there are social factors at play between the races and sexes, which lead to social problems, but at what level and by which groups? The answers to these questions are not simple, but sociology can definitely help find them.

Ostensibly, most popular understandings of these political movements rest more upon politically popular held beliefs than any grand, personal, systematic analyses of facts. Yet, sociologists do not accept something as a social fact just because "Everyone believes it is true." That might tickle the ears, but conscientious sociologists want to go even deeper into the reasoning centers of the brain.

Being social scientists, any question of social interest needs to be tested, analyzed, and verified utilizing the scientific method. Otherwise, the endeavor is in danger of being skewed, distorted, and doomed to failure—if scientific, intellectually-honest understanding is one's goal. This is the essence of *theoretical sociology*—using scientific approaches to evaluate social data obtained by methods based on systematic observation (such as surveys, interviews, demographics, and so on) and to formulate hypotheses leading to legitimate theories.

Of course, just having the scientific knowledge does little to disperse the malevolent effects of social problems. To solve a social problem, one must engage with it, fundamentally and purposefully. This is the essence of *applied sociology*, which seeks to yield practical applications for human behavior and organizations, through government commissions, environmental concerns, public misbehaviors, and the presence of toxic civil groups and gangs (Ward, 1906).

Additionally, oftentimes some specific environs receive investigation and treatment for social maladies. This is the essence of *clinical sociology*, which facilitates change by altering social relationships or by restructuring a social institution's organization (such as cultivating an anti-sexist or anti-racist atmosphere in the workplace).

DEALING WITH MATTERS OF THE DARK

In sociology, three main approaches to understanding social problems have been historically embraced: symbolic interaction, conflict theory, and the functionalist perspective. All three approaches are important and evidential in society. All three approaches deserve attention and contemplation, especially as they concern the various social problems addressed in future chapters. Yet, although the awareness of many social problems may be uncovered by all three approaches, not all three solutions are efficacious in solving social problems.

The *symbolic interaction* perspective suggests that society is the end result of individuals directly and personally interacting with other individuals. This approach assumes that "reality" is shaped by individual perceptions, evaluations, and definitions (Mills, 1959). Thus, it includes face-to-face, nominal activities; it focuses on how individuals treat, understand, and influence each other through symbols of expression and value. In religious circles, this could include the sacraments (baptism, marriage, communion or the Eucharist), hymnology (music), and iconography (religious/spiritual artistry).

The *conflict theory* perspective suggests that society consists of different groups of people competing and struggling against each other for scarce resources like food, domestic products, technology, information access, money, and power (Bartos & Wehr, 2012). Thus, society is constantly changing and shifting in response to social inequality and conflict (even within religious demesnes), in an overarching power struggle for social change, which communists like Karl Marx (1818–1883), assorted liberation theologians, and radical feminists assert is inevitable and beneficial for a society mired in the Haves and Have-Nots.

The *functionalist* perspective was initially established through the scholarly work of theorists like Herbert Spencer, Emilé Durkheim, and Robert Merton. This approach assumes that society is a complex system constructed of numerous interrelated forces and agents, with each part/person of the system performing a vital, needed function that contributes to the whole operation (like biological parts of an organism), which helps to maintain a sense of harmony and equilibrium within society (Berberoglu, 2017).

© hvostik/Shutterstock.com

While all three approaches are crucial, even inseparable from the diagnoses of social problems, they are not all equal to the task of solving social problems (Steiner, 1928). Each approach brings to the sociological table various tools and presuppositions about how society works and how to remedy social ills. There is some overlap between them; however, there are key differences in their philosophical assumptions and analyses of social problems.

For instance, symbolic interactionism may help sociologists understand the overall meaning of social constructs and artifacts in the lives of minds of people, but its reliance upon personal understandings and interpretations can leave social analysis perpetually in the theoretical or philosophical stage, with little to no direct effect upon public social problems. Likewise, conflict theory may help sociologists perceive real-life socioeconomic inequalities and abuses, but its reductionist emphasis on pervasive social exploitation and oppression, its de-emphasis on personal responsibility and logical consequences, and its narrow vision on certain social realities can leave people with only extended, perpetual conflict.

Ultimately, this textbook suggests that the functionalist approach is the one most likely to affect long-lasting, positive change in society, if employed fairly while utilizing scientific methodology. Functionalism works toward peaceful and productive unity while allowing for individual meritorious roles/options, real responsibilities and consequences, reasonable parameters for social protection, and addressing systemic dysfunctionality (often pointed out by conflict theory) in pursuit of a more harmonious, healthy society (Sharrock et al., 2003).

Perhaps no one has highlighted the differences and dynamics of these sociological approaches more than Jesus of Nazareth in his *Sermon on the Mount*, also known as "The *Beatitudes*" (Matthew 5:1–12). Although by no means a perfect effort, since its founding in the first century, C.E., Christian society has consistently lauded the analyses and applications of Jesus's words to the people of Israel on that mountainside, 2,000 years ago. With the aforementioned approaches in mind, one can see His sociological appraisal of the important social problems of His day.

In this passage (and touching upon elements of symbolic interactionism and conflict theory), Jesus enlightened His listeners on what it meant to be economically poor, emotionally distressed, culturally unimportant, intellectually curious, socially compassionate, and politically abused. He also explains how their social situations can (and will) be resolved.

Interestingly, Jesus ends the Beatitudes in quite a functionalist fashion, stating, "Blessed are the pure in heart, for they will see God. Blessed are the peacemakers [not conflict-makers] for they will be called children of God" (vss. 8-9). He continues this analysis even further later in the passage (vss. 14-16), pointing to His followers' beneficial presence in society, with their God-given ability to enact social change for the better (J. Stott et al., 2013).

Yet, more than just a charge for His Disciples, Jesus's words are universal and timeless, requiring much from those who call themselves "Christians." His followers are to be the salt and the light of the world, to help free all suffering souls from the matters of the dark with God's direction and assistance. Using the Beatitudes as the quintessential guide, His people (even the sociologists) are to honestly and fairly define social problems, determine their social parameters and impact, and to find kind, productive ways to bring light to others trapped in the darkness of the world.

INSIGHTS FROM THE EXPERTS

"Theology of Social Problems"

For over 25 years, while serving in local church ministry, many social issues have been encountered including assaults (sexual, domestic, etc.), relationship issues (marriage/divorce; dating, remarriage, parent/teen, etc.), elder care (assisted living, living wills, end of life directives, etc.), and adolescents in crisis (suicide, substance abuse, self-harm, etc.). The basis for these social issues produces challenges in many different disciplines from psychology to social work to education. *Pastoral care* is no different. There is a spiritual (or theological) aspect of social problems. In fact, social problems must be addressed from a spiritual basis in connection with the other disciplines.

The Beginning of Social Problems: A Biblical Understanding

God is no stranger to social problems. In the beginning of the biblical story, God pronounces, "You are free to eat from any tree in the garden; but you must not eat from the tree of the knowledge of good and evil, for when you eat from it you will certainly die" (Genesis 2:16–17). His design and intention for His image was to live in healthy relationships with Himself, fellow image, and creation. Yet, He understood the dire consequences of disobedience to this command. Three chapters later, it is recorded, that "Adam lived . . . and then he died" (Genesis 5:5) with subsequent declarations for each person mentioned in that chapter. The implication declares that each one must take God at His word.

According to Wolters (1985), the scope of Adam and Eve's disobedience of God's command had immense consequences. "[W]e must stress that the Bible teaches plainly that Adam and Eve's fall into sin was not just an isolated act of disobedience but an event of catastrophic significance for creation as a whole" (p. 44). He continued, "Everywhere we turn, the good possibilities of God's creation are misused, warped and exploited for sinful ends" (p. 45) and concludes "Sin introduces an entirely new dimension to the created order" (p. 47).

Sin's insertion into the created order changed how human beings viewed each other. J. R. W. Stott (2006) suggested, "All our human alienation, disorientation and sense of meaninglessness stem ultimately from this. In addition, our relationships with each other become skewed" (p. 62). And this reorganization leads to the theological basis for social problems. Walsh and Middleton (1984) declared the disruption of sin as a warfare and insisted,

> Two kingdoms are at war. A spiritual battle is going on, a clash of the kingdoms which permeates the entire range of human activities. Just as the two covenantal ways are cut through all that we do, so do the two kingdoms. Just as all our cultural life is *created* and thus under God's rule, and as we are called to serve him in all that we do, so all our life is now *fallen*. There is nothing in creation that sin has not touched: "The whole world is under the control of the evil one." (1 Jn 5:19)

Although God still calls us to obediently execute our cultural task, the usurper bids us to pledge allegiance to his renegade kingdom and so deny our true calling. The insightful words of C. S. Lewis cut to the heart of our post-Fall situation: "There is not neutral ground in the universe: every square inch, every split second, is claimed by God and counterclaimed by Satan" (p. 71). From a biblical perspective, this spiritual warfare or conflict is at the forefront of social ills.

The Question: Does God Care?

Many people, while experiencing social problems, ask "Does God care?" If a person is truly honest with themselves, the question really is "Why doesn't God do something about my _____?" (fill in the blank). The agony caused while experiencing an issue becomes overwhelming and help from God seems to be the only solution. But those matters are not always resolved by God. That is when the "Why" question is asked.

On a personal note, after my daughter's birth, it was discovered that she had a genetic disease called cystic fibrosis. Needless to say, this shook the foundation of our family and I immediately asked the question—Why? Why are You allowing our family to deal with this? Why are You letting my daughter face this debilitating disorder? And then as she began to grow, kind, caring people even began to ask—Why? Why don't you have more faith so that your daughter will be healed? Why don't you try this medication? I discovered after her diagnosis that the "why" question never gets answered, fully. One day, the question changed to "how" by asking God, show me how You care. How can cystic fibrosis in my daughter's body be used to bring You honor and glory?

In answer to the question, "Does God care?" it is important to look at Jesus. If you observe the life of Christ from an overall perspective, He did not solve, heal, or correct every ill, problem, or wrongdoing. Obviously, scripture does not record every moment of Jesus's life. Even the 3 years of ministry at the end of His life were not completely recorded. Still, with the stories recorded, Jesus did not solve every problem. Jesus did not heal each person He came in contact with. Jesus did not correct every wrong.

The Apostle Paul confronts the reality that God cares but does not remove every hurt.

> Three different times I begged the Lord to take it away. Each time he said, "My grace is all you need. My power works best in weakness." So now I am glad to boast about my weaknesses, so that the power of Christ can work through me. (2 Corinthians 12:8–9)

C. S. Lewis (2001) writes in *The Problem of Pain*, "God whispers to us in our pleasures, speaks in our conscience, but shouts in our pain, it is his megaphone to rouse a deaf world" (Ch. 6).

A Theology to Address Social Problems

The reality of social problems is undeniable. The response to the social issues must come from a theological foundation. First, it must be addressed from a *Christian mind* (J. R. W. Stott, 2006, p. 62). To think Christianly means that your focus always initiates with God (Colossians 3:1–2). The biblical story begins with God (Genesis 1:1) and so must the life of every believer. Our thinking is only transformed by the Holy Spirit working through scripture to show each one how to live. This personal responsibility will affect how a person lives but also demonstrates to others proper conduct in the midst of social problems.

Second, it must follow a *biblical prescription*. Even though the social issue may not be specifically referred to in Scripture, a biblical principle can address and be applied to that problem. The Bible conveys the opposite of what our selfish self would want to do amid personal social problems. Jesus states, "You have heard that it was said, 'Eye for eye, and tooth for tooth.' But I tell you, do not resist an evil person. If anyone slaps you on the right cheek, turn to them the other cheek also" (Matthew 5:38–39). The biblical principle is to do what is supernatural (*turn the other cheek*) instead of what is not natural (*eye for an eye, tooth for a tooth*).

Rob Van Engen
Associate Professor/Program Director
Liberty University

Contributed by Robert Van Engen. © Kendall Hunt Publishing Company

Case Study #1

For your first case study, write out the story of your life in two to three paragraphs. Include as many sociological details as you can about your socioeconomic background, family influences, passages of life (like getting your driver's license), peer pressures, cultural forces, religious upbringing, and any experiences with violence, racism, sexism, or any other -isms that you may have encountered. Share as much as you feel comfortable but be as honest as possible in your anecdotes. At the end of the book, you will revisit this essay, so DO NOT THROW IT AWAY! Save it somewhere so that you can easily recover it later.

Discussion Questions

1. What do you think about American society, in general? Is it cool? Troubling? Why?

2. How different is your perspective on American society compared to your parents? Your grandparents?

3. What was the best thing, socially, about junior high? High school? College?

4. Without looking at the readings (or your notes), define what "Society" means and includes.

Check out the Chapter 1 video at this link:

https://www.khpcontent.com/

Vocabulary

Applied Sociology

Beatitudes

Caste System

Clinical Sociology

Common Sense

Conflict Theory

Consequences of Difference

Evidentialism

Experientialism

Functionalist Perspective

Pastoral Care

Postmodernity

Scientific Methodology

Social Problems

Sociology

Symbolic Interaction

Theoretical Sociology

Women's Suffrage

References

Angelstam, P., Andersson, K., Annerstedt, M., Axelsson, R., Elbakidze, M., Garrido, P., Grahn, P., Jonsson, K. I., Pedersen, S., Schlyter, P., Skarback, E., Smith, M., & Stjernquist, I. (2013). Solving problems in social-ecological systems: Definition, practice and barriers of transdisciplinary research. *Ambio, 42*(2), 254–265.

Bartos, O., & Wehr, P. (2012). *Using conflict theory.* Cambridge University Press.

Berberoglu, B. (2017). *Social theory: Classical and contemporary—A critical perspective* (1st ed.). Routledge.

Kynard, C. (2018). Staying woke: Race-radical literacies in the makings of a higher education. *Urbana, 69*(3), 519–529.

Lee, B. H. (2018). #Me Too Movement: It is time that we all act and participate in transformation. *Psychiatry investigation, 15*(5), 433. https://doi.org/10.30773/pi.2018.04.30

Lewis, C. S. (2001). *The problem of pain.* Harper.

Mills, C. W. (1959). *The sociological imagination.* Oxford University Press.

Mills, K., & Mills, P. (Eds.). (2020). *C. Wright Mills: Letters and autobiography.* University of California Press.

Sharrock, W. W., Hughes, J. A., & Martin, P. J. (2003). *Understanding modern sociology.* Sage.

Shaw, I., & Lorenz, W. (2016). Special issue: Private troubles or public issues? Challenges for social work research. *European Journal of Social Work, 19*(3–4), 305–309.

Steiner, J. F. (1928). The limitations of a conceptual approach to the applications of sociology to social work. *Social Forces, 7*(1), 500–503.

Stott, J. R. W. (2006). *Issues facing Christians today* (4th ed.). Zondervan.

Stott, J., Larsen, D., & Larsen, S. (2013). *A deeper look at the Sermon on the Mount: Living out the way of Jesus*. InterVarsity.

Tastet, R. (2018). Anomie. *Le Télémaque, 53*(1), 21–30. doi:10.3917/tele.053.0021

Walsh, B. J., & Middleton, J. R. (1984). *The transforming vision: Shaping a Christian worldview*. InterVarsity.

Ward, L. F. (1906). *Applied sociology: A treatise on the conscious improvement of society by society*. Ginn.

Witt, J. (2009). *SOC*. McGraw-Hill.

Wolters, A. M. (1985). *Creation regained: Biblical basics for a reformational worldview*. William B. Eerdmans.

Ch 2 Cynicism and Imagination

INTRODUCTION

Anyone who has ever gone to the mall or a superstore knows that "people-watching" is one of the most interesting pastimes that a person can do. We stare out onto the sea of people, families, and individuals moving before us, and wonder what they are thinking (she chose to date him?), why they are there (especially wearing "that"), and guess about their backstories (must be their first time in a store). This is the essence of sociology—to consider the context and social forces in action (possibly at a Walmart, a school, a church, or a bar) that influence people's attitudes, actions, and outcomes.

This *sociological consideration* rests upon two very important functions of sociological studies: imagination and cynicism. In pondering the social possibilities and probabilities, sociologists use their *social imagination*—the awareness and ability to think outside of one's own social background—to consider other ways and forces influencing social interactions. Additionally, sociologists apply their *social cynicism*—reasonable suspicions regarding social realities—to scientifically analyze and evaluate people's social interactions, their causes, and their consequences.

Sociologists also assume that society is made up of three main parts: the micro-level, the middle-level (or meso), and the macro-level. As one would expect, the *micro-level* deals with individuals and private interactions, the *macro-level* deals with bigger groups and institutions, and the *middle-level* focuses on all the smaller groups and organizations in between the two extremes. While micro-level involves personal *agency* (the freedom to choose and act independently of others and to make their own free choices), the macro-level deals with public policy, and the middle-level focuses on diplomacy, pragmatically.

With these levels in mind, sociologists tend to ask three main questions (that almost sound Socratic): (1) How are people interacting with each other in this society and why? (2) What cultural era or philosophical mindset does this society embrace and which ones does it reject? and (3) How much deviance and conformity are evidentially demonstrated in this society?

SOCIAL IMAGINATION

Sociological imagination concerns both the private and the public in society and American Sociologist C. Wright Mills (1916–1962) is credited for defining the idea. In his pivotal book, *The Sociological*

Imagination (1959), he writes, "The sociological imagination enables its possessor to understand the larger historical scene in terms of its meaning for the inner life and the external career of a variety of individuals" (p. 5). For sociologists, this centered on their "capacity to shift from one perspective to another" (p. 7)—to not only think out of the box, but to try and think inside someone else's box.

This requires understanding the differences between "personal troubles" (also known as "private matters") and "public issues" (Roig et al., 2019). As one might expect, *personal troubles* occur at the intersection of an individual with some social problem. For instance, a young woman may drive up to an ATM, punch in her security code, and not be able to access her account. This is not necessarily a matter of sexism, ageism, or racism; probably, it is just a technological glitch in the system that affects only her. Yet, if all young women who drive up to the ATM and punch in their security code encounter the same problem, but all men (young and old) are able to access their accounts, then there might be a *public issues* (ageism or sexism) social problem with the bank's programming or programmer.

In either case, based on their suspicions that some bank ATM programmers are potentially sexist and ageist, a sociologist might recommend an experiment to investigate whether this particular ATM has a problem, if all the bank branches have the same problem, or if there is really a problem at all. The bank manager might say, "Well, that's absurd. ATMs cannot be sexist or ageist," but sociologists do not care about absurdity if they suspect that there is a sociological mystery to be solved. They want to find out if the social problem is the result of a *manifest function* (conscious or deliberate intention of a social policy) or a *latent function* (not a conscious intention, although still harmful/beneficial) (Cole, 2020).

SOCIAL CYNICISM

As one can see, social imagination is essentially the impetus
research. Things do not just happen in society without some
tional tenet of scientific methodology). Scientific speculation th
(imagination) creates doubts (cynicism) about sociological pre
logical investigations about the social reality surrounding a so
cynicism is important to get to the crux of the matter; otherw
personal opinion, which typically is self-serving and incomplete

It is the public nature of phenomenology and ethnomethodc
ogists find so fascinating and in need of investigation. The *phe*
social reality and "troubles" are very individualistic, centering on people's perception, thoughts,
linguistic activity, memory, imagination, emotion, desire, volition to bodily awareness, embodied
action, and social activity (Mills, 1959). Even more intriguing is people's *ethnomethodology*—the way
that people make sense of their everyday world and how they utilize practical, personal reasoning—in
greater society (Lynch & Sharrock, 2011).

Chapter 2   Cynicism and Im

This sociological
beings can disting
sorting, defining
especially wh
matters (T
This
cism

16

SOCIAL SCRUTINY

Prudent sociologists understand that influential forces shape people's lives (for better or worse)—
and that many social options are determined in the past but can still be molded by current social
structures and attitudes. This aspect of *social scrutiny* fights against oversimplified, often politicized
sociological notions of social realities with scientific inquiries. It requires that sociologists be willing
to ask any question—no matter how difficult or uncomfortable or annoying to people or groups.

…nvestigation involves *epistemology*, the study of knowledge, and how human …ish that which is public from mere personal opinion. It is the methodology of …, and valuing "the facts." Moreover, it acknowledges that society is a complex issue, …en it comes to social and cultural assertions, which reside in murky waters of personal …urri, 2014).

…is where research comes into the equation—to put the sociologists' imagination and cyni-
…o the test. So, as Mills (1959) puts it,

> Correctly or incorrectly, they often come to feel that they can now provide themselves with
> adequate summations, cohesive assessments, comprehensive orientations . . . They acquire
> a new way of thinking, they experience a transvaluation of values; in a word, by their reflec-
> tion and by their sensibility, they realize the cultural meaning of the social sciences (p. 8).

Far too often in postmodernity, the social sciences have slid into politics, anti-meta-narratives, and caved to the caprices of radical individualism more than pursuing academic rigor. The trend is to artificially promote personal troubles above public issues, pretending they are a legitimate topic, providing emotional coddling for the easily triggered and narcissistically entitled (Clawson et al., 2007). Furthermore, imagination is lauded, but sociological cynicism is scorned (Burgess, 2015), much to the disservice of the scholarly field (and humanity, in general).

Traditional sociology may be rude, but it is mostly beneficial because it asks the tough ques- tions, honestly analyzes valid and reliable data, and eschews politicizing sociological facts for political appeasements. Hard social science is often considered to be mean; *political sociology* is more palatable, even if false or anti-eviden- tial. The truth is that the sciences need to push back against presumptions and conclusions that prop up popular ideas of normalcy and social aesthetics—especially since sociology's particular brand of science can affect people's lives, dra- matically or even disastrously (Knox, 2019).

DEALING WITH MATTERS OF THE DARK

One of the joys of teaching Bible, history, and sociology over the years is being able to use my socio- logical imagination to evaluate the New Testament Gospels in regard to sociological thought such as conflict theory, functionalist theory, symbolic interactionism, and so on. Delving deeply into these historical accounts of Jesus's life, the social realities of Jesus, His Disciples, and the social problems surrounding Him, it is easy to read of individuals and organizations intersecting in typical human ways (with their consequential social problems) that all societies experience, historically.

For instance, according to most scholars, the first Gospel believed to have been written was the Gospel of Mark. Although the shortest Gospel, it is by no means the weakest, as it presents a powerful tale of Jesus of Nazareth, the Son of God, the mighty Messiah, a supernatural figure of unending strength. Its author, Mark, presents a condensed story of Jesus, with less liturgical expo- sition and application, due most likely to his Gentile audience who would have cared little to hear lengthy explanations of Judaism and its culturalisms. Instead, Mark endeavors to provide a quick and mighty biography on Jesus, leaving out other institutional details for stylistic or pragmatic reasons (Moloney, 2012).

The Gospel of Mark was most likely written somewhere in the West around 60–70 C.E. based on its lack of internal specifics, the translation of Aramaic terms, and the explanation of Jewish terms and festivals. Its descriptions and emphasis on suffering suggest that it may have been composed during or near a specific period of persecution and martyrdom—either by Jewish or Roman authorities. It was written as an intersectional bridge between two cultures—Jewish and Roman—with very different social presuppositions and parameters, relying upon the Gentiles' capacity for social imagination to flesh out the story.

The Gospel of Matthew, also known as *The Gospel of the Church*, has been the most used of the Gospels in the church institution, specifically regarding worship, preaching, and study. The longest of the Gospels (28 chapters), Matthew (Levi) provides clear guidance to the Christian community regarding expectations within and outside the church, especially concerning corruption, social obligations, and experiencing persecutions.

Demonstrating functionalist features, the Gospel of Matthew has a clear agenda from the start that focuses on the needs of a Jewish Christian community looking for confirmation, affirmation, and edification. Thus, Matthew begins with his explanation of Jesus being the Messiah foretold in the Hebrew scriptures, as seen in his genealogy and the words of the Prophets. Additionally, the Gospel is written as a liturgical tool, with instructions for both Christian worship and praxis.

In his Gospel, Matthew emphasizes several aspects to cultivate social unity and trust: genealogy, prophecy connections, strong Jewish themes, the leadership of Peter, community of believers' issues, the evil Jewish leadership, the addition of new discourses and teaching material, various magisterial titles, the followers as the new Israel, the Gentile Mission to come, Jesus as wisdom incarnate, Jesus as the new Moses, and Jesus as the long-awaited Jewish Messiah and Savior of all humanity (Love, 2009).

The Gospel of Saint Luke, also traditionally called, "The Third Gospel," provides for its readers a careful examination and analysis of the life and ministry of Jesus of Nazareth, based on all the Jesus narratives that Luke could find in first century Christianity. Less eschatological (focused on the end times) than the Gospels of Matthew and Mark, Luke emphasizes both compassion for the needy and patience in waiting for the end times (Rowe, 2006).

This Gospel displays a passionate interest in helping oppressed people such as the poor, the hungry, the hurting, women, and anyone generally in social trouble, which relates to conflict theory. Moreover, it emphasizes the duty of the rich and powerful to share from their wealth to help those lesser in society. Strauss (2007) even calls the Gospel of Luke, *The Gospel for the Outcast*.

One can also perceive symbolic interactionism in the Gospel as Luke also discusses ideas such as the Mosaic prophet, the suffering servant, the Prophet Elijah, among other allusions and connections within the Hebrew Scriptures. Additionally, Luke utilizes popular Greco-Roman cultural tenets such as philosophy, immortality, the benefactor relationship to aid in helping non-Jewish readers comprehend the story and significance of Jesus, the Christ.

Finally, the Gospel of John (also called the Fourth Gospel and the last to be written in the Gospel canon) is the centerpiece of the Johannine corpus. Within the work, readers can discover several different social perspectives on Jesus, the Son of God. One can find an ecclesiastical Gospel that, despite the word, "Church," not being used, assumes an ongoing, simpatico relationship between Jesus and the church. Readers can also find a sacramental Gospel with multitudinous references to liturgical traditions, feasts, and ceremonies, implying that the sacraments (such as baptism and the Eucharist) are rooted in Christ. The book also includes distinct features promoting an eschatological approach to the Gospel wherein Jesus is the "resurrection and the life" (v. 11:25) who provides present salvation with a merciful future judgment—the sharing of eternity in the temporal present.

John also presents the *Gospel of Symbolism* to his readers, where reality is more than just mere appearances. Jesus is God, but human, too; he is powerful and masterful; however, he can fatigue, he can weep, he can change his mind, he has friends and best friends (Koester, 2019). Others around him also share in this symbolic actuality; specific people often represent grand ideas and moral aspects—the brave, the committed, the wavering, the cowardly, the dastardly, and the wicked.

John's symbolism connects with Judaism in a very deep way. Jesus is the personification of all holy celebrations (Passover, Chanukah), he is the realization of all titles (Slain Lamb, Living Bread, Living Water, The Light, the Tent Where God's Glory Dwells, The New Temple), and His crucifixion means more than just the death of a righteous teacher (Kerr, 2002). It is the death of all sinful humanity; it is the lifting up of all people from Sheol; its acceptance and ownership is required for enlightenment and salvation.

Approaching these Gospels from a social scientific mindset, it is reassuring to see that the biblical stories align themselves well with accurate human presentations (both privately and publicly). The supernatural events and actions of Jesus may sound fantastical (only the Son of God could do what He did), but the social forces, constructs, and consequences involving Him fall well within the range of sociological thought and theory.

In fact, the universality of the Christian message seems to parallel the scientific axiom that good theories operate in macro- and micro-environments. With nearly two billion believers worldwide, the Gospels must contain something within their messages that resonant deeply with readers, allaying their cynicism and engaging with their imaginations to spark belief, even after 2,000 years of waiting for His return.

INSIGHTS FROM THE EXPERTS

"Resilience in Troubled Times"

The Scriptures are replete with the term, "Day of Trouble," beginning with 2 Kings through the Psalms, into Isaiah and Jeremiah, and landing on Jesus in Matthew 6:34. One reads, "So do not worry about tomorrow; for tomorrow will care for itself. Each day has enough trouble of its own." In Psalm 107, David alludes to such days of trouble on multiple occasions, applied to wanderers in the desert, prisoners, fools, and those who go down to the sea in ships. Regarding the latter, David describes the power over nature similar to Jesus on the Sea of Galilee when he writes, "He caused the storm to be still, so that the waves of the sea were hushed. Then they were glad because they were quiet, so He guided them to their desired haven." The same refrain is repeated after describing each Day of Trouble—"Let them give thanks to the Lord for His loving kindness, and for His wonders to the sons of men."

Within this Psalm lies a microcosm of *resilience—Resilience in Troubled Times*.

The first point to observe is the reality of trouble, suffering, tribulation, the "body slams of life." In erudite terms, we might describe it as the theology of suffering. In simpler terms, Jesus said "In the world you have tribulation . . ." (John 16:33a). This "tribulation" in Greek (*thlipsis*) conveys the notion of squeezing oil out of olives or juice out of grapes—an unpleasant experience. All of this is somewhat theoretical until it happens to YOU— then, it is raw, real, visceral, painful, unforgettable. Such tribulation ranges from the suddenness of a tornado to the slow march of an overwhelming hurricane, often compelling us to say, Why me? Why now? Why God?

In our current context, tribulation takes the form of a coronavirus, which is slowly visiting death across the globe. None of us chose the death, the isolation, the economic impact; but here it is on OUR doorstep, threatening OUR families. In light of such tragedy, we do best not to ask, "Why?" rather to ask, "What shall I do? How shall I respond? Who can I help?" Hence, a first tenet of resilience is not to be surprised by the reality of suffering, but to embrace it supernaturally as a "cleverly disguised opportunity."

A second tenet of resilience relates to the development of spiritual reflexes, which allow us to respond in healthy ways to the storms of life. The Swiss philosopher and theologian Paul Tournier said, "We fall the way we lean." Given that we know that we will have tribulation, it makes good sense to be leaning in the right direction—drawing nigh to God, knowing that He will also draw nigh to us in our time of need. Part of leaning in the right direction is clearly putting on the armor of God, maintaining comprehensive personal fitness, and developing the right spiritual, mental, and emotional reflexes that predispose us toward the healthiest possible responses to trauma.

Robert Preston Taylor was a Chaplain assigned to the Philippines in 1941, not a great year given the numerous Japanese invasions in the Pacific. Chaplain Taylor soon found himself on the *Bataan Death March* with 68,000 other Allied prisoners of war. On the march, he became a friend and helper to many, often carrying others to prevent the reality of a Japanese bayonet should they stumble to the ground.

Arriving at the POW Camp with less than half of the men that started the march, Chaplain Taylor continued to minister to his fellow prisoners, both physically and spiritually. He heard by the prisoner grapevine that there were guerillas outside the wire who could assist with medical supplies. Soon, he began sneaking out at night to obtain urgently needed medicines, particularly ointments to control the tropical infections which would afflict even the smallest cut. One night he was caught, thrown into the "hell box," a small pit in the jungle with bamboo thatch for a roof. Without food, he would catch drops of water from tropical rains to sustain himself—for days, then weeks. Finally, the Japanese pulled back his bamboo roof, blinding him with the bright daylight. Several of his fellow prisoners pulled him out of the pit, steadying him on failing legs (Riddle & Ceban, 2003).

In a moment that pastors and caregivers will understand, Chaplain Taylor's fellow prisoners gathered around him and one asked, "Chaplain, what's the good word?" Chaplain Taylor could have easily said, "Really? I've been in the hell box. Give me a break!" But he provided a much more gracious reply, "Men, do not doubt in the dark what you believed in the light." What's that Chaplain? "Do not doubt in the dark what you believed in the light."

This story highlights the importance of preparation, using the "light of day" to figure out what we believe, what is our calling, who are our true "911 friends," what is the opposition, what are our tools to fight future trauma, and ultimately what are our "actions on contact" (our Stop-Drop-Roll reflexes) to allow us to respond well to our day of trouble. When the car wreck happens, the diagnosis occurs, or the betrayal happens—it is too late. We must figure out what we "believe in the light" ahead of time, so we do not doubt in the dark of night, depression, despair, and even depravity.

A third tenet of *Resilience in Troubled Times* addresses how to *Weather the Storm*. Psalm 57:1b refers to "hiding under the shelter of God's wings until the destruction passes by." When the chaos of trauma hits us or those we love, this is sometimes all we can do—call out like David, "In my distress I called upon the Lord and cried to my God for help" (Ps 18:6a). Aligned with this appeal to God's protection in crisis is an equally important call for immersion in God's Word, which I refer to as "Put in the IV." In the midst of personal or collective crisis, a ten-minute devotional won't get it—we need continuous infusion of God's nutrients into our spiritual bloodstream . . . music, Bible study and reflection, inspiring and God-honoring books and movies.

As well, in crisis, we should seek to maintain routine: sleep, diet, exercise, human interaction. Finally, related to *Weathering the Storm*, it is important to *Remember Our Calling* and to continue to live it out, even in the midst of tribulation. While we all have distinctives to our individual callings from God, we hold in common the mandate to reach out to others in various ways ("comforting others with that which we have been comforted"—2 Corinthians 1:4) and to continue to grow in the Lord, even through adversity . . . or more aptly, particularly in adversity.

A post-Vietnam study conducted by Tedeschi and Calhoun at the University of North Carolina (2018) validated the proposition of "Post Traumatic Growth," a secular convergence with the truths of Romans 5:3–4— ". . . we also exult in our tribulations, knowing that tribulation brings about perseverance; and perseverance, proven character, and proven character, hope . . ." The point is that resilience is a critical life skill, and growth through adversity is a key part of resilient living.

Regrettably, the scope of this article requires me to land the plane. For now, we must defer discussion of resilience principles related to post-trauma recovery and learning and adapting in preparation for future storms. These concepts are further expanded in *Resilience God Style,* and are summarized in the *Resilience Life Cycle* (Resilience Consulting, 2020) shown as follows:

RESILIENCE LIFE CYCLE
← ← ← ← ← ← ← ← ← ← ← ← ← ← ← ← ← ← ← ←
**Building Resilience | Weathering the Storm | Bouncing Back
Before | During | After**

Finally, many resilience coaches urge one to run faster, jump higher, grit it out longer. Trauma by its very nature exceeds human bounds and capabilities—hence, the need for Resilience God Style—"'Not by might nor by power, but by My Spirit,' says the Lord of hosts" (Zechariah 4:6).

May each of us live resilient lives in troubled times, and may we help others to do the same—God Style!

Major General Bob Dees
U.S. Army
Retired

Contributed by Robert Dees. © Kendall Hunt Publishing Company

CASE STUDY #2

For the past 10 years, Judith Finch lived at the peaceful 221a Baker Street without incident. Then one day, everything changed. Two new tenants appeared, carrying boxes and bags into the flat upstairs. Not being unkind, Mrs. Finch considered baking her new upstairs neighbors some biscuits. That afternoon, a loud bang rang through the building. Then, another. Then, another. Judith quickly learned that her peaceful existence on this quiet London street had come to an end. Yelling at all hours of the day. Comings and goings at all hours of the night. Police officers appearing, time and time again. Mrs. Finch could hardly stand it; yet, her curiosity continued to increase as the weeks passed.

Over the next several months, Mrs. Finch speculated and spied with critical interest on her new neighbors. She even went so far as to rummage through their trash; her horrifying discovery of human remains shocked and traumatized her. Going directly to the police, she was shocked when a detective came downstairs and assured her that nothing was wrong, and everything was under control. One day, during biscuit and tea, Judith vents all of this to you.

DISCUSSION QUESTIONS

1. Based on the readings, how would a sociologist diagnose this situation?

2. What specific sociological factors are involved?

3. What might Judith Finch do to learn more or improve the situation?

Check out the Chapter 2 video at this link:

https://www.khpcontent.com/

VOCABULARY

Agency
Bataan Death March
Epistemology
Ethnomethodology
The Gospel of the Church
The Gospel for the Outcast
The Gospel of Symbolism
Latent Function
Macro-Level
Manifest Function
Micro-Level
Middle-Level
Personal Troubles

Phenomenology
Political Sociology
Public Issues
Resilience
Resilience Life Cycle
Resilience in Troubled Times
Scientific Cynicism
Social Cynicism
Social Imagination
Social Scrutiny
Sociological Consideration
Traditional Sociology

References

Burgess, S. (2015). The corrosive effects of social cynicism. *News: Nelson Mandela University Business School*. http://businessschool.mandela.ac.za/article/the-corrosive-effects-of-social-cynicism

Clawson, D., Zussman, R., Misra, J., Gerstel, N., Stokes, R., Anderton, D., Burawoy, M., Abbott, A., Burawoy, M., Collins, P. H., Ehrenreich, B., Glenn, E. N., Hays, S., Massey, D., Patterson, O., Piven, F. F., Smith-Lovin, L., Stacey, J., Stinchcombe, A., . . . Wilson, W. J. (2007). *Public sociology: Fifteen eminent sociologists debate politics and the profession in the twenty-first century*. University of California Press.

Cole, N. L. (2020). Manifest function, latent function, and dysfunction in sociology. *ThoughtCo.* https://www.thoughtco.com/manifest-function-definition-4144979

Kerr, A. R. (2002). *The temple of Jesus' body: The temple theme in the Gospel of John*. Sheffield Academic Press.

Knox, J. (2019). *Sociology is rude!: A conversation on sociological theory and thought*. Kendall Hunt.

Koester, C. (2019). *Portraits of Jesus in the Gospel of John: A Christological spectrum*. T&T Clark.

Love, S. L. (2009). *Jesus and marginal women: The Gospel of Matthew in social-scientific perspective*. James Clarke & Co.

Lynch, M., & Sharrock, W. (2011). *Ethnomethodology*. Sage.

Mills, C. W. (1959). *The sociological imagination*. Oxford University Press.

Moloney, F. J. (2012). *The Gospel of Mark: A commentary*. Baker Academic.

Raghunathan, R. (2011). Are you a social cynic? Giving others the benefit of the doubt enhances your happiness. *Psychology Today*. https://www.psychologytoday.com/us/blog/sapient-nature/201105/are-you-social-cynic

Resilience Consulting. (2020). *Resilience life cycle*. https://resiliencegodstyle.com

Riddle, J., & Ceban, B. J. (2003). *For God and country: Four stories of courageous military chaplains.* Barbour.

Roig, B., Weiss, K., & Thireau, V. (Eds.). (2019). *Management of emerging public health issues and risks: Multidisciplinary approaches to the changing environment.* Elsevier.

Rowe, C. K. (2006). *Early narrative Christology: The Lord in the Gospel of Luke.* De Gruyter.

Strauss, M. (2007). *Four portraits, one Jesus: An introduction to Jesus and the Gospels.* Zondervan.

Tedeschi, R. G., Shakespeare-Finch, J., Taku, K., & Calhoun, L. G. (2018). *Posttraumatic growth: Theory, research, and applications.* Routledge.

Turri, J. (2014). *Epistemology: A guide.* Wiley Blackwell.

Ch 3 Deviance

Part of the human condition includes the social reality that people do not always emulate the beliefs or actions of other people around them. People often express their unique beliefs through unusual actions, regardless of how everyone else believes or does it. They deviate from (or violate) a social norm or expectation—whether intentionally or not in a socially manifest way. The truth is that everyone has been deviant at some time or another in their lives and in their different attitudes and actions (Lemert, 1951).

Deviance depends much upon the historical time period, the existing and dominant cultures surrounding it, or in the level of individual freedoms of expression and behavior allowed in particular cultures. In academia, the definition of *deviance* is "a person's actions or attitudes that violate accepted, 'normal' standards of behavior, which can have a negative or positive connotation or significance" (Knox, 2018). Overall, deviance is the exception or the rarity in society that occurs for whatever reason.

The response to deviance could be just a *stigma*, which is cultural disapproval associated with disobeying expected norms. However, this deviance could be considered a more serious *crime*, in which legal institutions impose penalties upon the violators by the police or a judge.

Historically, most societies adopt two general approaches to dealing with social problems. The older mindset (and one less accepted in postmodernity) is the *medical model*, which asserts that social problems coexist with bad people and/or groups (Gabe & Monaghan, 2013). This presumes a universal criterion for health and normality, making all deviances or shortcomings "abnormal or harmful," socially. Thus, social problems occur because of mental deficiency or disorder, a lack of education, or a poor or incomplete socialization.

Alternatively, the *absolutist approach* suggests that a specific condition in society fosters particular social problems (Gabe & Monaghan, 2013). This model presumes a causal or catalytical effect of social relationships and social problems. For instance, one could make the case that unmarried, recreational sex in college leads to higher levels of sexually transmitted diseases within college communities. With this approach, sociologists look for pockets of social disorganization, dysfunction, or deviance to study and remedy (Goode & Nachman, 1994).

Interestingly, deviance is not always negative; sometimes, deviance is positive and is often ignored in many situations. Therefore, the circumstances surrounding deviant behavior are critical to understand. Some deviant acts are particular to the era or culture within which they occur; other deviances are more timeless and universal, stretching across history and cultures.

The definition of deviance is debatable. Some people take an *absolutist definition* wherein deviance is not a matter of social judgment, but one more of scientific certainty (Hills, 1977). This is true at a fundamental level, with deviance presumptuously condensed to a small percentage of the population, generally.

In the postmodern era, deviance is typically associated more with social harm than a statistical quality, which is why many former deviant acts such as homosexuality or transgenderism are no longer officially labeled as "deviant" because of the emotional and psychological harm that they are purported to receive from that label (Weitz & Bryant, 1996). Additionally, as mentioned earlier, sometimes deviance can be a positive social force, which seems to be oxymoronic (a word, term, or figure of speech that seems self-contradictory). Still, deviance can contribute to society (Andrews, 2015). For instance, examples of positive deviance include Germans who resisted the Nazi takeover in the 1930s, Rosa Parks sitting in a Whites-only section of a bus (on December 1, 1955), Christian adoption agencies ignoring pro-LGBTQ state mandates by only placing adopted babies in spiritually healthy homes, pro-life activists standing outside an abortion clinic, Mother Teresa touching the untouchables in Calcutta, and so on.

As mentioned earlier, some deviance is criminal (which is discussed in the next chapter), but deviance is more than just a violation of laws. Deviance can be proscriptive—what a person should not do—or prescriptive—what a person ought to do. *Culture* also plays a part in defining and determining deviance, as it concerns beliefs, values, norms, sanctions, and social symbols.

Beliefs are definitions and explanations about what is assumed to be true. *Values* are social agreements about what society considers to be good and bad behaviors and attitudes. *Norms* are socially defined rules of behavior. *Sanctions* are consequences for not conforming to accepted norms. *Symbols* concern the language, gestures, and objects whose meanings are commonly understood by members of a society.

There are many different social constructs concerning social norms although situations involving norms can change according to the varying contexts of any given situation. *Folkways* are the general customs and manners embraced in society. *Mores* are social norms with a moral basis or character. *Laws* are formal norms of behavior backed by police and judicial authorities. These typically originate with various social institutions such as family, church, government, the economy, and the educational system.

When considering the sociology surrounding deviance, one needs to consider several different factors. First, how many people consider a person's behavioral trait to be deviant? Second, who exactly is saying that a particular actor's behavior is deviant (what authority do they hold in society)? Third, how much does the deviance run against cultural norms and acceptance?

For instance, a pastor in Nampa, Idaho, might preach to his congregation that prostitution (which will be discussed in an upcoming chapter) is immoral, deviant, and should never be legalized—based upon a .5% cases per capita occurrence in that rugged Pacific Northwest state (Geoffrey G. Nathan Law Offices, 2018). Of course, in Washington, DC, which has the biggest incident rate of prostitution in the United States—6.1 cases per capita (Geoffrey G. Nathan Law Offices, 2018), a local shoe-salesman-turned-political-candidate might speak out for the legalization of prostitution ("It's a victimless crime") in his campaigning tour. Not surprisingly, the sociologist would question the authority of each person, their use of statistics to back up their claims, and then consider regional cultural norms to analyze their assertions on the subject.

An important question of deviance concerns the intentions or mindset of the individuals perpetrating the act(s). Deviance is not always about someone's lack of character, sanity, or morality (Heckert, 2002). Sometimes, it is quite the opposite and stems more from external socialization than inner demons.

With that in mind, sociologists have developed several specific theories over the decades regarding deviance and social problems. In 1938, Robert Merton came up with *social strain theory* (Merton, 1968). This theory asserted that social deviance occurs when a gap exists between cultural goals and personal achievements.

According to Merton (1968), five components make up *strain theory*: (a) *conformity*, which occurs when a person embraces cultural goals and standard methods of achieving them; (b) *innovation*, which occurs when a person accepts cultural goals but then uses illegal methods to achieve them; (c) *ritualism*, which occurs when a person rejects cultural goals, but then uses legitimate methods to achieve what he or she wants in society; (d) *retreatism*, which occurs when a person rejects cultural goals and legitimate methods, altogether; and (e) *rebellion*, when a person rejects cultural goals and legitimate methods, creating new goals and methods instead.

Another approach by Howard Becker, called *labeling theory*, proposes that rather than holding a preexisting condition of deviance, being labeled as a "deviant" actually leads to a person being more likely to engage in counter-normative (or anti-social) behavior (Becker, 1963). Moreover, the *labelers* who call out other individuals for deviant behaviors (who can be individuals, organizations, or whole social movements), are the *moral entrepreneurs* of the community or society.

For instance, a person, "Joe," might be walking down a school path when he sees a lit cigarette on the ground. Picking it up in curiosity, Joe may be seen by another person who finds smoking a dangerous pastime and spreads the word that Joe is a smoker and should be shunned. Then, when Joe is threatened by false accusations and is publicly belittled, he may begin to smoke in defiance—thus, accepting his new social role as a deviant "bad boy."

Deviance also touches upon many of the social "tendrils" involved in politics (especially in the postmodern era). Many governmental rulers across the globe fight deviance because of its inherent and historical potential for causing social disintegration and distress. During the 2020 COVID-19 outbreak, many people tired of the state-imposed quarantining and attempted to spend some relaxing, rejuvenating time at a beach or taking a jog on a mountain trail. Unexpectedly, for many of these people, they encountered—not just a social stigma or shunning for their actions—but police involvement, even arrest for the deviant acts (Smith, 2020).

Deviance is also controlled or dealt with through more subtle socialization from the higher controlling groups in society. Again, regarding the COVID-19 outbreak, many public announcements were delivered through the media outlets with messages like, "We're all in this together," "Don't be selfish—Stay at home," or "Freedom shouldn't come at the cost of another person's life." Besides the common sense of these statements (and the giant guilt-trips embedded in them), this methodology is called *priming* (Bargh, 2006), where repeated, subtle, social stimuli gradually produce a learned response that is eventually and unconsciously performed by participants in a social experiment or scheme. Television commercials are a clear example of this form of socialization.

In the coronavirus examples previously mentioned, external social control was in play (Goode & Nachman, 1994), with a system of rewards and penalties for violating the norms that were announced and expected by the state governors and city mayors. Additionally, steps to promote quarantining during the coronavirus outbreak and reducing any freedom-seeking deviant impulses could be advanced through the stimulus checks and other proposed "free public funding and resources" while society remained in lockdown an unknown duration.

I STAY AT HOME
TO FIGHT CORONAVIRUS

In these cases, the resistance to deviance is part of the political scene in postmodern America and the West. Ironically, in a period purported to cater to personal freedoms, under the aphorism of "public safety," many personal rights guaranteed to us by the Constitution of the United States (such as freedom to peacefully assemble and freedom to worship as Americans please) were set aside or ignored to enforce the quarantine (and informal house arrest) of all Americans (Sullum, 2020).

MAIN SOCIOLOGICAL APPROACHES

A *conflict theorist's perspective* asserts that all deviance comes as a result of economic inequalities in society (Griffiths et al., 2019). The conflict between compliance and deviance is generated by high society dictating what are "deviant acts or behavioral traits." Conflict theorists also see an unending and unavoidable battleground between deviances and norms especially considering sexism and capitalism's malevolent existence—a curious position considering that capitalism operates upon the idea of free markets and individual enterprise [thinking outside the box], which would logically lead to more options and choices that might be considered "deviant" by the economic power structure in control.

The *symbolic interactionist's perspective* of deviance rests upon personal perspectives, prioritization, and exchanges between people. It assumes or asserts that some acts (even those unbeknownst to the actor) can run against cultural norms while still being personally authentic, beneficial, and meaningful to the deviant person (Sutherland, 1942). A clear example of this is the current youthful trend of tattooing oneself, which used to be (ironically) taboo in most social circles in 20th-century America (Arp, 2012). Currently, the deviant act has lost its stigma (for many people) and has been transformed into an expression of the self that is shared in pride and admiration with others (tattooed and non-tattooed). Despite the dangers associated with tattooing (Mitchell et al., 2017), the artistry on these deviants' bodies mirrors the artistry of their life experiences and emotions, which they share with all to see and discuss in society.

Finally, the *functionalist's perspective* considering deviance is a two-faced coin, so to speak. On the one side, the functionalist considers deviance to be a potentially dangerous social force. Deviance runs against the smooth operation strived for in society. It splits and divides people-groups, leading to disharmony and antisocial behavior. It introduces social acts and attitudes that can create social problems, harming everyone in the social system (Thompson & Gibbs, 2016).

On the flip side of the coin, there are some positive aspects to deviance for the functionalist. *Positive deviants* can help recalibrate social settings and standards, bringing the hyper-rigid functionalist social environment back into reality with the truth that its former social presumptions of normalcy are more harmful than beneficial, more antiquated than relevant, and more artificial than organic (Ziyanak & Williams, 2014). Deviance can also trigger a refortification to protect the system from new and dangerous ideas introduced by unauthorized agents. This is especially true when it comes to generational disagreements and discord.

DEALING WITH MATTERS OF THE DARK

Deviance, as a social construct, has long been part of the human story, and its influence has been, at times, either negative or positive on society. As it is presently, people in antiquity also felt the need to push back against detrimental social norms or community beliefs to exercise personal convictions. One can easily trace its presence through the annals of time in both political and religious arenas.

In history, figures like *Socrates, Caractacus*, and *Sojourner Truth* all experienced what it was like to be labeled as "deviant." The Greek philosopher Socrates (469–399 BCE) rejected the political and vapid arguments of the sophists and the natural philosophers, leading to his execution by poisoning. Socrates's analytical, factual approach to social matters enraged the sophists, who were paid teachers of philosophy and rhetoric, and whom Socrates called "bad teachers . . . ignorant of the nature of general terms" (Plato, 1892).

Likewise, after Rome's Emperor Claudius Augustus Germanicus (10 B.C.E.–54 C.E.) took the reins of Roman rule, the British chieftain/king of the Catuvellauni tribe—Caractacus (15 B.C.E.–54 C.E.)—fought against their gigantic military forces in Britain with shrewdness, small numbers of warriors, and guerilla tactics until he was betrayed by Queen Cartimandua and turned over to Roman authorities. His defiant speech: "Think not, eagle-lord of Rome, and master of the world, though victory's banner is over your throne and in triumph unfurled, I would address you as your slave, but as the bold should greet the brave." Claudius was so impressed with his courage and poise that he pardoned him for his crimes in Britain (Church & Brodribb, 1942).

Isabella Baumfree (a.k.a. Sojourner Truth), an abolitionist from New York, lived a life that deviated dramatically from 19th-century standards for a Black person and a woman. Born a slave, she ran away from her slave owner when he demanded that she stay a year longer in servitude after slavery was banned in 1827.

In 1843, giving herself a new name—Sojourner Truth—she campaigned across the country, even meeting with President Abraham Lincoln, proclaiming the evils of slavery and the rights of women (Bernard, 2017). Despite the social darkness of that era, Sojourner vowed to walk in the light of God's truth in all her efforts to foster social equality for all people in America. Not surprisingly, her influence in society was significant, frequently meeting with other famous public figures such as William Lloyd Garrison, Frederick Douglass, Elizabeth Cady Stanton, and Susan B. Anthony.

History records many other positive deviants such as Macrina, the Cappadocian Teacher who fought for orthodoxy amidst the paganism of the fourth century C.E. (Johnson, 1998), the great reformer Martin Luther who pushed back against the despotic secularism of the papacy of the 16th-century C.E. (Hendrix, 2015), the Rev. John Wesley who strived to augment Anglican socialization with his own curriculum that would lead to the creation of the Methodist movement and church (Knox, 2017), German pastor and anti-Nazi dissident Deitrich Bonhoeffer who was eventually arrested by the Gestapo and executed for his involvement in an assassination attempt against

Hitler (Bethge & Barnett, 1999), Mother Teresa who ignored the caste system of Calcutta to rescue the untouchables, and so on.

The Bible also provides many examples of both good and bad deviants—from Rahab, the redeemed prostitute (mentioned in the biblical books of Joshua, Matthew, James, and Hebrews), to Matthew, the redeemed tax collector mentioned in the Gospels in the New Testament, and, of course, Jesus Christ, a carpenter from Galilee and the Redeemer of all humanity. Some might question Jesus's deviance, but in His time and culture, His words and actions upset many of the intellectual and spiritual leaders in Israel—the Pharisees and the Sadducees—who had a very different view of humanity's treatment of each other and God.

Ultimately, the Pharisees and Sadducees forgot that all God's ways are good, and so they deviated to other paths that only led people away from the one, true source of goodness. Jesus (and John the Baptist) merely pointed the crowds back to God's path for righteousness and told Israel to ignore the hypocrisy and vanity of the Pharisees and Sadducees (Matthew 16:6, New American Standard Version). This infuriated the religious rulers because (1) Jesus did not agree with or submit to their thoughts and their ways, and (2) Jesus made them look corrupt and sophomoric—like "wise fools."

Jesus's message (like all messages that have come from God through the ages) was straightforward and salvific: "Let the wicked forsake their ways and the unrighteous their thoughts. Let them turn to the Lord, and he will have mercy on them, and to our God, for he will freely pardon" (Isaiah 55:7). All people today have the same opportunity mercifully provided to them. We can follow the deviance of man, which leads to ever-increasing darkness, or the deviance of God, which leads to light and life and love.

INSIGHTS FROM THE EXPERTS

"An Ethic for Christian Deviance and Social Disobedience"

Many Americans have assumed that individual freedom is the highest expression of Christian expression in government. Syncretism notwithstanding, the American ideal of preserving life, liberty, and the pursuit of happiness is frequently given the same sacred reverence as Jesus's command to Love the Lord your God with all your heart, soul, and mind. In a culture that has produced both the courage of Martin Luther King, Jr.'s civil disobedience and the infamous hate-filled rhetoric of Westboro Baptist Church, many Christians are confused as to when it is appropriate to deviate from socially appropriate norms or act in civil disobedience within a democratic society.

Since the Christian faith must always embody the highest moral code in a believer's hierarchy of decision, moral choices must be regulated by an ethic defined primarily by Christian love. This essay establishes an ethic of Christian social deviance utilizing the tradition of just war theory. As *jus ad bellum* (part of the laws of war) and *jus en bello* (whether a war is conducted justly) dictate the rules by which one might deviate from the Christian ethic of love in the context of war, so too the same sorts of questions must be answered to justify deviation from the expected norm of civic obedience. This essay will discuss the basis for socially binding norms, the principles of deviation from peace between states, and apply those principles to a Christian ethic of social deviance and civil disobedience.

Humankind is bound by a contract that serves to preserve justice, freedom, and collective self-defense, and therefore must only be deviated from when the sovereign authority fails to uphold its contractual obligation. In the 17th century, the philosopher Hobbes theorized that the nature of man is to live free, yet the individual is bound by corruption. People choose to participate in society hoping to mitigate the consequences of societal injustice. Stating that life tends to be "nasty, brutish, and short," corrupted people tend to act out of self-interest. Because of this corrupted nature, the natural state tends toward anarchy and self-help. Whereas there is no worldly higher authority to regulate injustice, the world becomes insecure and unjust (Hobbes, 1615). Individuals opted to build collective societies to mitigate man's natural state of injustice with a sovereign (executive government) to ensure the maintenance of the *social contract*. The social contract between individuals served to provide security yet limited their freedoms.

Building on Hobbes, John Locke suggested that the authority of the executive component of government is necessary to protect the individual's property and well-being. However, if such protection is no longer present, or when the sovereign becomes a tyrant acting against the interests of the people, they then have a right to resist his authority. The contract can thus be dissolved or altered. Similarly, Jean-Jacques Rousseau proposed that individuals collectively must fulfill their responsibilities to the sovereign if they are to reap the benefits of citizenship, giving us the framework for living collectively under the state's authority (Celest Friend, 2020).

In a democratic society, individuals directly affect the power of the executive through voting, representative government, free speech, free press, and rule of law. In a truly democratic society, checks and balances exist to limit the government from having the opportunity for tyranny. Ultimately, none beside God has authority without permission of the people.

The Bible assumes that sovereign authority reflects the order appointed by God. Romans 13 declares: "Let everyone be subject to the governing authorities, for there is no authority except that which God has established. The authorities that exist have been established by God." As Christians living during a time of oppressive Roman rule, Paul mandated subjection to an ungodly authority. For Christians, the social contract serves a higher purpose than the needs of the individual. Peaceful society was preferable over individualistic anarchy despite the oppressive yoke of Roman rule. A social contract is the only way for collective justice, protection, and order to exist because man has been wholly corrupted by sin. Certainly, corruption is present in every form of government, yet the constraining nature of a sovereign authority affords it the only legitimate use of force in constraining evil.

Christians may only deviate from an ethic of love in order to restore peace. The question as to whether a Christian might deviate from societal order is no different than the criteria which must be met for sovereign states to use violence to mitigate aggression. Augustine of Hippo lived in the Roman Empire following the conversion of Constantine when most officials had converted to Christianity. Writing in response to Rome's recent sacking by barbarians, Augustine describes the nature of war in his day: Holy places were desecrated, there was no uniform treatment of those defeated, girls and boys were raped and kidnapped, people's homes were plundered and destroyed, innocents were killed, and there was no restraint in combat.

Augustine called Christians to a higher ethic. Christians were to confront evil, not for the sake of property, but rather to restore peace. Violence is only permissible for the agent upon whom the government has appointed to regulate justice. The only true agents permitted to act violently were soldiers and peace officers. For him, war was never just, but sometimes the lesser of two evils. Just war, he demanded, must have a just cause (jus ad bellum).

Thomas Aquinas later determined that for a war to be just its conduct must also be regulated by Christian principles. Aquinas assumed a steady state of peace and that war was permissible only when evil had disrupted that peace. War was sometimes necessary to preserve the republic and maintain the common good, but the authority to go to war fell solely upon the sovereign. Just war required three preconditions: right authority, just cause, and right intention. For a Christian nation to enter into armed conflict required that only the sovereign declare it as the sole "right authority." Furthermore, it must be for a "just cause" such as preservation of life or property. Finally, the intention must be to preserve peace rather than to harm others (Augustine, 2014, pp. 8–9).

Many times, the evils of war corrupt and injure the souls of those waging it, resulting in unjust measures. For instance, a war may be just; yet, targeting civilians in order to force a government to capitulate is unjust. Addressing this, Aquinas directed three principles of justice in war (jus en bello): necessity, proportionality, and the law of double effect. A society was to be collectively aligned with its sovereign in confronting evil; yet, it must do so according to a Christian ethic of regulation.

Conduct in war must serve a military purpose (necessity). The outcome of war must be proportional to the violence inflicted (proportionality). Finally, special care should be taken to ensure protection of the innocent while bringing justice to the guilty (law of double effect). The work of Aquinas presupposed a return to a steady state of peace and an ethic of Christian love. "By placing the locus on charity over justice, Aquinas' theory of just war addressed the inward state of emotion which might cause a Christian to go to battle seeking revenge (and) allowing for emotions like hatred, wrath, or cruelty" (Reichburg, 2017, p. 36).

War was bounded by peace and restraint, while regulated by right authority and intent. It protected the innocent while attempting to constrain evil, recognizing that the friction of war will sometimes produce unintentional second order effects. These foundations for just war became the basis for the Law of Armed Conflict and further serves to regulate Christian deviance from God's intended order.

Right authority has been determined in recent years to apply as a "right to protect" citizens of a sovereign nation when a tyrannical authority is imposing unrestricted abuse of basic human rights. While the international system recognizes the sovereign authority of each nation to defend its own territory and self-govern, it may be restricted when the state fails to uphold its contract to protect its own population. Similarly, the threshold for civil disobedience must be very high indeed if any group would challenge the common good, steady state of peace.

I am suggesting that the same weighty standard that lawful nations must apply in determining armed conflict be applied to the individual before a person is justified in deviating from the social contract with civil disobedience. One may argue that they were born into a contract, not of their own choosing. In truth, all of the benefits whereby an individual has benefited by living in a society becomes evidence that the individual is bound by the contract to governmental authority. For any Christian to deviate from their societal obligation requires just cause, right intent, right authority, necessity, proportionality, and sensitivity to double effect.

By applying the rules of jus ad bellum and jus en bello to social deviation, the Christian has an ethic by which to measure whether they should and in what manner they may deviate from earthly authority. There is no basis to subjectively reject earthly authority based on convenience or self-interest. The measure of just cause for civil disobedience must be to confront an evil so great that refusing to obey would make one complicit in that evil. To be clear, this must be an evil which threatens the individual's or innocent's safety, property, or well-being in a real and measurable way.

Second, right authority must remain unmoved by socially acceptable means for self-regulation. In a democratic society laws and politicians change on a regular basis. There are multiple avenues available to hold corrupt authorities accountable. To step outside of these boundaries for personal convenience or vanity is sin. The only "just cause" for stepping outside of "right authority" is when compliance becomes complicity in evil. This includes both the sin of commission (participating in evil directly) or of omission (failing to confront evil when it threatens the peaceful order). Thirdly, it must be for the "right intent."

It is not permissible for the Christian to deviate from lawful authority for the wrong reasons. The individual cannot confront authority simply on the basis of partisan interest. The reasons to deviate must be compelling and all other avenues of corrective accountability must either be exhausted or unavailable. Finally, the evil must be so great that failure to act would make the individual complicit with the sin.

If an individual disobeys civil authority, it must be necessary, proportional, and limited only to what is required to correct society to its peaceful state. One may only act in proportion to the wrong being confronted. A Christian must furthermore hold Christian love as a regulating force throughout. For instance, Martin Luther King, Jr. chose to disobey the laws of his day in order to confront the societal ill of racism. Yet, he did not resort to violence as this was neither necessary nor consistent with his goal to bring all races to peaceful coexistence. His disobedience was proportional to his objective. In fact, had he acted disproportionately to his objectives, he would have increased violence and undermined his objective.

Lastly, every individual must ask, "How will my action negatively affect those who are innocent of wrongdoing?" For instance, if a Christian chooses to block a roadway in protest to the government and their action blocks a fire truck from resulting in the death of an innocent person, it is therefore unjust and does not meet the standard of Christian love. The evil being confronted must be greater than the injustice resulting from the double-effect. Any deviation from lawful authority is weighted against social obligation, legal sanction, and Christian love.

Deviation from social contracts breaks the moral code implicit to any individual living within a society. It signals a return to humanity's natural state, but freedom to act comes with a price. The just war principles can serve as a guide for Christians to determine actions based on an ethic of Christian love. Ultimately, it is more effective to work democratically within a society to preserve peace and punish evil through collective action that is rooted in Christian love.

Rev. David R. Leonard
Master of Divinity
Master of Military Operational Art and Science

CASE STUDY #3

The bell above the door chimed softly as he entered the parlor. Even in a place such as this, all eyes darted towards Terree. Those waiting on the pews lined against the wall and sitting in parlor chairs in the middle of the room let their mouths gape just a little as he passed by. One of the workers stood, smiled, and called him by his name. He was a regular, and everybody knew it. Today, the young man would be finishing up a commission on his right foot, which was just a smaller project as he saved for larger pieces. Taking off his shoe and sitting in the parlor chair, the young man gushed with enthusiasm; for him, getting a tattoo was a euphoric experience. Sarcastically, the artist attending to him asked if he was sure he wanted one. The man gave the artist a wide smile, which twisted the two tattooed crosses on each side of his face affirming the procedure.

Terree had gotten his first tattoo in college and enjoyed it so much, he continued getting them. What started as a cool hobby with friends spiraled as his obsession with body art and piercings continued. After 3 years of body work, his face, neck, torso, arms, legs (and now feet) were covered in "art." All of this came at no small expense. Tattoos were expensive and a bit painful at time, (physically and socially). Supposedly (according to them), he lost his job and girlfriend because of his body art. His family called him a delinquent. Nevertheless, nobody could stop him from doing what he loved. The buzz of the tattoo pen jolted him back to the moment, and his heart began to beat faster as the needle began its slow but artist journey.

DISCUSSION QUESTIONS

1. Based on the readings, how would a sociologist diagnose this situation?

2. What specific sociological factors are involved?

3. How many tattoos is too many tattoos?

Check out the Chapter 3 video at this link:

https://www.khpcontent.com/

VOCABULARY

Absolutist Approach
Caractacus
Conformity
Crime
Culture
Deviance
Deviance, Conflict Perspective of
Deviance, Functionalist Perspective of
Deviance, Symbolic Interactionist Perspective of
Folkways
Innovation
Labelers
Labeling Theory
Laws
Medical Model
Moral Entrepreneurs

Mores
Norms
Positive Deviance
Priming
Rebellion
Retreatism
Ritualism
Sanctions
Social Contract
Social Strain Theory
Socrates
Sojourner Truth
Stigma
Symbols
Values

References

Andrews, M. (2015). Explaining positive deviance in public sector reforms in development. *World Development, 74*, 197–208.

Arp, R. (2012). *Tattoos—Philosophy for everyone: I ink, therefore I am*. Wiley-Blackwell.

Augustine, St. (2014). *City of God* (Marcus Dods, Ed. & Trans.). https://www.acatholic.org/wp-content/uploads/2014/06/The-City-of-God-Saint-Augustine.pdf

Bargh, J. A. (2006). What have we been priming all these years? On the development, mechanisms, and ecology of nonconscious social behavior. *European Journal of Social Psychology, 36*(2), 147–168.

Becker, H. S. (1963). *Outsiders: Studies in the sociology of deviance*. Simon & Schuster.

Bernard, C. (2017). *Sojourner Truth: Women's rights and activist and abolitionist*. Enslow.

Bethge, E., & Barnett, V. J. (1999). *Dietrich Bonhoeffer: A biography*. Fortress.

Celest Friend, C. (n.d.). Rousseau: Social contract theory. *Internet Encyclopedia of Philosophy*. https://www.iep.utm.edu/soc-cont/#SH2a

Church, A. F., & Brodribb, W. J. (Eds.). (1942). *Complete Works of Tacitus*. Random House.

Gabe, J., & Monaghan, L. F. (2013). *Key concepts in medical sociology*. Sage.

Geoffrey G. Nathan Law Offices. (2018). Top cities in America with the most cases of human trafficking. https://www.geoffreygnathanlaw.com/topics/most-cases-of-human-trafficking-in-america/

Goode, E., & Nachman, B. (1994). *Moral panics: The social construction of deviance*. Wiley-Blackwell.

Griffiths, H., Keirns, N., Strayer, E., Sadler, T., Cody-Rydzewski, S., Scaramuzzo, G., Vyain, S., Bry, J., & Jones, F. (2019). Theoretical perspectives on deviance. In *Introduction to Sociology* (2nd ed.). Pressbooks.

Heckert, A. (2002). A new typology of deviance: Integrating normative and reactivist definitions of deviance. *Deviant Behavior: An Interdisciplinary Journal, 23*(5), 449–479.

Hendrix, S. H. (2015). *Martin Luther: Visionary reformer.* Yale University Press.

Hills, S. L. (1977). Absolutist and relativist views of social deviance: Toward a humanistic perspective. *Humanity and Society, 1*(1), 147.

Hobbes, T. (1615). Leviathan (Andrew Cook: 1615). https://gutenberg.org/files/3207/3207-h/3207-h.htm, accessed on 05/19/2020.

Johnson, M. P. (1998). Daughter, sister, philosopher, angel: The life and influence of St. Macrina the younger. *Diakonia, 31*(3), 176–186.

Knox, J. (2017). *John Wesley's 52 standard sermons: An annotated summary.* Wipf & Stock.

Knox, J. (2018). *A lexicon of sociological terms and theorists.* Kendall Hunt.

Lemert, E. (1951). *Social pathology: A systematic approach to the theory of sociopathic behavior.* McGraw-Hill.

Merton, R. (1968). *Social strain theory and social structure.* Free Press.

Mitchell, L. V., Caruana, D. M., & Grant, W. (2017). Tattoo trouble. *British Medical Journal (Online), 356*, 1–2.

Plato. (1892). The dialogues of Plato, vol. 2 (Meno, Euthyphro, Apology, Crito, Phaedo, Gorgias, Appendix I—Lesser, Hippias, Alcibiades I, Menexenus, Appendix II—Alcibiades II, Eryxias). https://oll.libertyfund.org/titles/plato-dialogues-vol-2/simple

Reichburg, G. M. (2017). *Thomas Aquinas on war and peace.* University Printing House.

Smith, L. (2020). Couple arrested on honeymoon in Hawaii for ignoring coronavirus quarantine rules. *Newsweek.* https://www.newsweek.com/couple-arrested-honeymoon-hawaii-ignoring-coronavirus-quarantine-rules-1501744

Sullum, J. (2020). Will COVID-19 kill the Constitution? *Reason: Free Minds and Free Markets.* https://reason.com/2020/04/01/will-covid-19-kill-the-constitution/

Sutherland, E. H. (1942). *On analyzing crime (Heritage of society).* University of Chicago Press.

Thompson, W. E., & Gibbs, J. C. (2016). *Deviance and Deviants: A sociological approach.* John Wiley & Sons.

Weitz, R., & Bryant, K. (1996). The portrayal of homosexuality in abnormal psychology and sociology of deviance textbooks. *Deviant Behavior, 18*(1), 27–46.

Ziyanak, S., & Williams, J. (2014). Functionalist perspective on deviance. *Journal of Human Sciences, 11*(2). https://www.j-humansciences.com/ojs/index.php/IJHS/article/view/2791

Ch 4 Prostitution

Often called the *oldest profession, prostitution* is an oft-investigated social problem quite active all over the globe (including America). Although various types of prostitution exist (call girls, escorts, street-walkers, gigolos, fleabag, brothel, child), they all share the same definition: a person (male or female) who engages in normal or deviant sexual intercourse (with a customer or *John*), with no emotional or personal attachment, for a monetary (or other) reward as a regular part of their vocational profession, possibly under the management (or exploitational abuse) of a *pimp* (Flowers, 1998).

The catalyst for becoming a prostitute can be complex. Men and women may be predisposed to get into the sex business because of a sexual *addiction*, promiscuous nature, or sociopathy. There may be economic factors such as poverty, limited jobs, unwed motherhood, and so on, forcing them into prostitution. They might feel a compulsion to *hook* out of a psychological need for power, control, or attachment. Other forces might be at play, including social pressures, media promotion, a family pattern, or a religious obligation in some parts of the world (Scott, 2014).

Women make up the largest percentage of prostitutes (40 million); however, men still represent a sizeable percentage of prostitutes—at 8 million, or nearly one fifth of all sex workers (Lehmiller, 2018). Within male prostitution, a hierarchy exists with escort prostitutes working for a data agency holding the highest prestige, bar and hotel hustlers holding the middle position, and street hustlers and desperate drug addicts holding the lowest or bottom rung. Male heterosexual prostitutes are called *gigolos*.

All of these men offer their paid-for-sexual favors to both women and men. Homosexual men also service other men sexually, and they tend to come from peer-delinquent subcultures or from a strongly gay subculture. Homosexuals are thought to be the largest percentage of male prostitutes based on internet findings (Lehmiller, 2018), but again, all prostitutes are fearful or avoidant to voluntarily divulge their vocational practices for fear of punishment.

Historically, several factors tend to be part of the initiation process. First, the person might know another prostitute or pimp who beckons them to try out the profession. Second, the person has experienced younger sexual activity or promiscuity. Third, the person likely grew up in a home environment of poverty, drugs, and emotional or sexual abuse. Other factors include *truancy* (disinterest in school), *delinquency* (misbehavior outside of school), running away from home, homelessness, and general rebellion (Peterson et al., 2015).

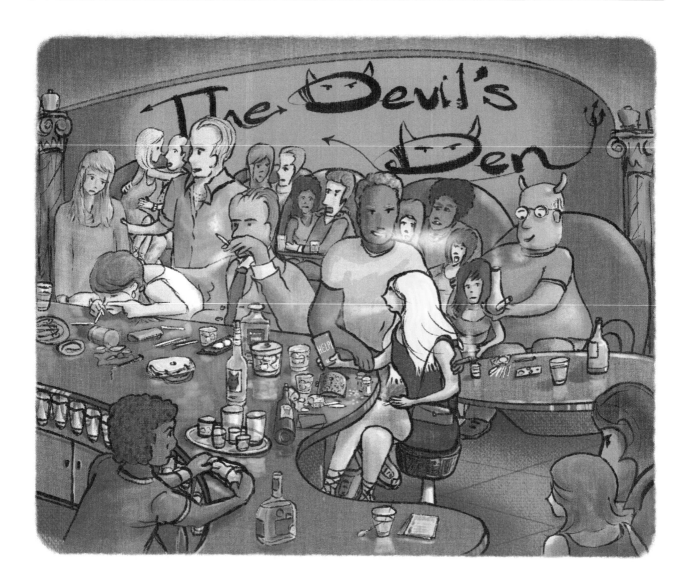

This is followed by three subsequent stages: (1) *drift*, where the person's promiscuity leads to the first prostitution job; (2) *transitional deviance*, where the person's role ambivalence turns into a normalization or rationalization of the act; and (3) *professionalization*, where the person surrenders to the deviant, sexual service lifestyle (Davis, 1993, pp. 1-14).

Despite the dangers and damages prostitution inflicts upon men, women, and children (Benoit et al., 2018), there is still some debate as to its merit. Arguing for its existence, some (incorrectly) claim that it is a *victimless crime*, that regulation of prostitution prevents sexually transmitted diseases, and pregnancies provide access to social programs that women otherwise would not have, and that it removes social taboo temptations, leading to a decrease in activity. Additionally, some extremists (including some feminists) assert that women should have the right to do whatever they want with their bodies, and prohibiting prostitution is both a violation of their civil rights and a stumbling block to women's financial autonomy and prosperity (Bell, 2009).

Countering this mindset (and with stronger evidence), the argument against prostitution asserts that it creates more victims, decreases public health, and increases crime rates, that it is a gateway to worse illegal activities, that it destroys families, and objectifies and enslaves women and children (Brock, 2009). In many ways, social progressives with pro-legalization of prostitution sentimentalities use the same rationale and fallacies as those who have pro-legalization of drugs sentimentalities.

Unfortunately, they seem unaware that increased usage of drugs and increased participation in prostitution has only created bigger and worse problems in society, globally (Adriaenssens & Hendrickx, 2012). Legalizing something harmful and exploitive will not suddenly make it healthy and equitable—logically, historically, and evidentially.

HOW BIG IS THE SOCIAL PROBLEM?

Just how many prostitutes exist worldwide is impossible to accurately ascertain (due to the illicit/criminal nature of the activity). A report from the *Fondation Scelles* (2012) indicated that at that time, there were 40–42 million prostitutes worldwide, with one million prostitutes potentially living and working in the United States. Another study from the 1990s suggested there were 25 prostitutes per 100,000 Americans, 70% of arrests for prostitution involved women, and that a typical prostitute services 690 customers in his or her lifetime (Monroe, 2005).

© Yupa Watchanakit/Shutterstock.com

Still, due to the murky nature of prostitution, valid and reliable data is nearly impossible to gather, but what is known is that the sex trade is a multibillion-dollar business (Kelly, 2019). Various community factors are involved, including the number of cheaper hotels/motels and sexually oriented businesses, and concentrated disadvantage, which is known as the *social ecology approach* (Mears et al., 2008). Succinctly, where you live either opens up or closes off social options.

A survey of national, federal, state, and international statistics on the sex trade provides a provocative yet disturbing view of just how deep and wide prostitution has become enmeshed within American and foreign cultures, sadly. Within the national milieu in the United States, data from the Central Intelligence Agency (the C.I.A.) suggests that nearly 50,000 people (both women and men) fall victim to sex *trafficking*, prostituting their bodies for personal financial gain or other benefits (Nichols, 2016). Additionally, the U.S. Department of Homeland Security and the U.S. Department of Justice opened nearly 3,000 sex trafficking cases that resulted in the arrest and prosecution of nearly 400 people convicted of prostitution and other related crimes (Rothman et al., 2017).

The incident rate for prostitution varies state-to-state depending much upon their population size, regional location, and collective cultural and legal standards. For instance, there were over 8,500 reported cases of human trafficking in the United States in 2017 and over 5,100 in 2018. The states with the highest number of human trafficking cases (from highest to lowest) were the District of Colombia (D.C.), Nevada, California, Ohio, Nebraska, and Oregon. The states with the least amount of cases (from lowest to highest) were New Hampshire, Idaho, Massachusetts, Maine, West Virginia, and Mississippi (Geoffrey G. Nathan Law Offices, 2018).

States like Virginia (26th highest) and Utah (25th highest) presently are ranked in the middle,

© Dmitrijs Kaminskis/Shutterstock.com

but all states had some incidence of prostitution within their cities. The numbers fluctuate and gravitate throughout the years, depending on population mobility, regional economic health, cultural events (such as the Super Bowl, etc.), and other political factors (Bluestone, 2015). For instance, in 2013, Norfolk, Virginia, had the highest number of prostitution cases per capita (Lopez et al., 2020), but by 2016, Richmond had the highest prostitution arrest rate per capita within that state. No cities in Utah even made the per capita list in 2016 (National Human Trafficking Hotline, 2017).

Internationally, the prostitution scene is even darker, more destructive, and more unknown. According to the World Population Review (2020), nearly four million adults and one million children were forced into prostitution and other sex trafficking activities. Most of these sex trafficking victims (70%) lived in Southeast Asia and the Pacific region. In Central Asia and Europe combined, prostitution and sex trafficking accounted for 14% of the practice; sex workers in North, Central, and South America accounted for just 4% (Kelly, 2019). Of course, such numbers are still speculative as most people involved in sex trafficking are unwilling or unable to honestly share their personal details without fear of legal or physical reprisal.

MAIN SOCIOLOGICAL APPROACHES

A *conflict theorist's perspective on prostitution* asserts that its presence is the result of economic inequalities in society (Benoit et al., 2018). People who enter into prostitution do so because they have been unfairly cut off or deprived of resources by others (especially men) using those resources to maintain their own bourgeoise positions of power through oppressing the lower working classes. The prostitute's surrender to the practice is driven by a patriarchal structure based on the objectivization of women and greed (Barkan, 2014a). Effectively, they have no choice because of the social structure suffocating them.

While there is merit to some of this argument, historically and evidentially, it does approach the topic in reductionist fashion with Marxist presuppositions that myopically focus more on the collective than the individual. Not all socioeconomic suffering is the result of systematic oppression and is more of a personal matter than a public one. People often make dumb and dangerous decisions that lead to bad straits.

To wit, not every prostitute has entered into that profession out of desperation or because they were forced; many women choose the lifestyle because they (incorrectly) think that it is the best that they can do considering their personal resources, that prostitution is a quick fix to get them out of financial trouble, or they enjoy the empowerment of being needed sexually. Finally, not all prostitutes are female, which pushes back against the patriarchy theory. As mentioned in Chapter 1, conflict theory is excellent at pointing out social inequalities, but its reductionist systematic approach is not always evidential or productive in solving social problems.

The *symbolic interactionist's perspective of prostitution* focuses on the social meaning of being a sex worker, which can go in different directions depending upon individuals' different prioritizations and judgments of the practice. Some people argue, "Sex work is essentially just work, and that it is not necessarily harmful to women" (Bell, 2009, p. 1). For feminists like this, moral condemnations regarding prostitution are based upon antiquated, irrelevant Puritanical ideals with which not everyone agrees.

While personal interactions and interpretations may seem to thwart the notion of an overarching evaluation of prostitution, experiential conclusions based on personal whims and perspectives are not as strong or persuasive as evidential conclusions based upon statistics and factual consequences. A person might say, "Well, I think prostitution is okay because the women don't get hurt, and it makes their lives better," but is that factually true and supported by the data? While some social matters are relative, many are not. Decades of studies indicate that prostitution is vastly more harmful to people than beneficial, regardless of one's opinion of it (Barkan, 2014b).

Finally, the *functionalist's perspective of prostitution* focuses on its effects upon the social "fabric" of communities "knit" together. Utilizing some questionable polemics, some say that it helps society by creating a source of income for the prostitutes, provides sexual pleasure for those feeling deprived, and helps keep the divorce rate down (Davis, 1937). Others consider it less of a crime or deviance and more of a social-sexual preference (Garsd, 2019).

Historically, though, many people have considered prostitution to be a vile and socially destructive profession. Only in postmodernity, with its hyper-focus on radical individualism and unfettered social choices (Knox, 2016), has prostitution been considered a socially acceptable practice (Bell, 2009). The evidential reality is that prostitution hurts the sex worker, his or her customer, his or her family, his or her neighbor, and the whole of society. It is not a victimless crime; rather, it turns everyone into a victim.

WHAT CAN BE DONE?

Rescue and escape are what prostitutes need most of all (Ross, 2014), and there are many different sources to help them find their sexual freedom once again. Their most immediate needs can be met by providing safe access to rescue homes and shelters. In these urban oases, the prostitutes can glean wisdom, insight, and alternative vocational training from skilled counselors to help them find other lines of work (Hunter & Humphries, 2011). They can also learn about options available to economically hurting families (such as social welfare programs) that can help them avoid bad choices made out of desperation (Wilson & Nochajski, 2018).

Additionally, more legal acts and measures can be developed and implemented at the federal, state, and local levels to protect these sex workers from physical and psychological harm from those who would coldly exploit them (Garsd, 2019). Along these same lines, some people have recommended providing licensing and regulation of the practice (Bell, 2009), which ostensibly would protect women from abuse, sexually transmitted diseases, and unwanted pregnancies; however, several recent studies suggest that legalizing prostitution only leads to more prostitution and greater health dangers for the prostitutes (Adriaenssens & Hendrickx, 2012).

Finally, greater efforts need to be made to dispel the myths and highlight the dangers of prostitution in the education of young people (grades 6-12), globally. Contrary to the sexy, exciting, empowering image that Hollywood and other media outlets often portray it, prostitution is a disgusting, disastrous, and disabling practice for all its workers. Careful socialization and resocialization can help people thinking about becoming prostitutes to see the darkness of the practice, to dismiss false and corrupt justifications, and to move toward safer, more beneficial opportunities—something everyone deserves in life.

DEALING WITH MATTERS OF THE DARK

While most consider the practice revolting, it is important to remember that all prostitutes are human beings, coming from various social contexts, and with limited personal resources leading up to their social deviance (and criminal activity). As such, they deserve to be treated with respect and dignity—especially since many/most of them are victims of circumstances or bad socialization. This is nothing new; a thorough examination of biblical texts (both the Old and New Testaments) displays a particular response from God when it comes to sexual social infractions.

Certainly, there are severe consequences and punishments set aside for those who wantonly promote and practice solicitation. Yet, what God desires most is a repentant heart, which He is happy to see and rewards with forgiveness and a second chance (again and again and again). These are the three 'Rs' that God offers to all people—Repentance, Redemption, and Renewal—whether His followers or pagans stumbling in the darkness.

Take, for instance, the story of a prostitute who turns from her life of crime to assist in the righteous plans of God's agents. In Joshua 2, two Israelites enter the house of a Jericho prostitute named *Rahab* and stay some time there reconnoitering the region. Under orders from Joshua, these men are to spy upon the Promised Land (and its inhabitants) and return to camp with a report regarding their findings and conquest prospects.

Unfortunately, the king of Jericho finds out about the scouts and demands that Rahab send them out. After hiding the men, she replies to the king, "Yes, the men came to me, but I did not know where they had come from. At dusk, when it was time to close the city gate, they left. I don't know which way they went. Go after them quickly. You may catch up with them." (vs. 2:4-5).

Once the king's messengers had left, she went up to the roof where the Israelites were hiding. Before the men climbed down a rope from a high window to escape their would-be captors, Rahab pleads with them to spare the lives of her family members, which they agree. They do, however, stipulate one item,

> This oath you made us swear will not be binding on us unless, when we enter the land, you have tied this scarlet cord in the window through which you let us down, and unless you have brought your father and mother, your brothers and all your family into your house. If any of them go outside your house into the street, their blood will be on their own

heads; we will not be responsible. As for those who are in the house with you, their blood will be on our head if a hand is laid on them.

When the Israelites return to conquer the land, Rahab complies with their instructions, tying the red cord in her window. Wood states (1986), "All the people of the city were killed, with the exception of Rahab and her family, whose lives were spared in keeping with the spies' promise, and the city was leveled by fire."

The heroine of this story is Rahab—an Amorite prostitute who eventually marries Salmon, one of the spies that she sheltered. From that marriage, Rahab then becomes the mother of Boaz, who marries Ruth, the ancestor of Jesus of Nazareth. Like Puah, Rahab's plotting became quintessential to the Jewish and Christian narratives. Without Rahab, there would have been no Boaz; without Boaz, there would have been no Obed; without Obed, there would have been no David. The overlapping threads in the fabric of God's story is mind-blowing sometimes.

In some Rabbinic writings, Rahab is considered one of the most beautiful women, and it is suggested by some scholars that she converted to Judaism. The author of the Epistle to the Hebrews places her in the list of the most faithful people in Israel's history, based on her faith and obedience to God, "By faith the prostitute Rahab, because she welcomed the spies, was not killed with those who were disobedient" (Hebrews 11:31, New International Version).

An important lesson from Rahab is that God loves, accepts, and forgives sinners out of His glorious nature—not just based on their family pedigree or social status. In fact, the biblical message is that all people can become noble children of the divine Father when they confess and repent of their ways (and not even perfectly). This message of hope is perhaps what prostitutes (and alcoholics and drug addicts and thieves) need to hear most of all. What they have done may have been tragic, but they are not rubbish to be discarded. Being part of God's creation, they are a treasure to the Lord, with the potential of a great destiny and beneficial social impact from their changed hearts and a renewed sense of mission on earth.

INSIGHTS FROM THE EXPERTS

"The Greatest Threat to Children and Youth"

My husband, Sheriff Brown, is known nationally and internationally for the work he has done (and is doing) to protect children from *online sexual predators*. His *Internet Crimes Against Children Task Force* (ICAC) received one of the first 10 grants from the Department of Justice in 1998. They have continued to receive this grant every year since and maintain a 100% conviction rate for the predators they arrest. Sheriff Brown founded the Safe Surfin' Foundation, a 501(c)(3) organization in 2000, to educate parents, children, and others on the dangers of the internet—especially in the social media platforms.

While Associate Professor of Psychology at Liberty University, I have also served on the Board of Directors of the *Safe Surfin' Foundation* since it was established. I have worked arduously to educate children and traveled extensively with my husband in support of these efforts. Last year, I was honored to be recognized for these efforts and I was appointed as Special Advisor to *the MOSAIC Foundation*.

The GSN is a registered charity in the United Kingdom and a growing private network of more than 900 leaders across Faith, Government, Business, Media, NGSs, and Academia. The GSN was founded by Monsignor Marcelo Sanchez, Chancellor of the Pontifical Academies of Sciences and Social Sciences, Rt. Rev. Bishop Alastair Redfern, Bishop of Derby, the Church of England, and Raza Jarar, Chairman Palazzo Versace, Dubai. The GSN has held conferences at the Vatican, the United Kingdom, United Nations in New York, and the Dubai Chamber of Commerce & Industry and Expo 2020 headquarters in Dubai. The GSN is committed to ending modern-day slavery and human trafficking.

After hearing of the work done by the *Safe Surfin' Foundation* and the *CyberSWAT* program, we were invited to speak at the Global Sustainability Network (GSN) Conference at the Vatican in April 2019. Sheriff Brown reported that one of the greatest threats to children and youth worldwide is carried in the palm of their hand—the ubiquitous cell phone—and the predators/human traffickers love it! They use social media to target, to manipulate, to lure, and trap their victims. Today, more than 95% of all young Americans between 12 and 17 years old are online. Some three in four teens access the internet on cell phones, tablets, and other mobile devices, rather than the home desktop computer of just a few years ago. Truly, young people today are carrying the internet around with them!

More than a third of teens are "friends" on social media with people that they have not met in person. Predators seek youths vulnerable to seduction, including those with histories of sexual or physical abuse, emotional instability and vulnerability, those who post sexually provocative photos/videos online, and those who talk about sex with unknown people online. Of online sex offenders, 65% used the victim's social networking site to gain home, school, and personal information.

Since 1998, the *Safe Surfin' Foundation* has been committed to tackling the problem head-on with the knowledge that an informed internet user is a safer one—helping to stop would-be predators right at their intended victims. They have employed a number of methods to reach young people—comic books, a day at the park, a celebrity speaking to people who did an excellent job—and have had some success. However, educating youth by conventional/traditional methods just did not appear to be working. Basically, they are not listening to adults.

The CyberSWAT program is truly a revolutionary paradigm shift. It eliminates traditional barriers in reaching young people, because the messengers are young people themselves. This peer-to-peer communication is a powerful and lasting means of reaching the young user of technology and stopping the predator right at the intended victim. It is a revolutionary, landmark, peer-to-peer educational breakthrough based on constructs of social cognitive theory.

Bandura's "Social Learning" was based on the premises of observational learning and imitation, then a cognitive piece was added—and it became known as *Social Cognitive Theory*. Children not only need to observe behavior, they need to pay attention to it, think about it, and be able to reproduce it. Researchers have found that ". . . similarity in age to the observed person (model) predicts the degree to which the behavior is integrated into a person's own actions" (Bandura, 1977; Schunk, 1987; Zmj & Seehagen, 2013, as cited in Burritica et al., 2013). This premise is part of the foundation of the CyberSWAT program.

As high school students learn principles of online safety, they take their message to middle- and elementary-school students. The CyberSWAT has made being safe and responsible online cool. A CyberSWAT Team Member becomes equipped—empowered—with a level of awareness that may possibly prevent the next tragedy from occurring. With technology, Safety and Responsibility go hand-in-hand. *S.W.A.T.—Safety While Accessing Technology.*

The CyberSWAT program was first tested and demonstrated to be effective in 2016–2017 at a high school in central Virginia, facilitated by a School Resource Officer. The team members at our first target school were enthusiastic from the beginning and have done an excellent job, and what they are doing is very powerful. One of their first endeavors was a presentation on the dangers of sexting for the entire student body. The team, school administrators, and teachers took note that every student in the auditorium was riveted to the message these young people were delivering. Much more so than if that message had been coming from adults.

These team members understand what it means to be a young person in today's world. They understand the culture and they understand the technology—better than parents and teachers do. Other young people listen to them and want to emulate them.

A related concept in Social Cognitive theory is self-efficacy–"I can." If a young person feels that with effort that they can accomplish a goal, they feel good about themselves, and their self-esteem increases. The team members feel very good about what they are doing, they are making a difference, and they know it. They are part of the solution, not part of the problem. In modeling this behavior, other young people watch them and think, "I can do that, too. I can be safe online, and I can teach others to be safe as well. I watched the 'cool kids' tell me how to be safe online. I can be cool, too." We want to replicate that confidence in other schools.

Eight target schools throughout the United States have been identified for the next step. The plan is to roll out this program in those schools in the Fall of 2019. I will be visiting the schools as part of research that I am conducting.

The research question(s) guiding this study will be: Do young people learn internet safety more readily from a similar-aged peer than from an adult? Does the data support the concepts of Bandura's Social Cognitive Theory? It is anticipated that data obtained from this study will improve the effectiveness of education in online safety and responsibility, enhance the CyberSWAT curriculum, and provide empirical evidence that the application of Social Cognitive Theory to the CyberSWAT program is effective.

The presentation was well received by the 100+ participants. Many people asked questions afterward and commented on the need for this program to be instituted in as many schools as possible to get this important message out to children around the world. As a result of our presentation at the Vatican, we were invited to speak at the GSN Conference at Columbia University and in Dubai, United Arab Emirates, in January 2020 and we will be going back to the Vatican in the future.

Dr. Janet Brown
Professor of Psychology
Liberty University

Contributed by Janet Brown. © Kendall Hunt Publishing Company

CASE STUDY #4

The border city of Brownsville, Texas, with its nearly 200,000 people and Gulf Coast beaches, is a fantastic place to grow up. At least, that is what 16-year-old high school sophomore Stacy thought. Growing up near the border, the opportunity for a little fun on the other side enticed more partiers in her high school to cross over and hit up the Mexican resorts. After one wild night in particular, Stacy awoke hungover in another student's room. Rumors quickly spread around the school. At first, Stacy hated the rumors, but then quickly realized that boys began to treat her, differently. Suddenly, Stacy had lots of guy friends who were willing to give her anything she wanted. While many in her friend groups disliked this new behavior, Stacy continued to attend parties and make more guy "friends."

Five years later, when home on break from college, a friend ran into Stacy. Even though both were the same age, Stacy looked weathered and sickly. She mentioned that her health hadn't been the best, and she needed insurance to cover her medical costs. The friend noticed that her face was covered in heavy makeup, obviously hiding bruising and sores. After high school, Stacy decided to stick around for the money and forgo higher education. She explained that one of her guy "friends" offered her a "job" in the film industry. It was good money, and she was hoping it would lead to brighter things.

DISCUSSION QUESTIONS

1. Based on the readings, how would a sociologist diagnose this situation?

2. What specific sociological factors are involved?

3. What might the future hold for Stacy?

Check out the Chapter 4 video at this link:

https://www.khpcontent.com/

VOCABULARY

Addiction
CyberSWAT
Delinquency
Drift
Gigolos
Hook
Johns
Oldest Profession
Online Sexual Predators

Pimps
Professionalization
Prostitution
Prostitution, Conflict
    Perspective of
Prostitution, Functionalist
    Perspective of
Prostitution, Symbolic
    Interactionist Perspective of

Rahab
Social Cognitive Theory
Social Ecology
Trafficking
Transitional Deviance
Truancy
Victimless Crime

References

Adriaenssens, S., & Hendrickx, J. (2012). Sex, price and preferences: Accounting for unsafe sexual practices in prostitution markets. *Sociology of Health & Illness, 34*(5), 665–680. doi:10.1111/j.1467-9566.2011.01400.x

Bandura, A. (1977). Self-efficacy: Toward a unifying theory of behavioral change. *The Psychological Review, 84*(2), 191–215.

Barkan, S. (2014a). *A primer on social problems. Lardbucket.org.* https://2012books.lardbucket.org/books/a-primer-on-social-problems/s12-04-prostitution.html

Barkan, S. (2014b). *Sociology: Understanding and changing the social world.* University of Minnesota.

Bell, K. J. (2009). A feminist's argument on how sex work can benefit women. *Inquiries Journal/ Student Pulse, 1*(11), 1–2. www.inquiriesjournal.com/a?id=28

Benoit, C., Smith, M., Jansson, M., Healey, P., & Magnuson, D. (2018). The prostitution problem: Claims, evidence, and policy outcomes. *Springer Link, 48,* 1905–1923.

Bluestone, D. (2015). Charlottesville's landscape of prostitution, 1880–1950. *Buildings & Landscapes: Journal of the Vernacular Architecture Forum, 22*(2), 36–61. doi:10.5749/buildland.22.2.0036

Brock, D. R. (2009). *Making work, making trouble: Prostitution as a social problem.* University of Toronto Press.

Buritica, J., Eppinger, B., Schuck, N., Heekeren, H., & Li, Sue-Chen (2016). Electrophysiological correlates of observational learning in Children. *Developmental Science, 19*(5), 699–709.

Davis, K. (1937). The sociology of prostitution. *American Sociological Review, 2*(5), 744–755.

Davis, N. (1993). *Prostitution: An international handbook on trends, problems, and policies.* London: Greenwood.

Flowers, R. B. (1998). *The prostitution of women and girls*. McFarland and Company.

Fondation Scelles. (2012). *Sexual exploitation, prostitution and organized crime*. Economica.

Garsd, J. (2019). Should sex work be decriminalized? Some activists say it's time. NPR.org. https://www.npr.org/2019/03/22/705354179/should-sex-work-be-decriminalized-some-activists-say-its-time

Geoffrey G. Nathan Law Offices. (2018). Top cities in America with the most cases of human trafficking. https://www.geoffreygnathanlaw.com/topics/most-cases-of-human-trafficking-in-america/

Hughes, D. M. (2004). *Prostitution: Causes and solutions*. Santiago de Compostela: Conference: Female Prostitution: Proposals and Interventions.

Hunter, R. L., & Humphries, M. (2011). Social enterprise: The rescue and rehabilitation of prostitutes—embryonic or false emancipation. *Third Sector Review, 17*(2), 87–106.

Kelly, C. (2019). 13 sex trafficking statistics that explain the enormity of the global sex trade. *USAToday.com*. https://www.usatoday.com/story/news/investigations/2019/07/29/12-trafficking-statistics-enormity-global-sex-trade/1755192001/

Knox, J. (2016). *Sacro-Egoism: The rise of religious individualism in the West*. Wipf & Stock.

Lee-Gonyea, J., Castle, T., & Gonyea, N. (2009). Laid to order: Male escorts advertising on the Internet. *Deviant Behavior, 30*, 321–348.

Lehmiller, J. (2018). Nearly one in five sex workers are men. *Vice*. https://www.vice.com/en_us/article/evm5vw/nearly-one-in-five-sex-workers-are-men

Lopez, J. J., Almquist, D., & Thomas, P. (2020). The geography of prostitution arrests in Virginia, USA, 2002–2013. *Crime, Law and Social Change, 73*(2), 133–157. doi:10.1007/s10611-019-09854-5

Luckenbill, D. F. (1986). Deviant career mobility: The case of male prostitutes. *Social Problems, 33*(4), 283–296.

Matthews, R. (2005). Policing prostitution: Ten years on. *The British Journal of Criminology, 45*(6), 877–895. doi:10.1093/bjc/azi046

Mears, D. P., Wang, X., Hay, C., & Bales, W. D. (2008). Social ecology and recidivism: Implications for prisoner reentry. *Criminology, 46*, 301–340.

Monroe, J. (2005). Women in street prostitution: The result of poverty and the brunt of inequity. *Journal of Poverty, 9*(3), 69–88. https://doi.org/10.1300/J134v09n03_04

National Human Trafficking Hotline. (2017). Ranking of the 100 most populous U.S. cities: 12/7/2007–12/31/2016. https://humantraffickinghotline.org/sites/default/files/100%20Most%20Populous%20Cities%20Report.pdf

Nichols, A. J. (2016). *Sex trafficking in the United States: Theory, research, policy, and practice*. Columbia University Press.

Peterson, S., Nachtman, C., & Roman, J. (2015). What are the risk factors for becoming a prostituted teen? *Purdue University*. https://www.purdue.edu/hhs/hdfs/fii/wp-content/uploads/2015/06/s_mifis06c06.pdf

Priceconomics Data Studio. (2019). The places in America with the most cases of human trafficking. https://priceconomics.com/the-places-in-america-with-the-most-cases-of-human/

Rothman, E. F., Stoklosa, H., Baldwin, S. B., Chisolm-Straker, M., Kato Price, R., & Atkinson, H. G., on Behalf of HEAL Trafficking. (2017). Public health research priorities to address U.S. human trafficking. *American Journal of Public Health, 107*(7), 1045–1047.

Ross, M. (2014). A diamond in the rough: The transnational duty to prevent human trafficking in the protocol. *Duke Journal of Gender, Law & Policy, 21*, 325–368.

Schunk, D. H. (1987). Peer models and children's behavioral change. *Review of Educational Research, 57*(2), 149–174.

Scott, G. R. (2014). *History prostitution: From antiquity to the present day (Kegan Paul library of sexual life)* (1st ed.). Routledge.

Wilson, B., & Nochajski, T. (2018). On the continuum of exit: Understanding the stages of change among women in commercial sexual exploitation. *Gender Issues, 35*, 98–112.

World Population Review. (2020). Countries where prostitution is legal 2020. https://worldpopulationreview.com/countries/countries-where-prostitution-is-legal/

Wood, L. (1986). *A survey of Israel's history.* Zondervan.

Zmj, N., & Seehagen, S. (2013). The role of a model's age for young children's imitation: A research review. *Infant and Child Development, 22*(6), 622–641.

Ch 5 Drugs and Alcohol

By definition, *drug and alcohol abuse* concerns the ingestion or injection of any substance that alters bodily function in some way, which when habitualized, hurts the individual, his or her family, or general society in a real and prolonged destructive way. For both, the abuse begins with an irrational, illogical, or unrealistic presupposition about the immediate and long-term consequences of alcohol or drug usage. The abuse ends with a psychological and/or physiological need for the drug to maintain a sense of well-being or an avoidance of withdrawal symptoms.

Regarding drug abuse, a myriad of drugs is available within the United States including marijuana, benzodiazepines, cocaine, and heroin. People also abuse prescription medicines (the average family has around 30 different drugs in their medicine cabinet or drawer). According to the latest statistics from the 2016 illegal drug report from the Centers for Disease Control and Prevention (CDC), nearly 11% of Americans over the age of 12 have used illicit drugs in the past month and 2.3% have taken nonprescribed psychotherapeutic or physio-corrective drugs in the past month.

According to the CDC (1999), some 104,000 people began using *heroin* for the first time—one of the most abused and rapidly active opiates; of those, 87,000 were 12–25 years old. Since then, there have been at least 80,000 new addicts every year, and 20% of all alcohol and drug-related suicides involved heroin dealers. From 1999 to 2017, in three waves (1990s, 2010, 2013), some 400,000 people have died from *opioid overdoses*. Not surprisingly, most doctors, researchers, and sociologists consider heroin to be one of the greatest evils in American history.

Alcohol is often played off as an innocuous drink, but although its immediate effects appear unremarkable compared to heroin or cocaine, its long-term effects can be equally devastating. According to the National Institute on Alcohol Abuse and Alcoholism (2017), over 15 million Americans had an alcohol drinking problem in 2015; and some 19% of kids ages 12–20 have had an alcoholic beverage in the past month (National Survey on Drug Use and Health, 2018). The average individual American consumes 2.5 gallons of wine, 32 gallons of beer, and 1.8 gallons of liquor per year. Alcohol acts as a depressant, suppressing the central nervous system, and, with habitual or unmoderated use, can damage brain and other vital organ functions.

Long-term drinking patterns include *social drinkers*, who imbibe occasionally at social events; *heavy drinkers*, who frequently imbibe and are often intoxicated; acute drinkers, who plan activities around their drinking and have trouble controlling their personal alcohol consumption; and *chronic drinkers*, who compulsively, secretively, and wantonly imbibe, leading to social dysfunction and physical impairment (McCune et al., 2015).

For both drug and alcohol abusers, numerous *treatment plans and programs* are available, including self-help groups, in-patient/out-patient programs, cognitive behavioral programs, group–family counseling, and addiction medication regiments. These plans and programs have experienced mixed results with very few people stopping their addictions on their own, a larger percentage with minimal help, but for the worst cases of drug or alcohol abuse, sustained and intense addiction therapy is required for any hope of rescue to be achieved (Murphy, 2015).

© Mars Brashok/Shutterstock.com

MAIN SOCIOLOGICAL APPROACHES

Concerning drugs and alcohol, the symbolic interactionist would consider them to be more of a symbol or a personal perspective influenced by various social forces than an objective reality. For instance, alcohol and drugs could be a symbol of social change or social freedom for an adolescent. Alternatively, alcohol and drugs could be a symbol of immorality or low cultural value for an elderly person. In other words, social climate and social interactions change the way that people perceive things.

Interestingly, in American society, alcohol has been a staple for centuries. Watching commercials (from a variety of alcohol vendors) suggests that after a hard day's work (or a hard week's work) people deserve a good stiff drink or a glass of beer to unwind and relax. Thus, it is associated with the "American way" (Schmidt, 2020). Unfortunately, while some people can imbibe with little social damage incurring, marijuana, excessive drinking, and other *illicit drugs* are clearly associated with vocational unreliability, questionable character judgments, irrationality, lack of education, infidelity, and risky life choices (Thomas, 2020).

For the symbolic interactionist, much of whether a drug should be used or not depends upon whom is the one dispensing or using it. The doctor clearly prescribes drugs in his day-to-day job as does a pharmacist or a pharmacologist; however, a *drug dealer* sells his illicit product(s) for profit, exploiting people's weaknesses. Additionally, a teenage college student might use it to have a good time (or for psychological escapism) or a grandma might use it to treat eye pain caused by her glaucoma (or for psychological escapism).

The problem is that such a sweeping, relativist approach toward the topic ignores the quintessential "middle truth" that exists, historically and evidentially. Drug and alcohol use matters because of the ways that they negatively or positively impact the family unit, community health and cohesion, and the function of everyday living for an individual. Although drinking and drug use (especially concerning marijuana, recently) at family and friends' get-togethers might be an ever-increasing occurrence, levels of drinking and drug use (as mentioned earlier) can dramatically rise to destructive heights, hurting both the alcoholic and those around him or her. Thereafter, alcohol and drug use become dysfunctional, debilitating factors, which left alone cause great personal and public harm (Stebbins, 2019).

In postmodernity, many people have come to equate alcohol and other illicit substances with the same or less social negative consequences. However, studies have shown that drugs like marijuana—and, of course, other harder drugs—are not physically or mentally healthy for adolescents, college kids, and adults to partake of, regularly (Wolff et al., 2014). They tend to impair the lifestyle conditions for the drug user, they deplete financial resources, and they are costly when it comes to the users' psychological and spiritual functionality.

Interestingly (and mistakenly), governmental groups set up to protect society from the horrible consequences of drug abuse (such as the drug enforcement agency [DEA]) are vilified and popularly seen as the "bad guys," who stop people from just having fun (Lo, 2003). In many ways, this echoes the social antinomianism or lawlessness of postmodernity and its worship of radical individualism and wide-open social avenues (Knox, 2016).

Speaking of which, a conflict theorist would consider drug use to be a two-sided affair, much as pornography is for many people. Conflict theorists assert that everyone in society should have open access to resources as drugs are just another resource for many people. Therefore, drug laws are frequently and politically used to oppress people's rights and to remove opportunities for happiness, relaxation, and escapism (Aseltine et al., 2000). Also, *drug prices* can be used and abused by pharmaceutical companies to garner profit through the exploitation of people's weaknesses. In a grander vision, economically, drug use and dependence can also be cultivated to control or to pacify certain social classes in a country (Mosher & Scott, 2014).

Besides illicit drugs such as marijuana, cocaine, heroin, opioids, and so on, other drug abuse occurs in "normal" society that is legitimate but no less dangerous (Goode, 2012). These include medicines for a variety of ailments: from nervousness to pain to neurological diseases and so on. This medicalization of human social problems can tread dangerously close to being more

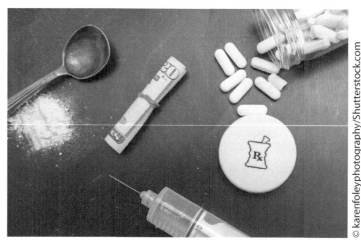

promotional than rehabilitational—especially so when drug companies and government officials are financial partners (whether legally or improperly).

Another social problem attached to medical drugs is that prescriptions for children are often given ostensibly as a medical solution for their "psychological problems," but sometimes they are more about a social engineering agenda than an authentic medical malady (e.g., tranquilizing boys for being too boisterous and aggressive) (D'Agostino, 2014). The misuse of drugs affects social life in many areas including the psychological state of people, their socioeconomic opportunities, and their social conditions.

Some people suggest that by *decriminalizing drug* use, the black markets for drugs will be eliminated. The current statistics show that the opposite effect occurs when societies follow that progressive mindset (Olinger, 2019). Ultimately, in pursuit of a progressive agenda pushed by radical individualism and toward open social avenues, some people would rather decriminalize drugs rather than rehabilitate people. Part of this is based on postmodernity's *culture of cynicism* and impatience, but another part is based on a self-serving mindset that considers narcissism to be a virtue and legal codes for social behavior to be despotic (Laursen, 2009).

Speaking of which, the *Tough Love Perspective* (Bhatt & Ogaki, 2012) asserts that strict parameters need to be set in personal and public spheres, and that appropriate action needs to be taken when people violate drug and alcohol laws. The *War on Drugs* (Mallea, 2014) definitely sees much social resistance and challenges in postmodernity, but too much "magical thinking" about the inherent dangers of drugs cannot change the necessity of their control and suppression. Most people with substance abuse issues started their experimentations at a very young age (Tolan et al., 2007). Therefore, beginning to educate children about the dangers of drug and alcohol use (and the causes of drug use) is beneficial and preventative for future addiction problems.

Unfortunately, the socialization of the pro-drug mentality owes much to the romantic, sexy, thrilling shows seen on media and in movies and television that provide viewers with examples of "cool" people using drugs and alcohol (Brumm, 2005). It may be unfashionable, but more censorship needs to be enacted to protect children and teens from these on-screen toxic presentations. Additionally, public responsibility and public programs centered on rehabilitation and treatment can be utilized in many different intersections of society, currently—especially considering the technological advances and benefits of postmodernity. Lastly, drug and alcohol abusers need to know about the numerous alternative social avenues (especially the religious ones) for finding personal fulfillment and dealing with their social fears and anxiety.

DEALING WITH MATTERS OF THE DARK

Biblically, *mind-altering substances* have been discussed and detailed from the very beginning of the scriptures. These verses are fairly straightforward—containing exhortations, prescriptions, and proscriptions. Even more, they provide anecdotes of alcoholism (and other addictions) leading to personal and social strife.

Sometimes, the Bible presents alcohol use in a morally proper and approved context: "He causes the grass to grow for the cattle, and vegetation for the labor of man, So that he may bring forth food from the earth. And wine which makes man's heart glad, oil to make his face shine, and the bread that sustains his heart" (Psalms 104:14–15); "Go then, eat your bread in happiness and drink your wine with a cheerful heart; for God has already approved your works" (Ecclesiastes 9:7, New International Version); and "Stop drinking only water and use a little wine because of your stomach and your frequent ailments" (1 Timothy 5:23, New International Version). Note that in each of these passages a positive outcome for the adult is associated with the imbibing (drinking), and that no sinful state results from it. The Bible never says, "Go and get wasted, dude! It doesn't really matter"—quite the opposite, actually.

Sometimes, the Bible directly addresses substance abuse: "Wine is a mocker and beer a brawler; whoever is led astray by them is not wise" (Proverbs 20:1, New International Version); "Do not get drunk on wine, which leads to debauchery. Instead, be filled with the Spirit" (Ephesians 5:18, New International Version); and "Envy, drunkenness, orgies, and things like these. I warn you, as I warned you before, that those who do such things will not inherit the kingdom of God" (Galatians 5:21, New International Version). Note that in passages such as these, a negative, sinful consequence occurs after drinking too much, leading to a worse social and spiritual state for him or her imbibing.

Sometimes, the Bible provides indirect admonitions regarding mind-altering substances: "But the fruit of the Spirit is love, joy, peace, patience, kindness, goodness, faithfulness, gentleness, self-control; against such things there is no law" (Galatians 5:22–23, New International Version); "Training us to renounce ungodliness and worldly passions, and to live self-controlled, upright, and godly lives in the present age" (Titus 2:12, New International Version); "Keep your conduct among the Gentiles honorable, so that when they speak against you as evildoers, they may see your good deeds and glorify God on the day of visitation" (1 Peter 2:12, New International Version); and "Be sober-minded; be watchful. Your adversary the devil prowls around like a roaring lion, seeking someone to devour" (1 Peter 5:8, New International Version). This is especially important for those who think

© LightField Studios/Shutterstock.com

that just because it does not say, "Weed" or "Smack" or "Stoned," God is fine with people ingesting, smoking, drinking, or injecting illegal substances, leading to them getting baked, faded, high, wasted, and so on.

Of course, the Bible also provides several historical examples and descriptions of people in the Bible who went too far in their drunken celebrations and lamentations. Two important ones, in particular, show the dangers of drinking too much and losing one's self-control (and consciousness). Both stories can be found in Genesis, the first book in the Old Testament.

After the Flood (Genesis 9:20–27, New International Version), Noah wasted little time getting back to old business and planted a vineyard and began farming once again. Perhaps very needy for some relaxation, Noah harvested the grapes and drank from the fruits of his labor, to the point where he became drunk. Soon thereafter, Noah decided to take off all his clothing (maybe to go back to the pre-fallen days of Adam and Eve) and passed out on the ground.

Noah's son, Ham, found his naked, drunk, unconscious father, and immediately went and got his brothers to show them his inebriated condition. Shem and Japheth, however, refused to look at their father's nakedness, and back up to him, eyes averted, to cover him up. When Noah awoke (and found out what had transpired), he cursed Ham's son (Noah's grandson), although the text does not say for what, explicitly (or why Ham was not the one being cursed).

Perhaps Noah thought Ham had disrespected his privacy, maybe Noah was mad that Ham had resumed the nakedness shame of Adam and Eve, or possibly Noah was angry over Ham's mocking response to his drunken nudity. Why did not Ham just cover up naked Noah? That is likely the question although the final answer is unknown. This is just another example of the Old Testament being descriptive and not overtly prescriptive—that is, the text tells you what happened, letting readers figure out what to do in a similar situation.

The second story is far more deviant and disturbing. The Genesis story turns dark and foreboding in Genesis 18. Lot's home, Sodom and Gomorrah, traditionally located east of Jerusalem and near the Dead Sea, in the Valley of Siddim, had become so vile and wicked that God was ready to pass judgment upon them, because "The outcry against Sodom and Gomorrah is so great and their sin so grievous" (v. 18:20).

Despite Abraham's bartering for leniency for the city of Sodom—"if only ten [righteous men] can be found there" (v. 18:32), God decides to carry out his punishment of them, but sends two angels to rescue Lot and his family. After being threatened with rape, the two angelic figures instruct Lot to flee from Sodom with his family and friends; however, his daughters' husbands ridiculed and mocked Lot, staying behind. The angels eventually grab him, his wife, and his daughters by the hands and lead them out of the city, which is about to be destroyed.

At that point, one of God's men commands, "Flee for your lives! Don't look back, and don't stop anywhere in the plain! Flee to the mountains or you will be swept away!" (v. 19:17). Instead of the mountains, they make it to a small town called Zoar, one of the five "cities of the plain" (vv. 14:2–8), but instead of submitting to the angelic instructions, Lot's wife looks back, presumably out of curiosity, and "became a pillar of salt" (v. 19:26).

Understandably, the whole affair has become a period of desperation and hopelessness for Lot and his daughters, who eventually flee to the mountains and hide inside a cave there. Perhaps thinking that the world was ending, perhaps thinking that it was their last chance to become pregnant, perhaps even just wanting to punish their father for offering them up as rape victims, "They got their father to drink wine, and the older daughter went in and slept with him" (v. 19:34). Later, the younger daughter followed suit, somewhat demonstrating the wicked and vile culture that they had escaped from before its destruction. Both young women become pregnant by their clandestine act of incest with their father (he was too drunk to know what had happened, clearly). Their children became the ancestors of the Moabites and Ammonites, who thereafter would carry the shameful reputation and stigma of incest—all because their father drank too much and lost consciousness.

Tales such as these help readers to understand the deeper ways of God. They demonstrate that faith makes people productive, but disbelief makes people paralyzed or perverted. Running from one's fears turns enemies into giants, but facing one's fears, with God at your back, makes them of little consequence (consider early church martyrs' reactions to emperors).

Drugs and alcohol are predominantly used as tools for mental and emotional escape by many who live outside of God. They do not know Him, but they need Him, desperately. In their drugs and alcoholism, they can only hide, embracing a depressing and destructive cycle of distrust, desperation, abandonment, dependence, weakness, fear, and infection that only leads to more sorrow.

Alternatively, people can (and do) live day-to-day in God's guidance and His love—trusting, surrendering, hoping, depending, strengthened, emboldened, and inspired to share the keys of their own joy, which comes from their relationship with God, with others in the dark. Like King David, they can honestly and gratefully say, "Truly, my soul finds rest in God; my salvation comes from him. Truly, he is my rock and my salvation; he is my fortress, I will never be shaken . . . Yes, my soul, find rest in God; my hope comes from him" (Psalm 62: 1–2, 5, New International Version).

INSIGHTS FROM THE EXPERTS

"Probable Effects of Cannabis upon Life Course and Quality"

As one would expect, the legalization and growing cultural acceptance of marijuana has led to many sociological studies on the effects of marijuana and has become a focal topic within the United States. To date, 33 states in the U.S. and the District of Columbia have passed *legislation* to approve some form of marijuana use (Governing, 2018). This includes *recreational* use, medical use, legalization of forms other than smoking, circumstantial use, or no legalization of marijuana at all. The National Institute on Drug Abuse (2018) has noted that within the U.S., marijuana consumption is more widely used by men than women and is used at a younger age than other drugs. Youth's perceptions of the risks associated with marijuana use have increasingly declined throughout the past decade—possibly due to the public debates on use and legalization for both recreational and medical use.

Positive Attitudes toward Cannabis

Prescriptions of tetrahydrocannabinol have been available for over a decade in the United States, and several studies have suggested positive therapeutic effects that cannabis use can have in advanced stages of illnesses such as cancer or AIDS (World Health Organization [WHO], 2018). The use of *medical marijuana* can be traced back to ancient and medieval texts (Conrad, 1997). Traditionally, cannabis was utilized to relieve childbirth pain, convulsions, fevers, insomnia, stimulate appetite, nervousness, and so on (Conrad, 1997).

Smoking cannabis can produce relaxation, decreased anxiety, sleepiness, increased sensory perceptions, and reduces inhibitions (Small, 2017). Additionally, cannabis is being used to treat symptoms of asthma, depression, appetite stimulant, anticonvulsant, gastrointestinal functioning, and is positively viewed by involved patients (WHO, 2018). Cannabis is thought by some to be a gentler alternative to common narcotics used to treat medical symptoms (Conrad, 1997). Rather than knocking clients out and subduing pain like an anesthetic, marijuana is purported to make the patient sleepy and reduces pain in like manner as an analgesic (Conrad, 1997).

Public opinion to legalize marijuana has drastically increased in all generations, with Millennials holding the highest approval. Wall et al. (2018) conducted a study to assess non-medical prescription opioid (N.M.P.O.) use among three generations in the United States; they found that Millennials were more likely to use heroin after the use of N.M.P.O. than Generation Xers or Baby Boomers. Wall et al. explains this progression to be affected by factors of greater availability and affordability of heroin, as well as high opioid use among Millennials.

According to a recent Gallup poll (McCarthy, 2018), one in four Americans between 18–29 years old record "regularly" or "occasionally" consuming marijuana. According to another analysis, 18% of these individuals noted they did not believe cannabis is harmful at all (Roberts, 2018). As of 2018, 62% of Americans believe that marijuana should be legalized (Pew Research Center, 2018). For comparison, in 2000, public approval of marijuana usage was at 31%. Clearly, public approval is rapidly expanding and can be seen in individual states' approval of marijuana's medical and/or recreational use.

Negative Side Effects of Cannabis

Although individuals in support of cannabis legalization argue that this drug provides harmless pleasure and pain relief, the data suggests that cannabis consumption can be harmful to the body. Negative side effects are particularly observed when cannabis is smoked and inhaled into the lungs. Countering public common sense, some studies have found negative correlations between marijuana use and subsequent health issues (as well as other life-course outcomes).

When assessing the chronic *health effects* of long-term cannabis use, the WHO (2018) observes the following physical adverse effects: epithelial injury of the trachea, airway injury, lung inflammation, symptoms of chronic and acute bronchitis, and an impaired pulmonary defense against infection. Additionally, Moore et al. (2007) note that within their pooled article analysis, some 40% of participants who have used marijuana had an increased risk for psychosis symptoms including disabling psychotic disorders—a number that grew with more frequent use.

Volkow et al. (2016) found high associations of marijuana use with abnormal brain development, addiction to other substances, *schizophrenia*, symptoms of chronic bronchitis, and other effects in accordance with long-term use starting in youth. The WHO (2018) claims that smoking cannabis impairs an individual's cognitive development, specifically affecting learning and recalling functionality and associated processes. Furthermore, dependent upon one's personality resources or stress threshold, smoking cannabis may initially result in increased anxiety to the point of panic, paranoia, or psychosis.

If a large dose is inhaled, the user may experience delusions, hallucinations, sensory distortion, or dysphoria (Small, 2017). Once cannabis is inhaled, it will produce temporary symptoms of higher heart rate, lower blood pressure when standing, dry mouth, lower body temperature, reduced bowel movement, and bloodshot eyes (Small, 2017). Even more serious, these marijuana usage side effects may worsen pre-existing psychotic disorders. For instance, the WHO (2018) recognizes cannabis to be a factor that can exacerbate symptoms of individuals diagnosed with schizophrenia.

Marijuana, Mental Illness, and Violence

Berenson (2019) analyzed the divide between insider and outsider knowledge surrounding marijuana use in the United States. He focused on the impact of cannabis on psychosis. In his studies, he found that teenagers smoking marijuana regularly are almost three times more likely to develop schizophrenia. Additionally, Boden et al. (2019) note in their New Zealand life course trajectory birth cohort study that long-term heavy cannabis use is associated with a substantially increased chance for drug dependency, poorer socioeconomic well-being, reduced incomes, increased chance of relationship violence and/or conviction, and mental health problems—including psychosis (Boden et al., 2019).

Possible Cannabis Effects on Youth

The average age of individuals smoking marijuana is 18–25 years old (Substance Abuse and Mental Health Services Administration, 2016). Use may vary depending on peer characteristics, availability, and familial factors (Boden et al., 2019). Considering that an individual's brain continues to develop until around age 25 (Arain et al., 2013), its usage can be considered specious. Cannabis is shown to be particularly attractive to youth (Small, 2017), with one in six people becoming addicted to regular marijuana use (Volkow et al., 2016). With heavy marijuana smoking, youth have also shown impaired neural connectivity in their brain, lower incomes, greater need for socioeconomic assistance, unemployment, criminal acts, and overall lower satisfaction with life in adulthood (Volkow et al., 2016).

Fergusson and Boden's research provides correlation evidence that cannabis is particularly used by individuals with anti-conventional attitudes. Thus, this possible linkage may be identified with individuals already discouraged by people regarding educational achievement and material success (2008). Yet, the causation between youth cannabis consumption and poorer life outcomes in adulthood is not fully accounted for regarding predisposing genetic or sociocultural aspects (Levine et al., 2017).

Levine et al. (2017) noted a strong correlation between youth exposure and consumption of cannabis to adverse neuropsychiatric outcomes in adulthood, but they were unable to conclude whether cannabis can act as a sole contributor on the youth brain for psychiatric outcomes. Furthermore, frequent cannabis use over a long period of time is associated with various harmful outcomes in adulthood (Boden et al., 2019).

What Can Be Done?

In 2018, some 21.2 million Americans needed substance use intervention (Substance Abuse and Mental Health Services Administration, 2018). At this time, there are no evidence-based drug treatment options for cannabis users (Walther et al., 2016). Thus, psychotherapeutic techniques remain the foundation of treatment options for individuals with cannabis dependence (Walther et al., 2016). Walther et al. found *cognitive behavioral therapy* (CBT) to be moderate to largely beneficial in lowering cannabis consumption and *systematic multidimensional family therapy* (MDFT) as beneficial for youth using cannabis who also have psychiatric comorbidities. As for short-term treatment, Walther et al. found motivational talk therapy to be valuable.

Gates et al. (2012) found that though there are beneficial cannabis treatment options, some 10 to 30% of dependent users will enter into treatment. These researchers found that the most commonly identified barriers for cannabis users to attend treatment is that users are not ready to stop, lack motivation, have fear toward beginning treatment, feel it is not necessary to stop using, have difficulty admitting problems that need to be addressed, and/or are unaware of treatment options. The most commonly reported facilitators to treatment include increasing and improving the information on treatment options, having treatment options specific to cannabis, increasing cannabis services (such as counseling over the phone), and creating an easier intake process (Gates et al., 2012).

Conclusion

The aforementioned data presented both positive and negative correlations between cannabis inhalation and subsequent health effects. However, considering the frenzy of cannabis use for recreational use in postmodernity and the possible correlations between consumption and mental illness, more studies need to assess the long-term effects of cannabis use, personal happiness, and correlated psychosis. Many environmental factors surround marijuana's recreational use for emerging adults. The draw to marijuana is primarily to achieve psychological escape or due to peer pressure, and frequent consumption is due to the campaign of disinformation in the U.S. regarding its ill effects and health risks. Fortunately, there are a growing number of treatment options and plans for people suffering from marijuana dependency.

Brooke Bragg
Social Worker

CASE STUDY #5

Keith leaned against the bed of his pickup truck, red Solo cup in hand. With the bonfire blazing bright before him and the music blaring behind him, he was thoroughly enjoying the night. It was his last night before heading off to college for his final year, and all he could think about was the fun he was going to have. Partying with sorority girls; nights out on the town with his fraternity bros—it was all he had dreamed about for years. His parents thought he was going to college for a degree when, in reality, he was going to escape. *Degrees are for nerds. I'll easily pass my classes anyway.* His hopes for the future burned as bright as the bonfire.

College was all he dreamed about and more, but he was still paying a terrible price. He had already been hospitalized twice for alcohol poisoning. During his sophomore year, he got in trouble with the administration (and the law) after a drunken night with an underage girl. And maybe worse—last weekend, he woke up in the city park in just his underwear with no clue how he got there from the night before. Even his frat bros had started making comments about him—"Hey, skipper. Where's your beer?" Still, his grades had started to slide, and his advisor warned him about "focusing on the important things." Just 6 more months and he would be free—if he passed his classes. He sighed and grabbed a bottle of brew (for later at home) and returned to the festivities.

DISCUSSION QUESTIONS

1. Based on the readings, how would a sociologist diagnose this situation?

2. What specific sociological factors are involved?

3. If you were Keith's friend/relative, what would you do?

Check out the Chapter 5 video at this link:

https://www.khpcontent.com/

VOCABULARY

Alcohol Abuse

Biblical View of Drugs and Alcohol

Cannabis

Chronic Drinkers

Cognitive Behavioral Therapy

Culture of Cynicism

Decriminalization of Drugs

Drug Abuse

Drug Dealer

Drug Prices

Heavy Drinkers

Heroin

Illicit Drugs

Marijuana Health Effects

Marijuana Legislation

Medicinal Marijuana

Mind-Altering Substances

Opioid Overdose

Recreational Marijuana

Schizophrenia

Social Drinkers

Systematic Multidimensional Family Therapy

Tough Love Perspective

Treatment Plans and Programs

War on Drugs

References

Arain, M., Haque, M., Johal, L., Mathur, P., Nel, W., Rais, A., Sandhu, R., & Sharma, S. (2013). Maturation of the adolescent brain. *Neuropsychiatric Disease and Treatment, 9*, 449–461. doi:10.2147/NDT.S39776

Aseltine, R. H., Gore, S., & Gordon, J. (2000). Life stress, anger and anxiety, and delinquency: An empirical test of general strain theory. *Journal of Health and Social Behavior, 41*(3), 256–275.

Berenson, A. (2019). Marijuana, mental illness, and violence. *Imprimis 48*(1). https://imprimis.hillsdale.edu/marijuana-mental-illness-violence/?fbclid=IwAR3wNOqAUPDw6C8zW_BzD09OAFM7vmCovOLnRUmq4Aj3hoEIL3QxeYUwa5w&utm_campaign=stripes&utm_content=02092019&utm_medium=social&utm_source=facebook

Bhatt, V., & Ogaki, M. (2012). Tough love and intergenerational altruism. *International Economic Review, 53*(3), 791–814.

Boden, J. M., Dhakal, B., Foulds, J. A., & Horwood, L. J. (2019). Lifecourse trajectories of cannabis use: A latent class analysis of a New Zealand birth cohort. *Addiction (Abingdon, England).* doi:10.1111/add.14814

Brumm, A. (2005). Heroin as hero: The 'heroin chic' film in European cinema (1995–2000). *Studies in European Cinema, 2*(1), 65–74.

Centers for Disease Control and Prevention (CDC). (2016). https://www.cdc.gov

Conrad, C. (1997). *Hemp for health: The medicinal and nutritional uses of cannabis sativa.* Healing Arts.

D'Agostino, R. (2014). The drugging of the American boy. *Esquire.* https://www.esquire.com/news-politics/a32858/drugging-of-the-american-boy-0414/

Fergusson, D. M., Boden, J. M., & Horwood, L. J. (2008). Exposure to childhood sexual and physical abuse and adjustment in early adulthood. *Child Abuse & Neglect, 32*(6), 607–619.

Gates, P., Copleand, J., Swift, W., & Martin, G. (2012). Barriers and facilitators of cannabis treatment. *Drug and Alcohol Review, 31,* 311–319. doi:10.1111/j.1465-3362.2011.00313.x

Goode, E. (2012). *Drugs in American society* (8th ed.). McGraw-Hill.

Governing (2018). *State marijuana laws in 2018 map.* http://www.governing.com/gov-data/safety-justice/state-marijuana-laws-map-medical-recreational.html

Knox, J. (2016). *Sacro-Egoism: The rise of religious individualism in the West.* Wipf & Stock.

Laursen, J. C. (2009). Cynicism then and now. *Iris; Florence, 1*(2), 469–482.

Levine, A., Clemenza, K., Rynn, M., & Lieberman, J. (2017). Evidence for the risks and consequences of adolescent cannabis exposure. *Journal of the American Academy of Child and Adolescent Psychiatry, 26*(3), 214–225.

Lo, C. C. (2003). An application of social conflict theory to arrestees' use of cocaine and opiates. *Journal of Drug Issues, 33*(1), 237–266. doi:http://dx.doi.org.ezproxy.liberty.edu/10.1177/002204260303300110

Mallea, P. (2014). *The war on drugs: A failed experiment.* Dundurn.

McCarthy, J. (2018). Two in three Americans now support legalizing marijuana. *Gallup.* https://news.gallup.com/poll/243908/two-three-americans-support-legalizing-marijuana.aspx

McCune, A., Patron, A., & Touquet, R. (2015). *ABC of alcoholism* (5th ed.). John Wiley & Sons.

Moore, T. H., Zammit, S., Lingford-Hughes, A., Barnes, T. R., Jones, P. B., Burke, M., & Lewis, G. (2007). Cannabis use and risk of psychotic or affective mental health outcomes: A systematic review. *The Lancet, 370,* 319–328.

Mosher, C. L., & Scott, A. (2014). *Drugs and drug policy: The control of consciousness alteration* (2nd ed.). Sage.

Murphy, J. (2015). *Illness or deviance: Drug courts, drug treatment, and the ambiguity of addiction.* Temple University Press.

National Institute on Alcohol Abuse and Alcoholism. (2017). *Alcohol facts and statistics.* NIH. https://www.niaaa.nih.gov/alcohol-health/overview-alcohol-consumption/alcohol-facts-and-statistics

National Institute on Drug Abuse. (2018). *What is the scope of marijuana use in the United States?* https://www.drugabuse.gov/publications/research-reports/marijuana/what-scope-marijuana-use-in-united-states

National Survey on Drug Use and Health. (2018). *2018 (NSDUH-2018) public-use file dataset.* https://www.datafiles.samhsa.gov/study-dataset/national-survey-drug-use-and-health-2018-nsduh-2018-ds0001-nid18758

Olinger, D. (2019). Collateral impact: The unintended consequences of the legalization of pot. *Colorado Springs Gazette.* https://gazette.com/news/collateral-impact-the-unintended-consequences-of-the-legalization-of-pot/article_ba1d857e-9161-5d07-8f57-1999162a1da4.html

Pew Research Center. (2018). *About six-in-ten Americans support marijuana legalization.* http://www.pewresearch.org/fact-tank/2018/10/08/americans-support-marijuana-legalization/

Prince, D. (2013). *Finding freedom and purging legalism from your life.* Baker Books.

Roberts, C. (2018). *One in four young Americans consume marijuana, survey finds.* https://www.marijuanamoment.net/one-in-four-young-americans-consume-marijuana-survey-finds/

Schmidt, A. (2020). Drinking in the US hits 30-year high: Here's how much the average American drinks. *Foxbusiness.com.* https://www.foxbusiness.com/lifestyle/alcohol-consumption-increase-in-us

Small, E. (2017). *Cannabis: A complete guide.* Taylor & Francis.

Stebbins, S. (2019). How much beer does your state drink? In the thirstiest, about 40 gallons a year per person. *USAToday.com.* https://www.usatoday.com/story/money/2019/09/14/how-much-beer-did-the-average-person-drink-in-every-state/40109241/

Substance Abuse and Mental Health Services Administration. (2016). *Marijuana (cannabis).* https://www.samhsa.gov/atod/marijuana

Substance Abuse and Mental Health Services Administration. (2018). *Key substance use and mental health indicators in the United States: Results from the 2018 national survey on drug use and health.* https://www.samhsa.gov/data/report/2018-nsduh-annual-national-report

Thomas, S. (2020). Alcohol and drug abuse statistics. *American Addiction Centers.* https://americanaddictioncenters.org/rehab-guide/addiction-statistics

Tolan, P., Szapocznik, J., & Sambrano, S. (Eds.). (2007). *Preventing youth substance abuse: Science-based programs for children and adolescents.* American Psychological Association.

Volkow, N. D., Baler, R. D., Compton, W. M., & Weiss, S. R. (2016). Adverse health effects of marijuana use. *The New England Journal of Medicine, 370*(23), 2219–2227. doi:10.1056/NEJMra1402309

Wall, M., Cheslack-Postava, K., Hu, M. C., Feng, T., Griesler, P., & Kandel, D. B. (2018). Nonmedical prescription opioids and pathways of drug involvement in the US: Generational differences. *Drug and Alcohol Dependence, 182*(1), 103–111. doi:https://doi.org/10.1016/j.drugalcdep.2017.10.013

Walther, L., Ganter, A., Heinz, A., & Majić, T. (2016). Evidence-based treatment options in cannabis dependency. *Dtsch Arztebel International 113*(39), 653–659. doi:10.3238/arztebl.2016.0653

Wolff, V., Olivier, R., & Bernard, G. (2014). Adverse health effects of marijuana use. *The New England Journal of Medicine, 371*(9), 878–879.

World Health Organization (WHO). (2018). *Cannabis.* http://www.who.int/substance_abuse/facts/cannabis/en/

Ch 6 Crime

Although *crime* is simply the violation of civil authoritative laws that reflect current legal opinions of what is socially acceptable or despicable behavior, its reality is far more complex and socially overarching. The causation, intent, concurrence, and the criminal act itself all carry with them great social significance and obstacles for social functionality and peaceful coexistence. Moreover, the etiology of crime is no small or trivial matter for some crimes are *consensus*, wherein members of society generally agree about the seriousness of the deviant act; however, other crimes are *conflict*, where one group passes a law over which there is profound disagreement or that disadvantages a particular social demographic group.

Adding to the complication, and touching upon symbolic interactionist theory, what is "deviant" may not be a crime, ontologically (Hall, 2012). Some acts are criminal and deviant, such as killing an elderly, defenseless woman, and some acts are deviant but not criminal, such as a dog wearing a dress or talking loudly during a movie. Additionally, some acts are criminal but not necessarily deviant as the vast majority of the public regularly violates the law, such as speeding in your car or jaywalking across the street.

Somewhere between the social sciences and law studies is *criminology*, the study of crime. *Criminologists* are concerned with how deviant acts become crimes and vice versa (and so are sociologists). They study when deviant behavior should be outlawed and when formal crimes should be decriminalized. Generally, criminologists are concerned with the impact of law on human behavior and the institution of criminal labels (Walsh, 2018).

© PRESSLAB/Shutterstock.com

Speaking of which, there are numerous official types of crime. These include predatory or street crime, hate crime, organized crime, cybercrime, white-collar crime, global crime, and so on. Crimes are also classified according to their severity. *Felonies* are more serious offenses, which carry with them longer imprisonment time in a federal prison and with the possibility of *capital punishment* (execution). *Misdemeanors* are less serious offenses, which carry with them shorter imprisonment time (less than a year) in a local or county jail, and which sometimes give people celebrity status—especially for Hollywood stars, apparently (Bucerius & Tonry, 2014).

People can also get in trouble for *larceny*, which includes grand theft or petty theft (depending upon the monetary value of the stolen goods), *burglary* (unlawful entry) and *robbery* (personal theft), *embezzlement or fraud* (stealing company money), *extortion* (a.k.a., "blackmail"), and knowingly receiving stolen property. *White-collar crime* is sometimes part of larceny, but is less publicized than other crimes; however, it is still quite damaging to the company, fellow employees, customers, and the general public (Gottschalk, 2016).

The more serious of crimes involve the taking of another's life (also called homicide). This can be classified as a *1ˢᵗ degree murder*, which is premediated killing; *2ⁿᵈ degree murder*, which is a non-premeditated, passion-of-the-moment killing; *felony murder*, which is killing someone while committing another felony; *voluntary manslaughter*, which is the intentional killing of a person without malice aforethought; and *involuntary manslaughter*, which is the unintentional killing during a nonfelony crime (Flowers, 2012). The latter are often classified as *3ʳᵈ degree murder*.

There are several responses to crime carried out by the *criminal justice system*: the police, the courts, the prisons (Terrill, 2016). Within this system (and sometimes outside of it), there are various responses to crime including *social protection*, which incapacitates and removes the criminal from social interaction; *deterrence*, which is meant to instill enough fear within the criminal that they abandon future deviant acts; *rehabilitation*, which is meant to re-socialize and reform the criminal; and *retribution*, which is non-sanctioned vengeance against the criminal—and a crime, in itself (Polaschek et al., 2019). Many conflict theorists accuse the judicial system of being more about socioeconomic oppression than management and application of laws to deal with the threat of social harm (especially considering minority arrests and convictions compared to the majority's experiences).

Ultimately, by relying upon functionalist theory, *prisons and jails* utilize total institutional control over prisoners' lives in order to remove dangerous individuals from society and to deter others from repeating the criminal behavior in the future (Johnson et al., 2017). There are alternatives to prison, though, including shock probation, which uses shorter prison times and intense therapy sessions to shock the prisoner out of his or her criminal habit. Additionally, *day treatment* and *halfway houses* are utilized for many of the nonviolent crimes to help rehabilitate criminals and help them rebuild social networks or find healthier people to associate with in general society.

Restitution is also sometimes employed to allow the criminal to work off or pay back what they have stolen or taken from others. This provides an opportunity for healing and balance to be regained for both the criminal and the victim. It also creates great social capital for the criminal, perhaps leading to resocialization, empathy, and self-pride that might keep him or her out of trouble in the future (Palmer, 2016).

DEALING WITH MATTERS OF THE DARK

Contrary to the postmodern religious approach of some that suggests Christians are free to live a life free of former biblical codes and Christian prohibitions (Hood, 2011), *antinomianism* (against the law or lawlessness) is nothing new. People might love the beginning of 1 Corinthians 6:12 (New International Version)—"I have the right to do anything," but forget about Paul's following response: "but not everything is beneficial . . . but I will not be mastered by anything." Time and time again, Christians are reminded in the Bible that we are free in Christ, free from death's power, but not free from our Christian obligation to follow Christ's example of righteous, lawful living (Grudem, 2018).

Of course, Jesus did not invent Jewish law or social-moral codes in the first century, C.E. Two thousand years earlier, in Exodus 20:21-24, Moses delivered the *Ten Commandments* of God for his people, Israel (and for all future believers of the Way). These were provided to help God's people understand how to get along with Him and each other. The decalogue included the following laws from God, directly:

1. You shall have no other gods before me.
2. You shall not make for yourself an idol in the form of anything in heaven above or on the earth beneath or in the waters below.
3. You shall not misuse the name of the LORD your God.
4. Remember the Sabbath day by keeping it holy.
5. Honor your father and your mother.
6. You shall not murder.
7. You shall not commit adultery.
8. You shall not steal.
9. You shall not give false testimony against your neighbor.
10. You shall not covet your neighbor's house.

The *Book of the Covenant* is the oldest record of Hebrew regulations and restrictions for the community. Within it, one can find ordinances on Israelite responsibilities to God and other members of the community. It also details the rules for religious worship and festivals, as well as civil/secular affairs. Dyrness (1977) writes,

> A proper understanding of the law leads one to see that all of life lies under the controlling will of God, whether one is getting up in the morning, sitting down to eat, walking along the way or going to sleep. (p. 138)

This *Law Code of God* displays many similarities to other ancient Middle Eastern and Mediterranean law codes; however, it is distinctly different in four important ways. First, the law code rests on the authority of God and not the king. Second, because Israel was a theocracy, there was no real division between civil and religious law. Third, there was supposed to be one universal application of the Law for all Israelites—if a peasant could not do it, then neither could the king. Finally, it utilized a one crime, one penalty philosophy—social status did not change the outcome of sentencing for a crime (Gane, 2017).

© Roman Motizov/Shutterstock.com

Regarding the presentation of these civil, social, and religious laws in the Hebrew scriptures, Exodus 20:22-26 provides instructions on worship, and the careful creation of altars; Exodus 21:1–23:13 expands upon the extents and limits of *civil laws*, such as the rights of servants, manslaughter and human life, property damage and theft, moral/religious duties, human rights, and Sabbath laws. Exodus 23:14-19 deals with festival seasons such as the requirement of unleavened bread, the harvesting of the *firstfruits*—the required participation of all men, and God's commitment to Israel.

The book of Leviticus focuses on the laws and regulations required of the Hebrews wandering in the Sinai Desert for 40 years, for both identification and survival. As Birch et al. (1999) state, "The Book of Leviticus is the center of the Pentateuch. This placement conveys the importance of worship for the life and well-being of the community" (p. 135). After the Pentateuch, no one could legitimately call themselves "an Israelite" if he or she did not follow the divine and civil injunction(s) from God through Moses. To be Israelite was synonymous with "the Law of Moses."

Some consider the cleanliness laws to be arbitrary and draconian, but besides some very real physical dangers of living in the desert/Middle East, God wanted his people to be set apart, as he is above all non-eternals. Thus, they were told to "maintain clean food (11), clean bodies (12–13), clean clothes (14), clean contacts (15), and to be a clean nation (16)." Even more so, they were to have clean hearts and consciences. This culminated in the *Annual Day of Atonement* (chapter 16)—"Presupposed in this ritual is that sin is not simply to be understood in individual terms; it is a reality which also has a corporate dimension. Thus, the ritual provided a means by which the community as a whole could deal with sin's potential communal destructiveness" (Birch et al., 1999, p. 138). In the present, radical, sacro-egoistical age of individualism (Knox, 2016) may seem unfair or absurd, but both the Hebrew and Greek scriptures promote unity of blessings (or guilt) as protectors of the faith (or promoters of wickedness).

The remainder of the chapters in Leviticus deal with following prudent steps to holiness and sanctification. Thus, Leviticus 18–19 could be considered the "Do not" chapters with their litany of sexual (and other) prohibitions—"Do not have sexual relations with your father's wife" (v. 18:7) or your sister (v. 18:9) or your grandchild (v. 18:10), or your aunt (vv. 18:12–13), or an in-law (v. 18:15), or a neighbor's wife (v. 18:20), or a member of the same sex (v. 18:22), or an animal (v. 18:23). Most likely, Leviticus 18:18 would have spared Jacob much marital strife and sorrow had it been explicitly clear, then—"Do not take your wife's sister as a rival wife and have sexual relations with her while your wife is living."

The rest of the chapters in Leviticus provide additional admonishments, rules, and consequences; however, they also include some happier instructions on festivals such as the Passover and the Festival of Unleavened Bread, the Offering of the Firstfruits, the Festival of Weeks, the Festival of Trumpets, and the Festival of Tabernacles, as Moses describes "the Lord's appointed festivals, which you are to proclaim as sacred assemblies for bringing food offerings to the Lord" (v. 23:37).

Additionally, the *Sabbath Year*, occurring every 7 years (at least, it was supposed to happen every 7 years) when all male slaves are set free. The *Year of Jubilee*, occurring every 50 years (at least it was supposed to happen every 50 years), when all land was given back to the original owner and all debts were canceled, was a very positive inclusion in the ordinances of the Lord (Fager, 1993). Just imagine the benefits for all people if this were implemented in Western society today.

Moses finishes the Book of Leviticus with numerous "I will" statements on the *benefits of obedience*, followed by numerous "I will" statements on the negative consequences of disobedience. For the former, he says, "I will look on you with favor and make you fruitful and increase your numbers, and I will keep my covenant with you" (v. 27:8). For the latter, he warns, "If after all this you will not listen to me, I will punish you for your sins seven times over" (v. 27:18). Clearly, this is a reminder for all people who think that their crimes against humanity will be unnoticed and unpunished. Quite the opposite, there will be a reckoning, eventually, for all people (Christians and non-believers, alike).

Some consider Leviticus to be indicative of a punitive, harsh deity, but unlike the fickle false gods of nearby nations whose main goal is self-pleasure and capricious whims, the God of Israel only has his people's best intentions in mind (and in his heart). This is why he put up so many "signposts" pointing to the path of holy righteousness. The 10 Commandments—really all the Levitical laws—are God's way of letting people know what it takes to return to an Edenic state.

Ultimately, all God really wants is to walk with humanity—"I will be your God, and you shall be my people" (vv. 26:12, 45). Sadly, many people do not want to walk or be with Him; they seal their own doom by rejecting laws of goodness for a life of pleasure and escape. Fortunately, this is why God sent Jesus to the world to pave the road to our redemption, reconciliation, and righteousness—if we believe and obey.

INSIGHTS FROM THE EXPERTS

"Criminology and Sociology"

For the past 4 years, my undergraduate career in the Helms School of Government focused on the scientific discipline of *Criminology*, which, stated simply, is the study of crime and criminal behavior. Criminologists seek to understand which elements of culture, society, and the economy relate to the development of criminal behavior. The importance of this scientific discipline cannot be understated. The nature and existence of crime significantly impacts all facets of culture and society.

As the Federal Bureau of Investigation's Uniform Crime Report shows (2020), current criminal trends within American society change over time. A plethora of factors (far too many to list here) comprise proper empirical research into crime. Successful criminologists take this empirical research and translate their findings into theories. These theories then shape new policies and public opinion. Therefore, understanding the nature of criminology as well as the nature of crime is the first step in solving the social problem of criminal behavior.

Two Branches of the Same Tree

For simplicity's sake, let us segregate the entire *field of criminology* into two subcategories; while not a complete picture of the science, these two facets of the discipline should provide a sufficient introduction to the field. The first category of criminology observes governmental order, control, and justice as a branch for study. This approach seeks to understand the responsibilities of government and the creation of law itself.

In essence, the archetypal government creates a productive and prosperous nation. Because prosperous countries increase historical legacy, further technological advancement, improve living standards, and grow the global population, it is the goal of every government to curtail any criminal actions that hinder this pursuit. Much like a sociologist studying symbolic interaction theory, criminologists studying natural law and governmental structures conceptualize in an attempt to order and structure society.

Second, criminologists study the behaviors of people to determine crime and criminal behavior. This textbook's earlier chapter on deviance highlights the fundamental sociological approaches to evaluating moral behavior. Criminology views the concept and study of deviance and criminal behavior as a keystone piece to solving the problem of crime.

Governing Crime

Who has the right to judge the actions of men and women? Considering the lot of human history, then the mightiest ruler makes all the rules. Humanity's earliest legal documents, such as the *Law Code of Hammurabi* (May, 2019), place all of the lower classes underneath the rule of a king. This system of governance existed with few exceptions (namely, the Israelites) for thousands of years until the Middle Ages. In any authoritarian society, crime is less about violations against human nature and more focused on behaviors the state deems "illegal." Obviously, this perceptive fails in today's modern republics and democracy thanks to the rise of a new religion—Christianity.

The world owes a great deal to the rise of Judeo-Christian values more than most postmodernists are willing to admit. For thousands of years, pre-Christianity, kings and tyrants alike operated with near impunity and were immune to all laws. The phrase, *might makes right*, functioned as the supreme law of the world. Ironically, most social justice warriors cite this power difference in modern society as a blight on Western culture when, in fact, it was the growth of Christianity that broke this barrier. Christian doctrine, at its core, states that all men and women are created in the image of their creator and have been endowed certain rights (Genesis 1:26-27).

Additionally, humans have within them the ability to distinguish right from wrong (Romans 1). This critical element of doctrine (when cultivated within a society) places all people—kings and peasants alike—before God's righteous judgment. Crime in the Judeo-Christian moral structure is less about the violation of the state's mandates and more about a person's failures to act according to natural law.

The creation of the *Magna Carta* was the first document to develop this doctrine into a legal framework (Magna Carta, 1215). In essence, the document placed the king and court within the sovereignty of the law. More than the Hammurabi code, Levitical law, or other ancient texts, the Magna Carta drastically advanced humanity's moral and legal structure by claiming that all people, regardless of social standings, have the potential to act unrighteous and required the intervention of a judicial system. This idea began to snowball later, creating *English Common Law*—arguably one of the greatest developments of Western society (Peterson, 2020).

The history mentioned above directly impacts a sociological analysis of crime. Pre-Christianity, crime had always been viewed within the context of the state. People who displeased or disobeyed the ruling class were punished; however, Christianity introduced a new standard of divine justice compelling all men to submit to God's sovereignty. It is no longer possible to discuss crime and criminal behavior outside the context of ethics or morals as all elements of crime are eventually subject to the righteous judgment of God.

The Balance between Conflict, Function, and Symbolism

All three sociological perspectives exist as lenses through which to interoperate criminological data. Conflict theorists, who often dramatize a single variable of analysis, seek to highlight the injustices between social groups as justification for criminal behaviors. Most commonly associated with race, conflict theorist highlights the different power structures and how the oppressed commit "crimes" as a result of a failed system (Schmalleger, 1999, p. 347).

Functional theorists (who often observe situations with general, overarching opinions) consider multiple points of intersection between members of society and shown behavior. Lastly, symbolic interaction, while the least popular method of analysis, attributes criminal actions to perceived norms within society. In truth, no one perspective paints a complete picture of criminality, and each lens should be used as a tool for critical analysis rather than a complete structure.

The Problem of Crime

From the previous discussion, the primary issue of crime should be summarized in the axiom, "All sins are crimes, but not all crimes are sins." Really, the problem with evil is not disobedience of the law, but instead wickedness within the heart of men and women. Murderers do not kill people because the law says not to but because there is something broken at the core of their being.

Criminologists seek to understand this brokenness and to develop theories that rehabilitate offenders. *Crime* is, at the core of the problem, brokenness within a person, group, or culture. It serves as a rip current for society, eroding the social fabric of culture beneath our feet. This erosion, visible in modern media, further increases the rates of violence and crime within our culture (Hagan, 2011).

People often celebrate entertainment that glorifies or rewards criminal behavior. Movies like *Oceans 11* or video games like *GTA5* all glorify criminal acts which, in reality, destroys the lives of both the offender and victim. To be clear, isolated instances of entertainment and art do not produce criminals; however, as society increases in immoral behavior and its duration, criminal actions will increase in tandem.

The Solution of Crime

Finally, at the end of this discussion, the question remains, "What is the solution to crime?" The answer is more straightforward than most researchers theorize. All three lenses of sociology indicate the same evil in the heart of every man. The solution, therefore, is returning to the *Judeo-Christian values* that our founding fathers set in place. Only a Christian nation can uphold true justice and peace. To wit, the Bible dictates in Micah 6:8, "He has shown you, O mortal, what is good. And what does the Lord require of you? To act justly and to love mercy and to walk humbly with your God" (New International Version).

It is our job as citizens of both this world and the next to walk in righteousness seeking to protect the innocent, bringing God's justice on the unrighteous, developing a society that rewards righteous actions, and instills our morals into social traditions for our future generations.

Quinn Weinzapfel
BS in Criminal Justice
Graduate Student Assistant and Researcher

CASE STUDY #6

Jim was a great dad. Admired by his coworkers for his wit and humorous nature, his demeanor appeared laid back and content. His marriage to office secretary Pam appeared blissful as well. Both worked side-by-side each day at their small regional paper company without much incident. However, as Jim's family began to expand and the cost of living began to increase, his pay became insufficient to meet the financial demands of his new life. This, in turn, was placing pressure on his marriage. One week at work, Jim began fudging his accounting and sales numbers in an attempt to increase his bonus amount. To his amazement, the fraud worked and went undetected, and after several months his salary was the largest in the office.

Jim's wife eventually found out, but while extremely disappointed, she said nothing about the fraud. After a while, she, too, began taking office supplies. Surprisingly, their marital problems did not dissipate, and, in an attempt to smooth things over, Jim took his family to Disneyland paid for with the stolen money. Jim's actions continued for the next several years as his kids grew. One day, his youngest daughter snagged a stick of gum from the checkout line and justified her action with, "Mommy does it." Jim stood in shock, wondering how their actions were impacting the kids. He wished he could stop, but if his numbers suddenly dropped, he would either be discovered or fired for poor performance.

DISCUSSION QUESTIONS

1. Based on the readings, how would a sociologist diagnose this situation?

2. What specific sociological factors are involved?

3. What should happen to Jim and his wife if they are caught?

Check out the Chapter 6 video at this link:

https://www.khpcontent.com/

VOCABULARY

1st Degree Murder	Conflict
2nd Degree Murder	Consensus
3rd Degree Murder	Crime
Antinomianism	Criminal Justice System
Burglary	Criminologists
Capital Punishment	Criminology
Civil Laws	Day Treatment

Deterrence
Embezzlement
Extortion
Felony
Felony Murder
Firstfruits
Fraud
Halfway Houses
Involuntary Manslaughter
Judeo-Christian Values
Larceny
Law Code of Hammurabi
Magna Carta

Might Makes Right
Misdemeanor
Prison and Jails
Rehabilitation
Restitution
Retribution
Robbery
Sabbath Year
Social Protection
Voluntary Manslaughter
White-Collar Crime
Year of Jubilee

References

Birch, B., Brueggemann, W., Terence Fretheim, T., & Petersen, D. (1999). *A theological introduction to the Old Testament*. Abingdon.

Bucerius, S., & Tonry, M. (2014). *The Oxford handbook of ethnicity, crime, and immigration*. Oxford University Press.

Dyrness, W. (1977). *Themes in Old Testament theology*. InterVarsity.

Fager, J. A. (1993). *Land tenure and the biblical jubilee: Uncovering Hebrew ethics through the sociology of knowledge*. JSOT Press.

Federal Bureau of Investigation. (2020). Crime data explorer. https://crime-data-explorer.fr.cloud.gov/explorer/national/united-states/crime

Flowers, R. B. (2012). *The dynamics of murder: Kill or be killed*. Taylor & Francis.

Gane, R. E. (2017). *Old Testament law for Christians: Original context and enduring application*. Baker.

Gottschalk, P. (2016). *Understanding white-collar crime: A convenience perspective*. Routledge.

Grudem, W. A. (2018). *Christian ethics: An introduction to biblical moral reasoning*. Crossway.

Hagan, F. E. (2011). *Introduction to criminology: Theories, methods, and criminal behavior*. Sage.

Hall, S. (2012). *Theorizing crime & deviance: A new perspective*. SAGE.

Hood, J. B. (2011). Heresy is heresy, not the litmus test of Gospel preaching. *Christianity Today*. https://www.christianitytoday.com/ct/2011/januaryweb-only/heresyisheresy.html

Johnson, R., Rocheleau, A. M., & Martin, A. B. (2017). *Hard time: A fresh look at understanding and reforming the prison* (4th ed.). Wiley Blackwell.

Knox, J. (2016). *Sacro-Egoism: The rise of religious individualism in the West*. Wipf & Stock.

Magna Carta. (1215). *The Avalon Project: Magna Carta*. avalon.law.yale.edu/medieval/magframe.asp

May, L. (2019). *Ancient legal thought: Equity, justice, and humaneness from Hammurabi and the pharoahs to Justinian and the Talmud*. Cambridge University Press.

Palmer, J. (2016). Restitution. *New Zealand Law Review, 2*, 435–457.

Peterson, J. B. (2020). *12 rules for life: An antidote to chaos*. Vintage Canada, 2020.

Polaschek, D. L. L., Day, A., & Hollin, C. R. (2019). *The Wiley international handbook of correctional psychology*. John Wiley & Sons.

Schmalleger, F. (1999). *Criminology today: An integrative introduction*. Prentice Hall.

Terrill, R. J. (2016). *World criminal justice systems: A comparative survey* (9th ed.). Routledge.

Walsh, A. (2018). *Criminology: The essentials*. Sage.

Ch 7 Wealth

Simply, *social stratification* is the classification of persons into groups based on shared socioeconomic conditions such as wealth or power. As Witt (2009) states, "Ever since people first began to speculate about the nature of human society, they have focused on the differences between individuals and groups within society" (p. 216). In stratification, groupings are vertical, based on social position or status superiority, and often include a criterion of economy, honor, and education. From top to bottom, distribution of goods and monies is based on perceptions of right, authority, or stereotypes.

Check out a video for more on this topic here:

https://www.khpcontent.com/

Most societies create ranks that place people into categories, influencing every part of human existence (for better or for worse). Some categories and ranks come with comforts and luxuries; others are more Spartan and austere. Although many politicians promise a utopian community where no one suffers and no one acts as "lord of the manor," the reality is that inequality is found in all societies and all economic systems. The axioms that it takes money to make money and that inequality begets more inequality are evidentially true, historically. Access is all about having the right social "key" to scarce goods and resources (Helms, 2006).

There are *four main principles of social stratification*. First, the stratification is a significant trait of society—not simply a reflection of individual differences. Second, the stratification carries over from past generations to future generations. Third, it is universally recognized, but still with some variance. Fourth, it carries with it some inequalities but also manifestations of personal or group beliefs also.

Throughout history and in cultures all over the globe, common social systems or groupings have been observed. Some cultures, such as India or in China, have a *caste system*, which is locked, hereditary, and ontologically divisive (Amaladoss, 1994). Some countries, such as France and England, have utilized the idea of estates to order political bodies and differentiate their social classes. *Slavery* too has been a severe form of inescapable stratification that has its roots deep within every continent, every race, every culture, and every people group. To be a slave is to be the property of another human being, without rights or self-autonomy. Incredibly, according to the *Global Slavery Index* (2018), some 40 million people in the world today are living in a form of slavery.

The fourth system is that of *class*, which brings with it the social dimensions of wealth, prestige, and power (or a lack, thereof). For instance, in Western society, there have been three main classes. The *upper class* includes individuals with considerable wealth in regard to personal property, real estate, stocks, bonds, or money. The *middle class* is the largest class in the United States, and includes people between the upper and worker classes, such as professionals and businessmen. The *lower class* includes individuals with the least amount of education and with the most employment problems.

In most Western societies, a huge rift exists between the classes (Henslin, 2018). For instance, in 2003, the 13,000 richest families in the United States had the same income as the 20 million poorest people. Even more, the richest 1% of the U.S. population owned as much property and goods as 96% of all other Americans' combined holdings. Sociologists (and economists) find questions on how much the richest person in the United States made in 2019, how many people are currently in the American middle class, and the salary ranges for each socioeconomic class to be intriguing at the least.

One of the most important factors in predicting future earnings for people relates to their family background. Sociological studies have shown that men from families with high incomes tend to make more money than families with low incomes. One can conclude that financial and social success is more about being born into a wealthy family than simply personal ambition or hard work. Succinctly, money and wealth open doors to occupations, lifestyles, education, housing, and legal protections (Wheelan, 2016).

This presents sociologists with some underclass realities. First, being in the lower classes severely hampers one's social life and chances of betterment. Second, although there are different types of poverty, *absolute poverty* occurs when people fall below the federally defined subsistence level. Third, most impoverished do not have access or money to acquire the resources they need to meet their basic necessities in life.

A central factor of being impoverished is the inability to escape from one's socioeconomic circle, which concerns *social mobility*—the ability to change one's social position. As Semuels (2016) writes,

> It's not an exaggeration: It is getting harder to move up in America. Those who make very little money in their first jobs will probably still be making very little decades later, and those who start off making middle-class wages have similarly limited paths. (online)

Mobility influences many social aspects including the growth of large corporations, an increased standard of living, an increase of urbanization, the development of advanced technologies, and the maintenance of the split labor market.

The *split labor market*, an economic theory suggested by Edna Bonacich in the 1970s, is a virtual community where people compete for jobs and their resources. Bonacich (1972) wrote, "The central hypothesis is that ethnic antagonism first germinates in a labor market split along ethnic lines" (p. 549). Bonacich theorized that some jobs afford upward mobility while others do not. This creates a job market split between the manual laborers and other white-collar workers. Moreover, this created greater obstacles for the minorities including the disabled and the aged—an aspect often pointed out by conflict theorists for decades.

DEALING WITH MATTERS OF THE DARK

In life, most people make ethical choices without knowing the foundations or theories leading them to those decisions. Whether dawdling at work instead of really working to fudging on your taxes or overcharging a customer for maximum profit, people face right-and-wrong choices every day throughout their lives. Too often, these choices are made impulsively or without much thought, leading to unnecessary and harmful social problems for all involved.

Through a careful analysis of approaches, though, four particular theories can be understood, observed, and implemented to possibly avoid negative social outcomes. These include the deontological approach, the teleological approach, the formal approach, and the situational approach. All four theories have clear positive and negative features that can aid people incorporating them into ethical choice-making. All four also can be observed in various subcategories or approaches leading to unique interpretations and manifestations of conduct and character.

The first theory, that of the *deontological approach*, focuses on the rightness of an actor doing such an act by virtue of factors besides its consequences (Hooker, 2012). Succinctly, it is a theory upholding principle over practicality. It asks questions like, "What ought I do in this circumstance?" and "What is the correct action to take?" One good example might be the early Christians' unlawful decision to refuse to worship the Roman emperor despite the fact that if they did not, they would be thrown to the lions or burned at the stake. Another example might be resigning from a well-paying job at a rich institution that habitually cheats their customers. In that circumstance, the principle of fairness and honesty is more important than personal financial gain.

The attributes of the deontological theory establish and sustain its stability. By focusing on the principle involved and disregarding the consequences, the deontologist avoids making any subjective rationalizations. The negative side is the obtuse rendering of the ethical judgment regardless of the circumstances surrounding the question. In such cases, elements of hypocrisy, insensitivity, and cruelty can be observed. For instance, abortion, scientifically, is infanticide, but somehow the humanity of the child "disappears" or "transforms to a blob of flesh" because of the principle of complete bodily freedom for women that is currently touted. Doing something "because of the principle of it" is good as long as the principle is good and beneficial.

The deontological approach has a variety of expressions such as pure, mixed, Kantian (Immanuel Kant's philosophy), social contractarian, pluralistic, and hierarchical. The pure deontological approach has already been explored earlier. A mixed deontological approach allows that some aspect of the consequences of an act can be relevant to its goodness or value. Kantian deontology stresses that the *categorical imperative* (Kant, 1785) is important in making ethical choices in that one is to choose an action only if it could be considered a universal law. For instance, "I'm not going to beat up and rob elderly women of their social security checks" could easily be considered a universal truth.

The *contractarian approach* grounds obligation in a social contract wherein a person acts conforming to a set of mutually advantageous rules agreed upon by members of a community. The pluralistic approach takes principles and finds ways to make them coexist such as permitting various actions as long as they do not violate the contract's parameters, such as Salvation Army volunteers collecting money for the poor—not to finance their next car. Finally, the hierarchical approach to ethics places certain principles above others in their rightness. Thus, the principle of not murdering far outweighs (in some people's minds) that of not cheating on one's taxes.

A second theory that many people incorporate into their ethical choices is the *teleological approach*. In this approach, the outcome or consequence of an action is vitally important to making one's decision (Levering, 2008). Basically, teleology aligns with the ends justifying the means. An ethical choice is good if it produces good or satisfaction for the people involved. This approach upholds beneficence over principle. A bank employee robbing the bank but equally distributing the funds to everyone who works in the bank (perhaps, say, the bank manager) would be a reasonable example—sort of a Robin Hood approach to robbery.

One good example might be whether or not it is ethical to smoke cigarettes in the toy section of a giant department store. The freedom to smoke is an important issue but not harming others (especially innocent children) is more important, so if smoking near vulnerable lungs could (and probably would) hurt innocent people, then the consequences of that act makes it unethical. Another current debate is that of wearing protective facemasks in public restaurants (because of the COVID-19 outbreak). If coronavirus exposure may kill many people (this is still under debate), then a teleological, consequentialism approach would assert that not wearing facemasks in public is unethical. The sum of satisfaction has not been met (Svensson & Padin, 2012).

The benefits of this approach are its relevance and effectiveness in dealing with specific ethical conflicts while at the same time providing some degree of satisfaction to the parties involved. The detriments of this theory are its subjective and unrealistic nature. A lack of knowledge or a naiveté can lead one's judgment far off the correct path of truth and rightness.

The *teleological approach* is expressed in a number of forms as well such as ethical egoism, act-utilitarianism, rule-utilitarianism, and the *Christian teleological approach*. *Ethical egoism* focuses on agent satisfaction for an act is right only if the agent is most satisfied by any one act. It is a rather self-serving approach because just one person's satisfaction is the most important aspect of making a decision. *Rule utilitarianism*, on the other hand, suggests that an act is right if it is required

by an optimal set of rules—such as being a good, friendly neighbor as everyone should be (Miller, 2009).

Unfortunately, this approach is limited by the inability of some to not work for that optimal set of rules. *Act utilitarianism*, however, focuses on doing the act that produces the least amount of dissatisfaction for all parties involved. This approach would suggest that driving safely is the best thing for all parties involved because it protects the driver's life and those on the road with him/her. Finally, the Christian teleological approach focuses on doing actions that best promote the kingdom of God and the welfare of others. This is, by far, the most higher-minded of the theories for it follows the codes of loving God and others above oneself.

The other two approaches to ethical choices, formal and *situationism*, focus on widely different aspects in concluding what is ethical or not (Cunningham, 1970). Formal ethics suggest that it is the form and not the content of an act that makes it good. A good example of this may be the inoculation of children against measles (still hotly debated in American society). True, the content of the shot may hurt the child in the immediate sense (sensory pain, short-time fever, etc.), but the lasting, beneficial value of the act overshadows that temporary pain—immunity to dangerous disease and protection of the innocent.

The benefits of this approach are seen in the Christian *virtue of love*. Love alone determines if an act is good as defined in biblical and not subjective terms. The negative side of this approach is in the differing interpretations of what the Bible calls loving and unloving actions. Some hold to a strict, literal interpretation of scripture while others take a more metaphorical and pragmatic approach (Newsome, 2019). The differences in character and conduct issuing from these interpretations are amazing. It leads some Christians to bomb abortion clinics and others (like John Wesley) to spend their entire lives and fortune taking care of the poor (Jennings, 1990).

The final approach of situationism takes a very loose approach to determining whether a choice is ethical. It suggests that there are no absolutes and that everything is relative, but choices must be based on agape love (Cochran & Calo, 2017). This type of love is the only universal principle to follow. A good example of this may be the firefighters and police officers who valiantly went into the burning buildings of 9/11 to rescue those in need. These men and women's only goal was to distribute love and compassion to the hurting regardless of the consequences or myriad of other factors involved.

The benefit of this approach is, of course, its other mindedness. In a way, it does parallel the example of Jesus Christ in the New Testament. Christ wholly incorporated the love of God and humanity into his actions. As Jesus revealed to His Disciples, "As the Father has loved me, so have I loved you. Now remain in my love. If you keep my commands, you will remain in my love, just as I have kept my Father's commands and remain in his love" (John 15:9–10, New International Version). The negative side of this theory is in the human subjective understanding of what love is. Jesus used a divine understanding of love and God on which to base his actions.

Humanity, however, is not so consistent. Being so multidimensional, love can be expressed in a myriad of ways. Not everyone has the same priorities or values and so what is considered loving for one person may not be for another. It is this subjectivity that may lead to rationalization or judgmentalness using situationism. Of course, *1 Corinthians 13* spells out love clearly and brilliantly, and carries with it the weight of our moral obligation to one another.

In studying ethics, it is clear that many different approaches to ethical choices are available (Baumane-Vitolina et al., 2016). Whether deontological, teleological, form, or situational, these theories reflect the multitude of personalities and values of humanity. In each circumstance, it is not always clear why one is chosen over another. What can be generally known, though, is that if one took the deontological approach, one would pick the good theory based on socially and biblically accepted principles; if one took the teleological approach, one would pick the theory with the most satisfaction for the parties involved; if one took the form approach, success would be in the correct, loving vehicle or manner of choice; and if one took the situational approach, it would not matter which theory was chosen as long as agape love was the guide and method of operation.

Each of these theories has their pros and cons but all, in some way, are interdependent as are we all. Perhaps understanding how people make ethical choices will eventually show us how interconnected humanity truly is and how much, how often, and how deeply our choices affect others. Maybe that is why Paul admonished readers to "work out your salvation with fear and trembling" (Philippians 2:12, New International Version).

INSIGHTS FROM THE EXPERTS

"Wealth: Good or Evil"

Growing up in a poorer part of the capital county in North Carolina, watching my parents frequently return to their even poorer roots in eastern North Carolina to visit family, observing how the rich and wealthy treated others, and even discovering the hypocrisy of the church and congregation in regard to money, wealth, and sin, it is no wonder that the first time that I heard the scripture, " . . . money is the root of all kinds of evil," I started to believe that only the poor and needy could find God's love. It was only years later that I learned about the nature of selective quoting, how context and meaning can be changed by dropping a few words or sentences before or after a quote, and how society and our fundamental beliefs are altered by our experiences and attitudes. In the intervening years, my understanding, knowledge, and beliefs about wealth, riches, and money have vastly changed. Today, I work as a financial advisor helping individuals save and plan for the future, protecting themselves from risk, and also contributing back to society.

For the record, Timothy stated, "For the love of money is a root of all kinds of evil, for which some have stray from the faith in their greediness" (1 Timothy 6:10, NKJV). If you notice, there is a fundamental difference between "_Money_ is the root of all kinds of evil" and "_the love of money_ is the root of all kinds of evil." Put simply, money (and by extension wealth) are not inherently evil, nor are they good. What Timothy was quick to point out was that our attitudes and beliefs toward wealth are what can lead us to a positive or negative outcome.

As a teenager in the late 1980s, I observed firsthand the social and economic changes brought about by the rise of business and finance and its inevitable social issues. If the 1980s could be summed up in a single quote, then the character of Gordon Gekko from the movie "Wall Street" (20th Century Fox,1987), sums it best: "The point is, ladies and gentlemen, that greed, for lack of a better word, is good. Greed is right, greed works. Greed clarifies, cuts through, and captures the essence of the evolutionary spirit. Greed, in all of its forms; greed for life, for money, for love, knowledge has marked the upward surge of mankind."

The movie, while designed to be an exposé on the excesses of Wall Street and its workers, instead became a cult hit inspiring Wall Street bankers, financiers, and business schools for years (Guerrera, 2010). These people then became the associates and principles who led the banks and investment houses and the CEOs and CFOs of corporations. If the stock market crash of 1987 was not enough, how about these scandals:

▶ Waste Management: In 1998, the new CEO and his team discovered they had reported more than $1.7 billion in fake earnings. Investors lost while the former owner and CEO reaped the financial benefits.

▶ Enron: In 2001, it was discovered Enron was using fake corporations and accounting loopholes to hide billions of dollars in bad debt and inflate earnings. In the end, owners of Enron stock, employees, pension plans, and retirement accounts all lost about $74 billion when the company went under. The employees of Enron and Arthur Anderson, Enron's accounting firm, all lost their jobs before it was over.

▶ WorldCom: In 2002, WorldCom was found to have been inflating their assets and using improper accounting to hide obligations and business failings. In the end, 30,000 lost their jobs and investors lost more than $180 billion.

▶ Tyco International: In 2002, it came to light that the CEO and CFO had stolen over $150 million from the company through unapproved loans and stock sales and inflated the company's earning by more than $500 million.

▶ HealthSouth: In 2003, it was discovered that the company had inflated earnings by more than $1.8 billion while the CEO was using inside knowledge to sell $75 million in company stock right before it would go down.

▶ Lehman Brothers: During the 2008 financial crisis, Lehman Brothers was found to have been hiding more than $50 billion in loans and the fake selling toxic assets—making the company look financially stronger and safer than it really was, to the tune of $100 billion. Again, shareholders lost billions during bankruptcy and the employees lost their jobs.

▶ Bernie Madoff: He was found in 2008 to have run the largest Ponzi scheme in history, bilking investors out of more than $64.8 billion.

While greed was "good" for the executives and criminals, it certainly was not for the investors, retirees, or employees in any of these companies. But let us face facts, those who had money wanted more and those who saw what others were getting had wanted in—until, like a house of cards, it falls. Some whole sectors of the economy have suffered for years due to a few bad companies, like the mortgage industry and financial services. People who expected to retire who were heavily investing in these companies lost everything. It is no wonder that trust among the mass population in financial services is at 55% while informed public trust levels stand at 67% (Edelman, 2019). So, we know that greed is not good and ultimately impacts wealth, but what about wealth itself?

The accumulation of money or wealth has been around since humanity developed the concepts of trade and basic economics. Over time, humans developed an amazing sense of how to make, keep, and use the financial resources available. In the 14th century, one of the most powerful and wealthy families in Europe was the Medici family. It is important to note that Machiavelli wrote *The Prince* to gain favor with Lorenzo di Piero de' Medici whose family motto put succinctly reads, "Money to get the power, power to keep the money" (Higgs, 2005).

Similarly, today we see the classism and separation of the have from the have-nots. The rich get richer and the powerful continue to wield power. This is just like the corporate scandals we can observe when justice moves against elected leaders embroiled in scandals involving financial corruption (Jim Traficant in 2002), bribery (Duke Cunningham and William Jefferson in 2005), tax evasion (Michael Grimm in 2015), money laundering (Rick Renzi in 2013), and so forth. This is by no means an exhaustive list of wrongdoers; you can find more with a simple internet search. So, we know that wealth enables those in power to do things that keep both power and wealth in their hands until they are caught.

At this point you might be thinking that wealth is evil or at least begets evil. However, let us look at what wealth has accomplished. The United States of America was based on the foundations of life, liberty, and the pursuit of happiness. A person could become anything he or she wanted if they worked hard. While it is true that for a long period of time groups have had to fight for equality and rights that would enable them to pursue the same wealth building opportunities as have been afforded to others, today they enjoy access to capital, banking, investments, education, freedom, and a standard of living that is more than many countries.

Can more be done? Absolutely. Should more be done? Absolutely. However, money and wealth do change lives and that change can be positive. Today, we can look at what micro-finance is doing in Asia, as it lifts families out of poverty and creates new opportunities. We can see what public education is doing for people all over the world by enabling an educated society to develop and grow. We can watch as technological developments and medical innovations extend people's lives.

The arts and the humanities are driven by the contributions of those with means and the desire to be involved. Charitable organizations are largely funded by people and groups with the resources and shared passion for the mission. All these are driven by wealth and investment. Wealth, not even at the level you may think is rich, affords grandparents time to spend with grandkids, parents the ability to see their kids more successful than they were, families to spend time together, cultures to be explored, history to be recorded, inventions to be developed, the aged to be cared for, lives to be saved, shelter to be shared, and most of all life to be lived.

Gordon Gekko was wrong, "Greed is _not_ good." Greed does not make us better, sharper, or richer. Greed is what destroys wealth. Greed is what destroys our soul. Greed is, as Timothy stated, the root of evil. So, as you pursue wealth (or even a modest savings), you must ask yourself: Do you seek wealth just to have more or do you seek it for a higher purpose?

Craig Brigman
Financial Advisor
Virginia

Contributed by Craig Brigman. © Kendall Hunt Publishing Company

CASE STUDY #7

Kim Lin grabbed her designer purse and exited her Aston Martin. Suddenly, the world exploded, with flashing bulbs, screaming people, music playing faintly in the distance. Kim smiled wide and waved as she stepped onto the red carpet. It was hot under the lights as celebrities glided up and down the promenade, smiling and shaking hands with each other, moving slowly toward the gala's entrance. Kim, a movie star of the highest class, ignored the paparazzi and headed toward people of her social echelon. Everyone had come out tonight, and the event was pasted with the rich and famous. Maybe, if Kim was lucky, she would snag the eye of a producer or director. But for now, it was time to look good for the cameras.

The remainder of the event was boring as all of the rich, beautiful people droned on about how honored they were to give awards to other rich, beautiful people. The receiving actor would then, in turn, stutter and stumble over how honored they were to receive the award, shaming the public for how they were killing the environment. For a bunch of actors, nobody seemed to know their lines. Kim saw right through the glitz and glamour of the event. Growing up with nothing in a trailer park in Madison Heights, Virginia, Kim saved up enough money to travel across the United States, where she caught a break. From nothing, she managed to land a key role in a TV drama and snowballed her success into major motion pictures. Now she had achieved her dream of dining with the rich and shaking hands with the powerful, leaving her poverty-stricken trailer park.

DISCUSSION QUESTIONS

1. Based on the readings, how would a sociologist diagnose this situation?

2. What specific sociological factors are involved?

3. How might Kim's new celebrity status affect her relationships with her relatives and older friends?

Check out the Chapter 7 video at this link:

https://www.khpcontent.com/

VOCABULARY

1 Corinthians 13
Absolute Poverty
Act Utilitarianism
Caste System
Categorical Imperative
Christian Teleological Approach
Class
Contractarian Approach
Deontological Approach
Ethical Egoism
Four Main Principles of Social Stratification
Global Slavery Index

Lower Class
Middle Class
Rule Utilitarianism
Situationism
Slavery
Social Mobility
Social Stratification
Split Labor Market
Teleological Approach
Upper Class
Virtue of Love

References

Amaladoss, M. (1994). *A call to community: The caste system and Christian responsibility*. Gujarat Sahitya Prakash.

Baumane-Vitolina, I., Cals, I., & Sumilo, E. (2016). Is ethics rational? Teleological, deontological, and virtue ethics theories reconciled in the context of traditional economic decision making. *Procedia Economics and Finance, 39*, 108–114.

Bonacich, E. (1972). A theory of ethnic antagonism: The split labor market. *American Sociological Review, 37*, 547–559.

Cochran, R. F., & Calo, Z. R. (Eds.). (2017). *Agape, justice, and law: How might Christian love shape law?* Cambridge University Press.

Cunningham, R. L. (1970). *Situationism and the new morality*. Apple-Century-Crofts.

Edelman. (2019). *2019 Edleman Trust Barometer: Financial services*. https://www.edelman.com/sites/g/files/aatuss191/files/2019-04/2019_Edelman_Trust_Barometer_Financial_Services_Report_1.pdf

Global Slavery Index. (2018). https://www.globalslaveryindex.org

Guerrera, F. (2010, September 24). How 'Wall Street' changed Wall Street. https://www.ft.com/content/7e55442a-c76a-11df-aeb1-00144feab49a

Helms, B., & Consultative Group to Assist the Poorest. (2006). *Access for all: Building inclusive financial systems*. World Bank Publications.

Henslin, J. M. (2018). *Social problems: A down-to-earth approach*. Pearson.

Higgs, R. (2005, October 1). The economic policy of Machiavelli's Prince. https://www.independent.org/news/article.asp?id=1662

Hooker, B. (2012). *Developing deontology: New essays in ethical theory*. Wiley.

Jennings, T. W. (1990). *Good news to the poor: John Wesley's evangelical economies*. Abingdon.

Kant, I. (1785). *Groundwork of the metaphysics of morals*. Cambridge University Press.

Levering, M. (2008). *Biblical natural law: A theocentric and teleological approach*. Oxford University Press.

Miller, R. B. (2009). Actual rule utilitarianism. *The Journal of Philosophy, 106*(1), 5–28.

Newsome, C. A. (2019). *Rhetoric and hermeneutics: Approaches to text, tradition and social construction in biblical and Second Temple literature*. Mohr Siebeck.

Semuels, A. (2016). Poor at 20, poor for life. *The Atlantic*. https://www.theatlantic.com/business/archive/2016/07/social-mobility-america/491240/

Svensson, G., & Padin, C. (2012). Teleological approaches from complexity sciences in services. *International Journal of Quality and Service Sciences, 4*(3), 224–237.

20th Century Fox. (1987). *Wall Street*.

Wheelan, C. J. (2016). *Naked money: A revealing look at what it is and why it matters* (1st ed.). W.W. Norton & Company.

Witt, J. (2009). *SOC*. McGraw-Hill.

Ch 8 Poverty

Few social problems have been as historically prevalent than that of poverty. In society, *poverty* refers to the social condition of consistently lacking the basic necessities in life, such as food, water, shelter, clothing, communication, education, medical care, social services, and so on. Poverty is a multidimensional issue (Greve, 2019). Defying reductionism, it is a complex, cyclical, social reality that hurts millions, if not billions, of people in the world (Human Development Reports, 2019).

Poverty transcends all social, economic, and political boundaries and rests upon a variety of social and environmental factors. According to the World Bank (2020), "The majority of the global poor live in rural areas and are poorly educated, employed in the agricultural sector, and under 18 years of age" (worldbank.org). Most of the impoverished live in southern Asia or greater (sub-Saharan) Africa. According to Worldvision.org (2020), nearly a billion people live in *extreme poverty*, making less than $2.00 (U.S.) a day. Additionally, nearly 75% of the world's population live in *developing countries*, with many of them lacking basic sanitation, clean water, or modern health or affordable medical services.

Although poverty levels have globally decreased percentage-wise in the last 50 years (Chen & Ravallion, 2004), with a booming world population and other globalization factors, poverty remains in effect for most regions in the world. Although there are several subcategories (situational, generational, urban, rural, and so on), there are three basic types of poverty: biological, relative, and the official poverty line. These levels of poverty range from the extreme to the political, although all poverty still inflicts painful wants and needs upon its victims.

Biological poverty (also known as absolute poverty) refers to the starvation, malnutrition, and a lack of proper housing for people in a region (whether due to man-made or environmental factors). The effects of biological poverty are profound, creating serious health and personal safety issues for the afflicted, as well as other cognitive and developmental problems without proper nutrition and protection (Jensen, 2009).

Relative poverty refers to people living below economic standards of their society or social group. This is more common and, as the name suggests, is more subjective, political, and environmentally specific within the society or community. While still based on a serious lacking of resources, this may relate more to people feeling economically restricted rather than actually being dangerously impoverished (Dunn, 2017). In other words, people are unable to purchase or acquire the accoutrements of society that more affluent people can, which leads to great frustration and *anomie* (a social disconnect and neglect within a social environment).

The *official poverty line* (also known as the poverty threshold, limit, or breadline) is based on a governmental financial equation that was established in the mid-1960s (under *President Lyndon Johnson's "War on Poverty"*) to make sure that all citizens in the U.S. could have at least their basic financial needs met (Haveman et al., 2015). The government determines the poverty line through a presumption of a typical American income food budget (about one third of a family's monthly food costs). Once they've determined that, they multiply it by three, with those above the line being economically self-sufficient and those below the line being economically lacking.

Although definitely needed across the world (United Nations, 2020), this figure is somewhat artificial and can be influenced by domestic and global politics on either side of the aisle. Understandably, the higher developed countries will have a higher poverty line than the lower developing countries. For comparison, the 2020 poverty line for Americans amounts to about $35 a day; across the globe, the poverty line is $1.90 a day—a huge difference but understandable considering the vast differences in foreign countries' economies. Still, a sobering question is "Could you survive on $1.90 a day?"

Poverty falls upon people in many different ways (Sarlo, 2019). One of the biggest *causes* is the system of trade, work, and globalization (which will be discussed in a future chapter) that results in low-paying jobs, unfair agreements, and low technology. Poverty can also come from war or military conflict, which interrupts most services and social norms. Additionally, people can build up too much in debt, paying back a very high interest rate that depletes their financial reserves. Additionally, people can also have restricted access to land to own and to utilize for financial gain. In fact, in many countries, large tracts of land are owned by large businesses, which hoard and exploit them for production purposes.

One of the more powerful teaching tools that I use in my "Social Problems" class is to show students a *cycle of poverty* chart created from information gleaned and combined from other sources collected over the years. The top of the chart begins with "Born into poverty," and it is one of the most significant factors for why people live in poverty. Much less a matter of the will or a deficit in industriousness, poverty is brought on from one's location or environment.

The next box on the chart states, "Malnourished & Ill Health in Family," which many people can relate to as they have had to take off "sick days" to recover. Once better, they return, but what if they could not? What if the disease or sickness never left their home? That is what it is like for many people in the world today.

Other boxes follow such as "Children help with work" (because their parents might be too sick to work, or even dead), "Children miss school" (because the family cannot afford for them not to work), and "Children less qualified," which pushes them to the bottom of the hiring pool behind others with parents well enough to afford for their children to learn and play and socialize, upping their chances for a brighter future.

Without much money, the child turns into an adult, but finds only *closed social avenues*, which creates a sense of "desperation and hopelessness," leading them into risky, criminal environments to survive yet another day. Perhaps they fall in love, but they cannot afford condoms or other contraceptives, so they become "very young parents"—too immature to know how to parent well.

Their children grow up in the same sort of environment that they did, and the whole cycle begins again—year after year, generation after generation (Blandón et al., 2017). This is how poverty gets perpetuated and even how caste systems ensnare their social prisoners. Questions abound: How can people break this vicious cycle? What can people do to remedy this sad reality for nearly half the world's population? What should people's attitudes in First World countries be concerning the impoverished in the Third World countries?

MAIN SOCIOLOGICAL APPROACHES

As mentioned in the previous chapter, one's social status and class directly influence one's social opportunities and comfort level in life. Whether earned or inherited, wealth is the great door-opener for social opportunities and poverty is the deep pit for social restrictions. As mentioned earlier, though, there are a variety of presumptions and conclusions regarding the causes and cures for a social problem as vast as poverty.

For the symbolic interactionist, the biggest issue concerns how to objectively and fairly define what poverty is, across the globe. Rather than pure scientific inquiry, often public sociology (a.k.a., political sociology) is employed to create a one-sided definition of poverty for social engineering purposes. For instance, Reeves et al. (2019) admit,

> We propose the utility of a phenomenological conceptualisation of poverty that is grounded in the first-hand experiences of individuals who experience poverty and thus has the potential to drive a social and policy agenda that meaningfully reflects their perspectives and sense-making. (p. 2)

It goes without saying that this is a rather myopic approach to a monumental problem. Moreover, it approaches this social problem as a systematic issue, without regard to cultural and personal values that might be influential or precipitate economic hardships. As poverty is very much dependent upon regional contexts, governmental policies, cultural behaviors, and other interactive constructs, it is important to expand one's vision to what could be its cause.

For the conflict theorist, poverty is the direct result of a *capitalist economy*. Relying a great deal upon Marxist ideals, they hold to the notion that world history provides a chronicle of class con-

flict played out between the oppressed and the oppressors, with poor people suffering the brunt of the rich people's self-serving financial schemes. As Losurdo (2016) remarks, "No one should be indifferent to the polarization of wealth and poverty inherent in bourgeois society" (p. 64). Thus, poverty occurs because the middle class cannot be trusted to be concerned with or make effort to take care of the poor and downtrodden in society. Only when the state controls the economy and private ownership has been dissolved and redistributed will economic hardships like poverty cease to be a social reality, theoretically.

Yet, as seen in the economic histories of all countries that have embraced *communism* or socialism, the functionalist would point out that the "haves" in communist/socialist societies continue to hold most of the wealth and the *have-nots* continue to suffer, despite political promises of shared wealth. Pethokoukis (2019) notes,

> What about the terrible history of centrally planned economies? Apparently, the great lessons from those experiences must be relearned. I mean, clearly the message isn't getting through when some folks—as I've seen on Twitter—can look at a chart showing the steep decline in global poverty and view it as an endorsement of the Chinese communist party rather than market reforms and decentralization. (Web)

The loss of freedoms that are exchanged for promised financial comforts are enticing but are not very realistic or pragmatic, evidentially. Still, poverty carries with it a tremendous negative social impact for everyone in society. Regardless of one's socioeconomic status, *poverty's toxic effects* such as increased crime, homelessness, child abuse, increased physical and mental health issues, and a general social decline must be addressed to protect and preserve as many people as possible in society. Economic aid (along with food, clothing, medicine, water, and shelter) definitely helps manage the symptoms of poverty in the present, but for any long-term improvements, educational and skill-building intersections for people suffering at any part of the cycle of poverty must be offered and utilized for poverty's malevolent grip to be broken (Mihai et al., 2015).

DEALING WITH MATTERS OF THE DARK

Throughout history, humanity has been constantly seeking after the accumulation of goods and money. It is this acquisition that each human strives for, relentlessly—an assertion that Scottish philosopher and theologian John *Macquarrie* refers to when he speaks of the *dehumanization* of not *having* (Macquarrie, 1985). The pursuit of "having" is more than a simple function (or dysfunction) of society. In many ways, it displays who we are and who we are not.

Macquarrie asserts (1985), "One who possesses nothing—not even the clothes on their backs—experiences a dehumanizing, but the opposite is also true" (p. 80). Possessing nothing can lead to feelings of inadequacy, worthlessness, and lack of character. People need a modest amount of possessions for emotional security and identity. Without them, they can become desperate and cynical in life.

Of course, on the other end of the spectrum, people who have much wealth sometimes display feelings of superiority, irreplaceability, and nobility. Although there are many exceptions, such rich people (and especially those who inherit their wealth from their parents' hard work) may overestimate their social capital or (ironically) can also become desperate and cynical in life, but for different reasons.

© Janos Levente/Shutterstock.com

Their desperation comes out of insecurity created by a life of "vanity." Their identity is lost in a turbulent sea of possessions and this fills them with sadness, for their life lacks meaning. A simple analogy of this would be a woman living next to a lake and has less reverence for water than say, a man living in the desert. For one, it means nothing; to the other, it means everything. In this, they share a commonality of desperation in "having."

As an alternative, one of the Hebrew names of God that seems to be of great value in our world today would probably be *El Roi*. The first person recorded to have ever called God this name was Hagar, the slave and servant of Abraham and Sarah, who fled from an abusive, exploitative relationship with Patriarch Abraham's wife, Sarah, into the desert (Genesis 16:6, New International Version).

At a distant spring, surrounded by wildness, with little to no possessions to protect or provide for herself, Hagar waited and hoped for rescue from her circumstances (and she was not disappointed). In dismal environments of isolation and indignation such as this one, people need a God who watches us as we are, where we are, and yet still counts us worthy of His love. Thus, this name of God, meaning "The God who sees me," is quite relevant to people's transcendent needs of acknowledgment, acceptance, and love (Hrichi, 2017).

Yet, we live in a world which is growing rapidly in population and shrinking in free space. People are becoming a cheap commodity. We are assigned numbers and made to stand in line after line to get everything. Our schools, banks, stores, and freeways all create a sensation of moving livestock around. Worse yet, as too much product drives the price down, so does too much humanity lessen our value.

Bums and runaways on the streets are ignored as if they were phantoms. People are laid off at work due to downsizing and are quickly forgotten by their peers. Families rarely talk to each other as the television creates a vacuum of communication. Nations, too concerned with their own domestic problems, cease to cultivate international relations and shut down lines of communication (Turku, 2016). In this dismal environment of isolation and indignation, people need a God who sees us as we are, where we are, and yet still counts us worthy of His love.

Of course, God could ignore us all. We do not deserve recognition in our sinfulness, but God does not just see His fallen children on Earth. He reaches out to us in holy love and wraps His loving arms around us. Moreover, He calls His beloved children in Christ to do likewise with our broken brothers and sisters. We are to see people as God sees them—with loving, compassionate, considerate eyes of redemption and rescue. Fear, anger, and low self-esteem cannot resist the powerful love of *El Roi*.

As the slave Hagar experienced unmerited mercy and mission from a real and relational deity (Genesis 16:13), as Moses thought himself unworthy of God's noble call to free the Hebrew slaves (Exodus 3:11), as the Prophet Isaiah was devastated by the social environment that surrounded and pervaded him (Isaiah 6:5), as John the Baptist was flabbergasted that the Savior of the world needed his assistance (Matthew 3:13), or as the Prodigal Son was overwhelmed by his own father's forgiveness and acceptance of him despite his rebellion, so all people—the whole wretched mass of humanity—are warmly embraced by God giving us priceless value in a valueless society.

INSIGHTS FROM THE EXPERTS

"Family Dysfunction"

Theories and research on what constitute a family (or even just the definition of family) are inconclusive. Taylor (2011) suggested there is no precise definition and characteristics of "family." The definition of family goes beyond a structure that serves to stabilize society, as suggested by functionalist theory or the Marxist perspective of serving as a distraction from other realities (Wilson, 1980).

Some have suggested that the family is a vitally important institution (Haskey et al., 1999) for the socialization of children and a place of safety for adults, which results in the overall well-being and social conformity (Bogenschneider & Corbett, 2010a). To a child, family represents a secure environment that facilitates emotional and intellectual skills, while adults look to family for care, love, and mutual support (Haskey et al., 1999). Societally, family serves as a structure from which children cultivate social skills to engage in healthy interaction with others and eventually develop into well-balanced adults who can assimilate into society (Haskey et al., 1999).

What happens when this family unit is not functional? This question is one of the reasons why family dysfunction is an important topic in the field of sociology and psychology as this dysfunction can have long-lasting psychological and behavioral effects which negatively impacts individuals, families, and society (Forward, 1989). All families may, at some point, have elements of family dysfunction. However, when several negative signs of a dysfunctional family are evident without intervention, this could lead to a constant state of dysfunction for that family (Becvar & Becvar, 2002).

Common Signs of Family Dysfunction

According to Kaslow (1996), dysfunctional families typically present certain common signs and behavior patterns, and this dysfunctional behavior is often reinforced by enabling or perpetuation. Kaslow (1996) identified these common signs:

1. Lack of empathy, understanding, and sensitivity (e.g., one family member may repeatedly be favored, while another is marginalized).
2. Denial (e.g., the "elephant in the room" syndrome, whereby families fail to normalize abusive behaviors and refuse to acknowledge the occurrences).
3. Unhealthy self-boundaries (inadequate or missing boundaries) (e.g., enduring inappropriate treatment, physical, emotional, or sexual abuse; and a failure to express or define acceptable and unacceptable behaviors/treatments).
4. Disrespect of others' boundaries (e.g., intentionally violating expressed physical or other boundaries, and unreasonably breaking promises).
5. Conflict extremes (e.g., excessive hostile feuds or the lack of peaceful disagreeing amongst family members).
6. Privileged family member (e.g., one or more family members may receive unequal or unfair treatment based on birth order, gender, age, family role (father, etc.), abilities,

race, or caste which may lead to the concession of one member, while others are marginalized or selective application of rules).

7. Emotional love is often conditional, and support may often be pathological (Al Ubaidi, 2017).
8. Violation of personal privacy and suppressed autonomy (Al Ubaidi, 2017).
9. Role reversal or role confusion (e.g., both parent and child change their roles; Al Ubaidi, 2017).
10. Perfectionism and unrealistic expectations of children (e.g., parent's expectation may exceed the child's developmental level, abilities, or skills). Perfectionism is not only unrealistic but toxic to the family life (Al Ubaidi, 2017).

Effects of Family Dysfunction on Society

Functional and healthy families are foundationally essential to society. Society looks to functional families as a source of sustaining the labor force needed for a robust economy (Bogenschneider & Corbett, 2010b). Functional families also serve to facilitate the environment for the nurturing of caring, altruistic, and committed citizens needed for a stable democracy. On the other hand, family dysfunction is the antithesis to promoting the healthy development of children, adolescents, and adults, as well as achieving healthy societal goals (Bogenschneider & Corbett, 2010b).

Education and Labor Force

According to Reynolds and Temple (2005), amongst a worldwide economic transformation, nations' competitiveness relies more and more on its human capital. This reliance on human capital is particularly dependent on the education and social skills of its labor force. Children growing up with family dysfunction have no control over their toxic life environment, and the emotional scarring from repeated trauma and pain shapes their identity and life choices.

During the transition from victimized children into victimized adults, these individuals attempt escaping past trauma/pain by practicing even more destructive behaviors and finding biochemical coping solutions (Vannicelli, 1989). These behaviors and coping solutions may include alcohol abuse, drug abuse, high-risk sports, risky behaviors, over-eating, and proliferation of sex partners (Reynolds & Temple, 2005). These behaviors and coping solutions only serve as a catalyst for negative outcomes, such as academic deficiencies, school dropouts, juvenile delinquency, crimes, physical and mental health decline, gambling, and unemployment (Al Ubaidi, 2017; Reynolds & Temple, 2005).

Based on a 30-year longitudinal study, researchers Sroufe et al. (2005) used one variable to predict which children would be most likely to drop out of school. Using the variable of "quality of care up to age 42 months," Sroufe et al. were able to make these predictions with 77% accuracy. With this tool, researchers could predict the probability of becoming a high school dropout before a child started school. The variables of family dysfunction, whereby parents who were neglectful or disengaged have shown to increase the odds of children dropping out (Sroufe et al., 2005). Al Ubaidi (2017) confirmed that deficient or absent parent(s) is often found in dysfunctional families, which usually involves the neglect of children's physical and emotional needs.

Sroufe et al. (2005) also found that by age 23, educational attainment was contingent on young adults' early care and cumulative history, which focuses on the family environment of nurture. It was found that the early experiences of children were robust predictors of later development, returning to high school, and peer relationships (Sroufe et al., 2005).

Family and the Role of Quality of Citizenship

Certain parenting styles lend itself to secure attachment relationships, which have been found to predict qualities that societies value in their citizenry (Sroufe, 1988). These styles included parents that were reliably available and sensitively responsive. In a longitudinal study, Sroufe (1988) indicated that the mother-infant secure attachment was shown to result in children that were less hostile to peers, more empathetic, and self-reliant.

Likewise, Englund et al. (2000) found that the mother-infant attachment relationship was significantly linked to the qualities found in good citizenship by ages 15 and 16. These qualities included social aptitude in problem-solving, leadership, involvement, and self-confidence (Englund et al., 2000). Additionally, healthy parenting at age 2 in the first generation predicted healthy parenting at age 2 in the second generation (Conger & Conger, 2002; Sroufe et al., 2005).

Fejes-Mendoza et al. (1995) interviewed incarcerated juvenile female offenders in three states to obtain profiles of certain dysfunction. The participants were asked to self-report their criminal, educational, and family histories. Fejes-Mendoza et al. (1995) found that juvenile female offenders characteristically reported the following:

1. "Failed one or more grades in school
2. More than one serious arrest
3. Used drugs prior to crimes and as part of a daily lifestyle
4. Acted intentionally, and most often with others, to commit crimes." (p. 309)

Significant factors that served to hinder these juvenile female offenders from becoming functional adults were geared around dysfunctional family and relationships, siblings who were criminal offenders, academic deficits, and substance abuse (Fejes-Mendoza et al., 1995).

In summary, family dysfunction rubs against the grain of society and the psychological well-being of individuals. The benefits of belonging to a functional family are evident. To a child, the family represents a secure environment that nurtures secure attachment relationships and emotional and intellectual skills. For adults, the family is a source of care, love, and mutual support (Haskey et al., 1999).

Socially, when the family is dysfunctional, children lack the social skills to engage in healthy interaction with others, and they struggle to cope and assimilate into society (Haskey et al., 1999). Hence, these behaviors and coping solutions that result in negative outcomes, such as academic deficiencies, school dropouts, juvenile delinquency, crimes, physical and mental health decline, gambling, and unemployment are thrust upon communities and society (Al Ubaidi, 2017; Reynolds & Temple, 2005).

Dr. Margaret Gopaul, PhD
Clinical Psychologist
Institute Review Board Member

CASE STUDY #8

Little Timmy did not know why his mommy and daddy fought so much. His grandma was nice, though, and was always around to watch him as he waited for someone to get home. She always said both parents were either at work or in school and couldn't be home much. Even though there wasn't anything to eat, play with, or wear, Timmy always found something to do in their absence. Most of the time, his thing was television. He didn't like to play outside because he didn't have a bike, skateboard, or basketball. His one pair of tennis shoes were too small for him and broken in the heel and toe.

One day, his grandma sat him down at lunch and talked to Timmy about money (or more accurately, the fact his parents had none). Timmy asked if he could work because he wanted to make money for the family and his grandma began to cry. She made him promise to do good in school. Timmy hated school, and his dad always told him it was stupid, but he still promised to try. Later that night, his parents came home and were watching television on the family couch. Sheepishly, Timmy asked why they were poor. This created a massive fight between his parents. That night as Timmy fell asleep to the sound of his parents fighting, he dreamed of life when they were home and could play together.

DISCUSSION QUESTIONS

1. Based on the readings, how would a sociologist diagnose this situation?

2. What specific sociological factors are involved?

3. What would break the cycle of poverty for this family?

Check out the Chapter 8 video at this link:

https://www.khpcontent.com/

VOCABULARY

Anomie	Have-Nots
Biological Poverty	Having
Capitalist Economy	Macquarrie
Causes of Poverty	Official Poverty Line
Closed Social Avenues	Poverty
Communism Economy	Poverty's Toxic Effects
Cycle of Poverty	President Lyndon Johnson
Dehumanization	Relative Poverty
Developing Countries	Solutions
El Roi	War on Poverty
Extreme Poverty	

References

Al Ubaidi, B. A. (2017). Cost of growing up in dysfunctional family. *Journal of Family Medicine and Disease Prevention, 3*(3), 1–6.

Becvar, D., & Becvar, R. (2002). *Family therapy: A Systemic Integration.* Pearson Education.

Blandón, E. Z., Källestål, C., Peña, R., Perez, W., Berglund, S., Contreras, M., & Persson, L. (2017). Breaking the cycles of poverty: Strategies, achievements, and lessons learned in Los Cuatro Santos, Nicaragua, 1990–2014. *Global Health Action, 10*(1), 1–11. doi:http://dx.doi.org.ezproxy.liberty.edu/10.1080/16549716.2017.1272884

Bogenschneider, K., & Corbett, T. J. (2010a). *Evidence-based policymaking: Insights from policy-minded researchers and research-minded policymakers.* Taylor & Francis Group.

Bogenschneider, K., & Corbett, T. J. (2010b). Family policy: Becoming a field of inquiry and subfield of social policy [Family policy decade review]. *Journal of Marriage and Family, 72,* 783–803.

Chen, S., & Ravallion, M. (2004). How have the world's poorest fared since the early 1980s? *The World Bank Research Observer, 19*(2), 141–169.

Conger, R. D., & Conger, K. J. (2002). Resilience in Midwestern families: Selected findings from the first decade of a prospective, longitudinal study. *Journal of Marriage and Family, 64,* 361–373.

Dunn, A. (2017). Relative poverty, British social policy, writing, and public experience. *Social Policy and Society, 16*(3), 377–390.

Englund, M. M., Levy, A. K., Hyson, D. M., & Sroufe, L. A. (2000). Adolescent social competence: Effectiveness in a group setting. *Child Development, 71,* 1049–1060.

Fejes-Mendoza, K., Miller, D., & Eppler, R. (1995). Portraits of dysfunction: Criminal, educational, and family profiles of juvenile female offenders. *Education and Treatment of Children, 18*(3), 309–321.

Forward, S. (1989). *Toxic parents: Overcoming their hurtful legacy and reclaiming your life.* Bantam Books.

Greve, B. (2019). *Routledge international handbook of poverty*. Routledge.

Haskey, J., Kiernan, K., & Morgan, P. M. (1999). *The fragmenting family: Does it matter?* St. Edmundsbury.

Haveman, R., Blank, R., Moffitt, R., Smeeding, T., & Wallace, G. (2015). The war on poverty: Measurement, trends, and policy. *Journal of Policy Analysis and Management, 34*(3), 593–638.

Hrichi, S. (2017). *Hagar: Rediscovering the God who sees me (Bible study)*. Leafwood.

Human Development Reports. (2019). *The 2019 global multidimensional poverty index* (MPI). http://hdr.undp.org/en/2018-MPI

Jensen, E. (2009). *Teaching with poverty in mind: What being poor does to kids' brains and what schools can do about it*. ASCD.

Kaslow, F. W. (1996). *Handbook of relational diagnosis and dysfunctional family patterns*. Wiley-Interscience.

Losurdo, D. (2016). *Class struggle: A political and philosophical history*. Palgrave Macmillan.

Macquarrie, J. (1985). *In search of humanity: A theological and philosophical approach*. Crossroad.

Mihai, M., Titan, E., & Manea, D. (2015). Education and poverty. *Procedia Economics and Finance, 32*, 855–860.

Pethokoukis, J. (2019). An economic lesson worth remembering: Communism was pretty terrible. *American Enterprise Institute*. https://www.aei.org/economics/an-economic-lesson-worth-remembering-communism-was-pretty-terrible/

Reeves, L. S., Parsell, C., & Liu, S. (2019). Towards a phenomenology of poverty: Defining poverty through the lived experiences of the 'poor.' *Journal of Sociology*, 1–16.

Reynolds, A. J., & Temple, J. A. (2005). Priorities for a new century of early childhood programs. *Infants and Young Children, 18*, 104–118.

Sarlo, C. (2019). *The causes of poverty*. Fraser Institute.

Sroufe, L. (1988). A developmental perspective on day care. *Early Childhood Research Quarterly, 3*(3), 283–291.

Sroufe, L. A., Egeland, B., Carlson, E. A., & Collins, W. A. (2005). *The development of the person: The Minnesota study of risk and adaptation from birth to adulthood*. Guilford.

Taylor, C. (2011). Foucault and Familial Power. *Hypatia Wiley Online Library 27*(1), 201–218.

Turku, H. (2016). *Isolationist states in an interdependent world*. Routledge.

United Nations. (2020). Ending poverty. UN.org. https://www.un.org/en/sections/issues-depth/poverty/

Vannicelli, M. (1989). *Group psychotherapy with adult children of alcoholics: Treatment techniques and countertransference*. Guilford Press.

Wilson, W. (1980). *The declining significance of race* (2nd ed.). University of Chicago Press.

World Bank. (2020). Poverty: Overview. *Worldbank.org*. https://www.worldbank.org/en/topic/poverty/overview

World Vision. (2020). Global poverty: Facts, FAQs, and how to help. *Worldvision.org*. https://www.worldvision.org/sponsorship-news-stories/global-poverty-facts

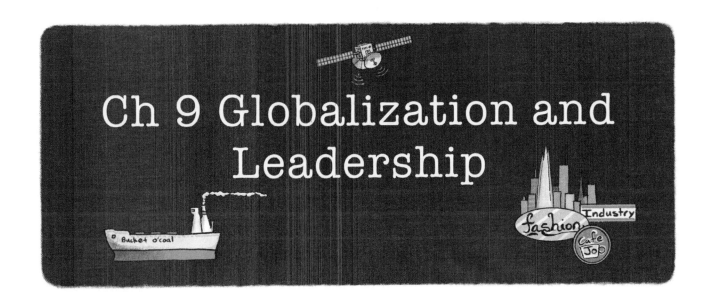

Ch 9 Globalization and Leadership

The *globalization movement* is ubiquitous, and it has been a social force for centuries. Although slow in its beginnings, globalization, since the 1950s and 1960s, has caused a social explosion of *trade, people, investments, technological advancements,* cultural awareness, and influences, as well as a blending of ideas between foreign countries previously separated by long distances. It is not an understatement to say that globalization has created a more integrated and dependent *world community.*

Historically, scholars have evidence of globalization as far back as the 15th century C.E., with *European explorers* and colonists being credited for starting the globalization movement. Yet, there are archaeological hints that ancient maritime activities connected distant countries together long before previously thought in the historical timeline. Rather than living in isolated regions, speculations and suspicions abound on whether the Egyptians visited Central and South America (or vice versa) or if the ancient Chinese explorers made it to North America (Jairazbhoy, 1974).

As most Western civilization scholars will attest, after the thousands of years of hunter-gatherer existence, the rise of organized agriculture communities aided in the development and building of nation-states and empires, who frequently reached out into the known world to accumulate more goods and ideas to profit the state (Collyer, 2017). Although the movement saw its share of inactivity, after the Dark Ages (459–1350 C.E.), the emergence of the *Renaissance* (1350–1600 C.E.) saw an incredible increase of new thought and investigation. Ultimately, this led to new, better technologies and economic options, which in turn boosted international trade and financing exploration into the New World by countries like England, France, and Spain, who sought to increase and protect their global reach. While their goals may have been fundamentally political in nature, these countries' *empire-building* efforts helped to spread new ideas, products, and communication across the globe via the resources and forces of *imperialism.*

The driving force of globalization in the 20th century began with the decline of *socioeconomic barriers* after World War II (Kozarova, 2013). Before the second great war, most countries had innumerable international trade and foreign investment restrictions. Many countries, in order to thrive or even remain in existence, adopted less isolationist, friendlier international policies to avoid future wars and to reap the *benefits of globalization.* The threat of a communist takeover was real, and joining the Western *global community* helped in political protection and economic provision (Dubinsky, 2012).

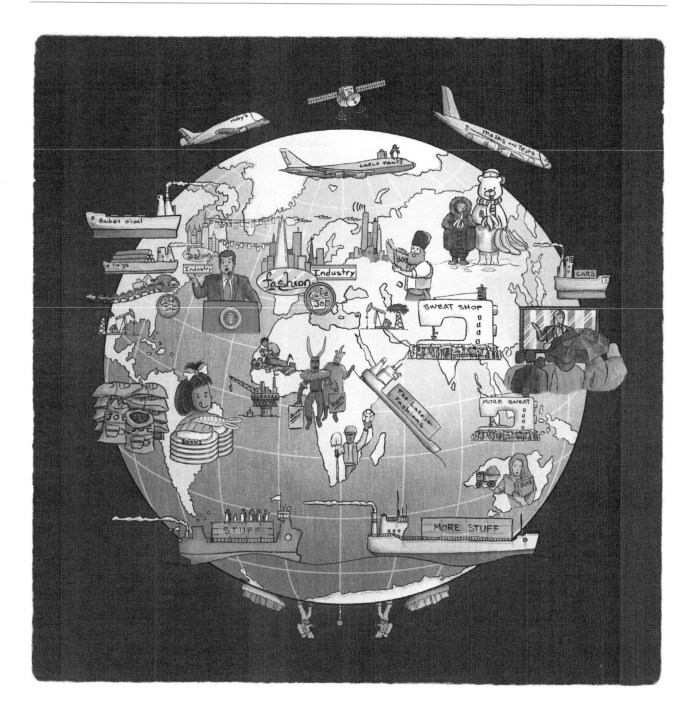

Additionally, the technological advancements after WWII positively influenced globalization. New inventions and new technologies assisted in worldwide production (commercial and agriculture), better health and medical options, an easier shipping of goods, and the facilitation of faster communication between the nations of the world. Decade after decade, globalization, with the powers of technology, brought the traditional spheres of social influence (economics, politics, culture) into greater and more unified alignment than ever before in human history.

One of the biggest spheres of influence in society is that of our leaders, who come to their positions with greater or lesser skills and talents, generally. There are different types of leaders. *Instrumental leaders* mainly focus on helping the group they lead meet its agreed-upon goals. On the other hand, *expressive leaders* promote group unity and harmony, focusing upon their group's emotional needs and social problems.

Authoritarian leaders are the most hostile and aggressive, ruling with an iron fist and myopic view of their position in society. *Democratic leaders* typically let the entire group decide what and how things will get accomplished. There might be criticism, but it is objective and fair (especially compared to the authoritarian's approach). The *Laissez-faire leader* basically acts as a facilitator, requiring little from the group members and giving even less of themselves, involvement-wise. Allowing any collective to decide matters can be a risky venture because *groupthink* tends to override critical thinking and "thought-police" begin to stamp out political dissent and enforce conformity (especially with those deviants!).

Generally, *self-interest* is the major motive behind the way that people behave toward each other (Homans, 1961). Still, there are several forms of interaction between people, historically. An *exchange relationship* occurs when a person acts in a certain way toward another to receive a reward or return. *Spontaneous cooperation* can occur when people are in need of aid, *traditional cooperation* can become a fixture of social customs, *directed cooperation* is one managed from outside a group, and a *contractual cooperation* occurs when groups formally agree to work together for a certain time period in a certain way (Ross & Nisbett, 1988).

MAIN SOCIOLOGICAL APPROACHES

The majority of sociologists today would agree that the most influential factor in the globalization movement, currently, is technology. Very few people would have known how deep, how far, and how wide the World Wide Web (a.k.a., the internet) would affect human society. The inventor of ethernet actually wrote, "I predict the Internet will soon go spectacularly supernova and in 1996 catastrophically collapse" (Metcalfe, 1993), which is somewhat ironic since I researched his prediction this year (2020) . . . well . . . on the web. The *internet* provides immediate access to financial data and immediate communication abilities, making transactions that formally took hours, days, or years to complete, done in minutes—if not seconds. The speed of technological advancements is staggering as the world launches into the 21st century.

Many sociologists do a reasonable job in summing up the connections between technology, *social change,* and social meaning (a.k.a., symbolic interactionism). Ogburn (1947) was astute in his assessment of the influence of technology upon society in regard to social desires and needs for increased production, an accompanying infectious usage of technological products, and these products' overall influence upon social activity and norms—both productively or destructively (pp. 81, 86). Shipp et al. (2012) additionally affirm that the relationship between technological products and social change is intertwined and catalytic in many ways (p. 72).

One can envision society and technology "leapfrogging" over each other, with human needs creating opportunities for advancements, which in turn lead to new needs or wants, in an endless cycle—for better or worse. As such, Ogburn (1947) suggests that a population reduction could influence both technology and social change (p. 84), and Shipp et al. (2012) suggest that the social changes brought on by technological advancements and offers will require new rules, regulations, and guidelines to protect moral and safety standards in society (p. 79).

Also, few if any companies can exist without computers anymore. In fact, the functional nature of computers has become a social force of its own, with speed and hard drive size being quintessential components for an efficient, productive company. However, with the advent and development of the virtual world, some technologies (like hard drive size) have been supplanted through virtual hard drives, making the old technology obsolete. Still, computers are the equivalent of financial capital, with Silicon Valley in California becoming one of the largest economies in the world (Segarra, 2018).

All global societies utilize technology and all global societies pay millions (or billions) of dollars to develop the best technology. Thus, in many ways, globalism and technology are integrally joined, with each pushing the other onward into new frontiers. This prompts the questions of how far human society will change and what will follow the current postmodern era. The old central narratives that surrounded vocations no longer exist in *postmodernity*. Currently, personal choice and diversity are a nominal part of work life.

With industrialization and the facilitation of production being more automated and inexpensive than ever before, knowledge and service for workers/owners have become primary economic products. Most people have more than one job and expect to do more than one duty while at work. Furthermore, the work that people do often reaches far beyond the confines of their office or business (Fekete, 2016). One can write a book and get it published in Eugene, Oregon, and then discover it advertised online in England, China, and Australia.

Presently, one can easily find the evidence of globalization in the media outlets, television and movies, in music and literature, and in day-to-day living. Of course, not everybody appreciates globalization, but everyone benefits from it to a greater or lesser degree. The evaluation of this grand social change is a complex and hotly debated topic, which Kellner (2002) discusses in his article (pp. 287–290); however, the social "tendrils" of globalization affect all aspects of human existence—from continent to continent, and culture to culture—and thus challenge blanket statements of condemnation or commendation.

Certainly, there are profound benefits to globalization, not least of which is the increased availability of goods and services for Third World countries that formerly were available only to select First World countries in Europe and North America. Presently, globalization has brought advanced technology, communication, goods, comforts, and cultural freedoms to areas of Asia and Africa that previously were shut out or ignored. New markets have opened, new international connections have been established, and new channels of sociological exchanges have been created (Archibugi & Pietrobelli, 2003). This is a definite benefit of globalization and definitely connected to functionalist theory.

That being said, as Caldwell (2004), Satterthwaite (2009), and Westley et al. (2011) point out in their articles, not everything about globalism is positive when it comes to the realities of such intense global exchange, integration, and interdependence. In the past 5 years, a countercultural, anti-globalization movement has arisen, pushing back against the homogenization of national identity and distinctives. Examples of this can be seen in England's *Brexit* from the European Union as well as the handful of countries resisting the mass Islamic immigration/invasion into European lands and, in the opposite direction, the introduction of any Western progressive culturalisms in more radically Muslim Middle East countries. Eschle remarks, "Clearly, 'the *anti-globalisation movement*' does not operate outside globalized economic, gendered, racialized and geopolitical power relations but is bound up within them and reflects them" (2004, p. 68).

Satterthwaite (2009) suggests that globalization, with its encouragement of *consumerism*, carries with it a danger-ous threat of damaging the climate even more than it already has been since the Industrial Era (p. 564). Caldwell (2004) questions what will ultimately transpire in the world by 2050—economically, educa-tionally, and environmentally—because of the increase in world population and the limitation of planetary resources (p. 313). Finally, Westley et al. (2011) point out that technological advancements accom-panying globalization have a great poten-tial to harm natural environments across the globe (pp. 763–764).

© nEwyyy/Shutterstock.com

Effectively, globalization is a two-edged sword (Westley et al., 2011, p. 763); yet, contrary to some Utopian dream of humanity living in perfect harmony with nature and each other, human existence before globalization had its pros and cons, humanity during globalization will have its own share of benefits and detriments, and people after globalization will no doubt have its own slides and speed bumps to contend with in life (as we move out into the cosmos, perhaps).

Regarding *global inequality*, I can think of nothing more important in the future of our planet. So much fighting, bloodshed, and conflict come from people perpetually suffering because of their social circumstances (a concept relating to conflict theory). As Witt (2009) states, "One of the things we learn from sociology is that we are embedded in larger networks in which decisions and events that happen far away, and about which we may know little or nothing, shape our daily life experiences" (p. 261).

This is such a powerful, unrecognized notion in the world today. People live in what they think are disconnected social bubbles, but in truth, we are all fighting the same battle to stay alive or to live our lives well. My life does affect people in Africa and China, and their lives affect me too. With such sociological awareness, I can make good choices so that I contribute positively to the world society.

DEALING WITH MATTERS OF THE DARK

A *worldview* is exactly what it states: a personal perspective on how the world generally operates—physically, philosophically, socially, and religiously (Bavinck, 2019). Considering a world population currently over seven billion people, there are innumerable personal worldviews from all countries and regions of the world. These worldviews are overarching in what they influence and/or affect, normally not in agreement with each other.

Worldviews include innumerable concepts, attitudes, and beliefs; however, in his book, *Deliver Us From Evil* (1997), Ravi Zacharias suggests four main questions that a worldview addresses: questions of origin, questions of meaning, questions of morality, and questions of destiny (p. 219). In other words, a worldview embraces or enforces quintessential ideas about where and how human beings came to be as a species on the Earth, what it means to be a fully-functioning human being, what limits people should and can have on the way they treat each other, and what final outcome awaits everyone in life and the afterlife (which might include the possibility of no post-death existence).

All worldviews impact or influence people's understandings of the supernatural, biblical authority, and the Christian faith. For instance, Entwistle states, "For the Christian, Christianity provides a worldview from which to understand the nature of the world and the nature of humanity" (2015, location 355/10377). Thus, the traditional Christian worldview suggests that God is an eternal figure who created the universe and the Earth (and all its inhabitants), that human beings were created for His pleasure and for His worship (because He is so awesomely wonderful), that humans ought to live in loving harmony with God and each other (sounds like functionalist theory to me), and that despite our fallen nature, we can restore our relationship with God on Earth through a holy relationship with Jesus Christ and subsequently regain our lost perfect existence after we die in Heaven with God (again through a holy relationship with Jesus Christ).

Of course, not all worldviews affirm or approve of the Christian faith. As Romans 8:5 (New International Version) concludes, "Those who live according to the flesh have their minds set on what the flesh desires; but those who live in accordance with the Spirit have their minds set on what the Spirit desires." The Christian worldview mandates that followers live according to the priorities and prohibitions set down in the biblical texts 2,000 years ago, which have been followed in the Christian community faithfully (but not perfectly, of course).

Other non-Christian (or anti-Christian) worldviews promote living by the flesh in hedonism, permissiveness, and violence. The Christian worldview operates on the premise that the healthiest and happiest people are those who deny their fleshly impulses and seek to reform themselves with Jesus and God as perfect models of holy living (MacArthur, 2003). Other worldviews operate on the premises that feed human weaknesses and lusts, all too frequently at the detriment of those around us.

Thus, a strict worldly approach to the social sciences is dangerous and to be avoided. As McMinn states, "Because we are sometimes too eager to import psychological techniques into Christian counseling, we overlook the troubling theoretical and worldview implications of the techniques we use" (2011, location 425/6260). Therefore, great care must be undertaken in protecting a Godly worldview in philosophy and praxis—lest one's attempts to solve social problems be infected with *wisdom from below* causing even greater harm.

INSIGHTS FROM THE EXPERTS

"Divine Social Distancing"

Would it surprise you to know that one of the earliest stories of humanity is one of *urbanization* and globalization? In Genesis 11, we read an account of the surviving population of Earth gathering together in a large city instead of spreading out and repopulating the Earth as God had told them to. This really is a fascinating story in light of this course because:

1. Great production value and opportunities were found by gathering and working together, urbanization (v. 1), and
2. God separated (socially distanced) them by creating the major linguistic groups, an intriguing argument against evolution (v. 6), as all the groups are distinctively different and just as developed, but regarding this course, it was the major break-up of globalization.

Particularly in the undeveloped world, cities are exploding in size. People move to these urban centers because:

1. Resources are becoming tapped out in rural areas
2. The rumor has it that better employment can be had there, and
3. Because of better nutrition and medicine, they have a higher birth rate, and a lower rate of death.

The five largest cities are all over 20 million in size: namely—Tokyo, Seoul, Mexico City, New York, and Mumbai. All these cities have different languages and cultures, but as they gather millions into them, like great social magnets, the differences tend to homogenize. Geographically, transportation technology and information streams bring the world to them at the touch of a button. Economically, they all trade on the same stock exchange and purchase from each other with instantly processed credit lines.

Though politically of different governments, a close study of at least these top five show little difference. Socially, entertainment grows the same, celebrities look alike, and favorite foods export. Culturally, the populations grow alike. In short, to see globalization in today's world, just look to the major centers of urbanization.

Urbanization is a great thing. It can bring large numbers of people together where if life is planned well, they can have more time, goods, and services than they could have had in small villages. Globalization can also be a great thing. With increased trade, everyone theoretically comes out with more of what they want. Opportunities increase for all education and health advances are available to all.

Check out a video for more on this topic here:

https://www.khpcontent.com/

As I write this, most of the world trade has stalled due to the worldwide coronavirus pandemic. The hardest hit areas are the big cities where services can only be maintained with huge influxes of borrowed money. Most of the globalized people groups are staying at home, avoiding the rest of their large populations for fear of contagion.

The *dark side of globalization* and urbanization seems to run on two levels. The first is huge conglomerations of impoverished people urbanizing out of fear, globalizing on only the most basic horrors of fear and hunger. The second is that large groupings of humans brings with them scary threats like pollution and influenza.

China and India have done a really good job with urbanization. Whole courses could be taught on why this is. They would touch on a common culture, great bureaucracies, strong central governments, and a well-educated populace. When we talk about globalization in the Third World, we tend to think of these countries, but compared to the world population as a whole, these countries are more the exception than the rule. Baghdad, Iraq; Bangui, Central African Republic; Sana'a Yemen; Port Au Prince, Haiti; and Khartoum, Sudan, are the five cities in the world with the worst quality of life (Martin, 2018).

Most of Africa, large portions of South and Central America, and huge portions of Asia all have newly enlarged cities where violence and hunger are a way of life, and none of the above touted benefits of globalization and urbanization are helping at all. The populations of these cities are helpless to care for themselves, and as the governments lack structure, life spans are short, many die, and whole populations become refugees.

Political inequality; tribal and class struggle; lack of water, food, and employment; and environmental mismanagement all are terrible things exacerbated by globalization, but the prevalence of disease is even a scarier prospect. In January of 2019, the World Health Organization listed the top six population threats facing the world (World Health Organization, 2019). These included the following:

1. Air pollution—respiratory systems of humans in this environment weaken, making them die quickly.
2. Non-communicable diseases—things like diabetes, alcoholism, and heart disease.
3. A global influenza epidemic—this study came out before the coronavirus.
4. Fragile and vulnerable settings—famine, drought, and conflict.
5. Antimicrobial resistance— to pneumonia, tuberculosis, and STDs.
6. Ebola and pathogens—at the time MERS and SARS.

As the world has seen in the past few months, population centers, urbanization centers, are the world danger centers simply because they have a lot of humans living there. Sociologists constantly study this reality and inspire articles like (with my favorite title), "Dengue, Urbanization, and Globalization: The unholy trinity of the twenty-first century" (Gablur, 2011). Perhaps now we can see God's wisdom in spreading out the world's populations at Babel.

German sociologist Max Weber wrote much on this topic in the early part of the last century. With Prussian simplicity, he touted bureaucracy laced with social capitalism built on the tenants of the bible, actually positing that cities ran best who used biblical principles. Weber reminds us that our faith is eminently practical on the aforementioned sociological problems. The tenants of free markets and capitalism only work well when tempered with honor to God and love toward others. Clean cities, good health care, industrious workers, a rule of law—all make urbanization work; otherwise, globalization will happen, only in a monstrous way.

John Knaus
Masters of Religious Education
Government and Economics, Secondary Ed.

Contributed by John Knaus. © Kendall Hunt Publishing Company

CASE STUDY #9

Byron McKeeby and his wife, Hattie, spend the early and middle years of their life on a potato farm in central Iowa. Schoolhouse sweethearts from when they were young, both never left the small home-town of 3,000. The aging couple decided it was time for a change after 50 years on the farm and rais-ing nine bright, beautiful children. Desiring to be closer to their grandbabies, the duo sold the farm and moved into a small retirement community in Florida near some of their children. The change, shocking at first, came at great expense but with new discoveries. Hattie had never seen the beach before, and Byron experienced his first megachurch service. Both were happy for a time but began to miss what they had given up at "home." For the first time in forever, they had neighbors—some of whom were quite obnoxious and loud. The traffic also scared them as neither were accustomed to stoplights, four-lane freeways, or busy intersections.

Over time, the Florida heat and congestion began to wear on Byron and Hattie. They didn't know anybody at their megachurch and going shopping and running errands was always stressful. The additional stress of urban life hurt the couple's health and reduced the number of visits from their children. One day, Byron discovered Hattie looking at home listings in Montana. Not 3 years after moving to the sunshine state, Byron and Hattie had placed their retirement home on the market and moved to a one-bedroom cabin in the mountains of Montana.

DISCUSSION QUESTIONS

1. Based on the readings, what would a sociologist make of this situation?

2. What specific sociological factors are involved?

3. Which place (Iowa, Florida, Montana) would it be healthiest for you to live? Why?

Check out the Chapter 9 video at this link:

https://www.khpcontent.com/

VOCABULARY

Anti-Globalization Movement
Authoritarian Leader
Benefits of Globalization
Brexit
Consumerism
Contractual Cooperation
Dark Side of Globalization
Democratic Leader
Directed Cooperation
Empire Building
European Exploration
Exchange Relationship
Expressive Leader
Global Community
Global Inequality
Globalization Movement
Groupthink

Imperialism
Instrumental Leader
Internet
Laissez-Faire Leader
Postmodernity
Renaissance
Self-Interest
Social Change
Socioeconomic Barriers
Spontaneous Cooperation
Technological Advances
Trade
Traditional Cooperation
Urbanization
World Community
Wisdom from Below
Worldviews

References

Archibugi, D., & Pietrobelli, C. (2003). The globalization of technology and its implications for developing countries: Windows of opportunity or further burden? *Technological forecasting and social change, 70*, 9, 861–883.

Bavinck, H. (2019). *Christian worldview* (Sutanto, N. G., Eglinton, J., & Brock, C. C., Trans.). Crossway.

Caldwell, J. (2004). Demographic theory: A long view. *Population and Development Review, 30*(2), 297–316.

Collyer, B. (2017). The real roots of early city states may rip up the textbooks. *NewScientist*. https://www.newscientist.com/article/mg23631462-700-the-real-roots-of-early-city-states-may-rip-up-the-textbooks/

Dubinsky, V. (2012). How communism took over eastern Europe after World War II: Book review of Anne Applebaum's book, *The Crushing of Eastern Europe*. *The Atlantic*. https://www.theatlantic.com/international/archive/2012/10/how-communism-took-over-eastern-europe-after-world-war-ii/263938/

Entwistle, D. (2015). *Integrative approaches to psychology and Christianity: An introduction to worldview issues, philosophical foundations, and models of integration* (3rd ed.). Wipf and Stock.

Eschle, C. (2004). Constructing "The Anti-Globalisation Movement." *International Journal of Peace Studies, 9*(1), 61–84.

Fekete, É. G. (2016). A postmodern employment model on the peripheries. *Theory, Methodology, Practice, 12*, 41–54. http://ezproxy.liberty.edu/login?url=https://search-proquest-com.ezproxy.liberty.edu/docview/1899435310?accountid=12085

Gablur, D. (2011). Dengue, urbanization and globalization: The unholy trinity of the 21st century. *Tropical Medical Health, 39*(4), 3–11.

Homans, G. C. (1961). *Social behavior: Its elementary forms*. Harcourt, Brace & World.

Jairazbhoy, R. A. (1974). *Ancient Egyptians and Chinese in America (Old World origins of American civilization)* (1st ed.). Rowan and Littlefield.

Kellner, D. (2002). Globalization. *Sociological Theory, 20*(3), 285–305.

Kozarova, I. (2013). Driving forces of globalization. *European Journal of Geopolitics, 1*, 5–36.

MacArthur, J. (2003). *Think Biblically!: Recovering a Christian worldview.* Crossway.

Martin, W. (2018). The 23 major cities with the worst quality of life in the world. *Business Insider.* https://www.businessinsider.com/worst-cities-in-the-world-to-live-2018-4

McMinn, M. R. (2011). *Psychology, theology, and spirituality in Christian counseling* (Rev. ed.). Tyndale House.

Metcalfe, B. (1993). Wireless computing will flop—permanently. *InfoWorld, 15*(33), 48.

Ogburn, W. F. (1947). How technology changes society. *The Annals of the American Academy of Political and Social Science, 249*, 81–88.

Robert, N., & Douthat, R. (2010). *The quest for community: A study in the ethics of order and freedom.* ISI Books, 2010.

Ross, L., & Nisbet, R. E. (1988). *The person and the situation: Perspectives of social psychology.* McGraw-Hill.

Satterthwaite, D. (2009). The implications of population growth and urbanization for climate change. *International Institute for Environment and Development (IIED), 21*(2), 545–567. doi:10.1177/095624780934436

Segarra, L. (2018). California's economy is now bigger than all of the U.K. *Fortune.* http://fortune.com/2018/05/05/california-fifth-biggest-economy-passes-united-kingdom/

Shipp, S., Gupta, N., Scott, J., Weber, C., Finnin, M., & Lal, B. (2012). Advancing manufacturing to new frontiers: Increasing opportunities for society. *Innovations: Technology, Governance, Globalization, 7*(3), 71–81.

Westley, F., Olsson, P., Folke, C., Homer-Dixon, T., Vredenburg, H., Loorbach, D., Thompson, J., Nilsson, M., Lambin, E., Sendzimir, J., Banerjee, B., Galaz, V., & van der Leeuw, S. (2011). Tipping toward sustainability: Emerging pathways of transformation. *Ambio, 40*, 762–780. doi:10.1007/s13280-011-0186-9

Witt, J. (2009). *SOC.* McGraw-Hill.

World Health Organization. (2019). Ten threats to global health in 2019. https://www.who.int/news-room/feature-stories/ten-threats-to-global-health-in-2019

Zacharias, R. (1997). *Deliver us from evil.* Word.

Ch 10 Race

Racial and ethnic differences have been part of the human condition since the beginnings of time. Be it Cro-Magnon man, Neanderthals, Denisovans, or modern humans, all racial formations are the product of a bio-socio-historical process in which categories are created, established, inhibited, transformed, and destroyed. Thus, although current racial types include the Asian, African, Caucasian, and Indigenous peoples of the world, the racial mixture was quite dissimilar thousands of years ago.

According to the U.S. Office of Management and Budget (1997), America's population is made up of the following *racial groups*: American Indian (or Alaska Native), Asian, Black (or African American), Caucasian (or White), and Pacific Islander (or Native Hawaiian). There are other ethnic categories such as Hispanic or Latino, which include people of Central or South America or any other Spanish culture or origin.

Within the countries of the world, people in these categories fall into either the majority or minority categories. *Majority groups* may be larger in population, but more importantly, they dominate societies in regard to cultural standards, political control, and economic stability. *Minority groups* are those whose members have less control or power over their own lives than people within the dominant group. The terms, majority and minority, refer not as much to population size, though, as about political power and access to resources (Yetman & Steele, 1971).

As a subset, racial groups exist that are set apart because of physical differences that have taken on social significance within the culture over time. *Ethnic groups* are set apart because of national origins or distinctive cultural patterns. Historically, all races have received fear responses from another people group because of an unusual appearance—an otherness that is perceived as threat, and presumptions that looking different can and should be equated with being "uncivilized."

Much of this assumption of inferiority and/or threat is based on projection, transference, and political posturing. This can lead to negative attitudes and responses to people of other races including stereotypes, prejudice, discrimination, and racism. *Racism* is the fallacious belief that all members of each race possess characteristics or abilities specific to that people group so as to distinguish it as superior or inferior to another race (Fredrickson & Camarillo, 2015).

Thus, some racist accusations have been made over the centuries that are not backed up with any scientific evidence or research. The following aphorisms can be considered to be myths based upon irrational perceptions:

"American Indians are the most environmentally friendly."
"Asians are the best at math."
"Black men are naturally the best athletes."
"Jewish people are the shrewdest with money."
"White men are automatically born privileged."
"Hispanics cannot rule themselves well."
"Middle Eastern people are all unreasonable."

None of these statements can be considered scientifically true or valid. They are opinions based on limited perspectives and personal opinions. Much of this comes from *stereotypes*, which are widely held but fixed and oversimplified ideas or images of a particular racial or ethnic group or person (Sethi & O'Flaherty, 2019). For example, most American women are not vain, not all gay men dress well, and not all Italian women are feisty or fierce. These are just shallow accusations that have been used, historically, to justify political attacks, defend against shifts in cultural power, or just because of personal character flaws and/or neuroses.

Nevertheless, attitudes like those earlier can lead to prejudice and discrimination. *Prejudice* is the negative attitude toward an entire category of people for irrational reasons (and not a reasonable, fair judgment). Prejudice can be individual or communal, and not necessarily acted out despite having the opinion. *Discrimination* is the denial of social opportunities and equal rights to individuals and groups because of prejudice, bigotry, or other arbitrary reasons.

Discrimination typically starts with petty, greedy, and self-serving assumptions and ends with unfair, mean, and destructive behaviors and judgments (Haugen & Musser, 2014).

Racial bias is not limited to or concentrated with one racial group. Historically, all racial groups have employed bias, bigotry, and discrimination against other groups within and outside their societies. Still, no one likes to receive or perceive negative treatment regarding their race, gender, and economic backgrounds, which appears to close or restrict the professional doors more open to their (majority) counterparts (Glenn, 2012).

Sometimes, this is more of a pretentious attitude, as with *ethnocentrism*, which conveys the message that "our culture is better than your culture." While this can be true (cannibalism, female circumcision, and infant sacrifice are hard to defend, culturally), most of the time, it is the result of cultural myopia and obtuse reasonings.

Other forms of racial bias are more apparent and socially damaging such as racial profiling, institutional discrimination, and hate crimes. *Racial profiling* occurs when a person in authority presumes assumption of guilt or evil solely because of a person's personal appearance (while ignoring clear evidence or observational realities). *Institutional discrimination* has occurred often throughout history, with a systematic denial of opportunities of normal social benefits or operations because of one's race or ethnicity. Perhaps the worst concerns *hate crimes*, which combine bigotry with violence, typically because of a person's race, religion, gender, or socioeconomic class.

Sociologists have noted six general patterns of intergroup relations when racial or ethnic tensions are high within a society or between cultures. Regarding negative responses, *segregation* is employed, which is the physical separation of groups in terms of residence, workplace, or social events. *Expulsion* sometimes happens, which is the forced removal of a hated people group in society. The worst is *genocide*, which is the deliberate, systematic killing of entire people or nation.

Critical Race Theory attempts to address this social issue through the advancement of social justice and cultural awareness in the public forum and in governmental policies at the city, state, and federal level. It examines the intersections of people (particularly those affecting and involving minorities) regarding race, ethnicity, gender, and sexual orientation. It seeks to understand the social forces at play that benefit or hinder traditionally oppressed social groups. It approaches the problem solely from the perspective of the minority—regardless of counterevidence from the majority perspective. Additionally, it focuses on how mass media has influenced the popular perception of minorities in the past (leading to unequal distribution of social and economic power), and how it can be utilized to socially engineer a more equitable or politically advantageous position for minorities.

Concerning positive responses to intergroup relations, an *amalgamation* often occurs, which is the combining of a majority or minority group to form a whole new group. At the individual level, *assimilation* is quite common, when a person forsakes his or her own culture to become part of another one. Last, *pluralism* can occur, which had been a hallmark of American society up until the last decade, which previously aided racial and ethnic relations through mutual respect for another's culture despite significant philosophical differences.

Speaking of differences, within the American population, while Whites make up 72.4% of the American population, several minority groups stand out. The Latinos (or Hispanics) is the largest minority group in the United States (16.3%), with 43.2 million people claiming Latino ethnicity (from both legal and illegal immigration). Few people realize that America is one of the largest Spanish-speaking nations in the world. It is not a race but an ethnic group with origin roots in Mexico, Puerto Rico, Cuba, the Dominican Republic, and Central and South America. Many refer to Mexican Americans as *Chicanos*, which carries with it both positive and negative associations.

The second largest minority group is that of Blacks or African Americans. Although most Black people live in the American South, other centers of Black population include the Chicago area and the central Eastern seaboard. In 2010, Blacks made up 42 million people in the United States (13.6%). Despite experiencing huge civil rights gains since the 1960s, Blacks still lag behind in political power, economic prosperity, and personal education although those trends are shifting. In 2008, some 3.2 million Blacks were enrolled in college, and 80% of African Americans had high school diplomas.

Asian Americans may be the fastest growing minority group in the United States, making up 4.8% of American society. Their origins are from China, Japan, Korea, and Vietnam (among others). They have the highest incomes, and they have experienced a more stable family life regarding divorce and two-parent families than any other minority group.

Native American Indians make up the smallest minority group at 1% (besides Pacific Islanders at 0.2%). Called the *invisible minority* (Garrett et al., 2015), they have the highest educational dropout rate of any minority group, as well as cultural issues with alcoholism and suicide. There is no clear consensus on how many Native Americans (also called First Nations People) were in America when the colonists arrived. Based on cursory evidence, their population could have been as high as 1.5 million, but by 1776 that number had dropped to 200,000 because of disease and warfare. They do have the largest number of dialects with over 500 tribes.

To combat against what is perceived as minority oppression, political progressive activists have pushed for affirmative action programs to be implemented in educational institutions, federal organizations, and big businesses. *Affirmative action* is the policy favoring people groups who tend to suffer from discrimination, especially in relation to employment or education (Pedrick & Scham, 2018). Also called *positive discrimination* by some, it is a controversial and somewhat philosophically contradictory program that calls for artificially selecting some people groups over others in society because it was wrong for the majorities to select some people groups over others in society for jobs and appointments, regardless of personal qualifications.

Affirmative action is also sometimes connected to the *glass ceiling*, which is the presumption that the minorities (including women) encounter a behind-the-scenes cultural barrier blocking their promotions of qualified people in a work environment based on their gender, race, or ethnicity. Although there is some historical evidence to back up the glass ceiling theory, current studies suggest more nuanced, gender-specific reasons for salary differences and hiring practices.

Wagley and Harris (1958) called out several key responses to minorities that have been observed, sociologically. Minorities have been the targets of unequal treatment by the dominant group, which is discrimination. They are demeaned because of some physical or cultural trait of low regard by the dominant group, causing prejudice. The minority groups find group solidarity because of their

physical or cultural traits. They usually marry within their own people group (endogamy) finding cultural resistance to intermarriage with the majority group (racism). Finally, they experience a form of a caste system being born with an ascribed status connected to their race or ethnicity.

Many people in America are unaware as to the extent that their race opens or closes social opportunities to them. Moreover, many have never personally experienced institutional discrimination or overt racism (although most have observed ethnocentrism—ever been to a sports event?). The question remains on how people can actually overcome racism and prejudice.

Sociological studies have shown that the best way to end racism and prejudice is to bring divergent racial groups together (Wax, 2004). Dialoguing often breaks down the walls, soothes fears, and generates utilitarian brotherhood and an awareness of our shared humanity. Education also reduces stereotypes and bigotry, bringing mysterious culturalism into context and connection.

Considering how "small" our world is becoming (check out Chapter 9 for more information on globalism), fostering better personal relations, compassion, and brother/sisterhood between the races and countries seems like the wisest and most beneficial of paths to take for all people on our beautiful planet.

DEALING WITH MATTERS OF THE DARK

One of my favorite reads is the short story, "The Man Who Would Be King," which was written by Rudyard Kipling (1865–1937) in 1888. Although I read it first as an undergraduate English major, I have revisited it a few times since then (Kipling, 2014) and I have also seen its 1975 movie adaption (Columbia Pictures). The author, Kipling, was born in Bombay, India, and aside from his formal education in England from ages 5–17, he spent much of his life abroad engaging with the various indigenous cultures that he encountered and writing about them. I find Kipling's approach in this story (as in other stories of his) to be excellent and moving depictions of both the indigenous peoples and his fellow countrymen in the *Imperialism Era*.

In particular, Kipling's portrayals of the protagonists (the Narrator, Peachy Carnehan, and Daniel Dravot) present them in an honest fashion, showing their ethnocentric attitudes and myopic optimism. Yet, Kipling also shows their dark sides, their weaknesses, their latent racism, and their equality to the Central Asian people whom they are trying to conquer and exploit (and to whom they feel superior) on their way to Kafiristan. Likewise, Kipling provides readers with numerous examples of non-Western cultural conventions, customs, and conscience of the peoples that Carnehan and Dravot bump into (sometimes literally), demonstrating the advanced social structure of the locals, despite being non-Western and somewhat "barbaric" in existence.

This anecdote relates to the era of *colonialism*, a historical movement that had been in process for centuries, which Kipling's story affirms. Although Great Britain's chief goals in India were predominantly political and economic in nature, their empire-building efforts ended up helping socially connected nations far apart from each other—culturally, technologically, and morally. Whether they ever were aware of it, in Kipling's story, protagonists Carnehan and Dravot brought English customs to the Kafiristanis and received new socialization from the Kafiristanis, themselves (Gopalakrishnan, 2019). Despite their "superiority," they still needed something from the indigenous people, which indicates an inferiority, logically.

Additionally, Carnehan and Dravot might have considered themselves to be heroes in their epic journey, but that perspective was mostly driven by ethnocentrism, ego, and imperfect objective realities. Rather than being heralds of enlightenment and civilization, for many people in the story, these British men were only invaders from the West who brought death to their people and exploitation of their resources. I just kept thinking, instead of holding out their hands in friendship (like Carnehan and Dravot did with the Narrator), these men held out threatening and menacing fists, which did little to foster international community and much to promote international conflict.

This reminds me of Goffman's "Dramaturgic Sociology," where human interaction is comparable to that of actors in a play (1959); however, in this case, the roles of the actors in the global theater are not fixed and can be simultaneously held by more than one person at a time. Thus, at home and in the classroom, people need to strive to gently open people's eyes regarding what life is like at home and abroad across the globe. We are all diverse when taking the whole of the world into context.

The important factor to consider here is that while such cultural exchanges were rarer in the past, in postmodernity, with its powerful increases in technology, transportation, and communications, people are "bumping" into other global communities more often and more deeply than ever before in history (Turku, 2016). Thus, people in all countries need to recognize that, due to this globalism hyper-connectivity, we are all citizens of the world and that we have the potential to share both good and bad things with each other. Cut off from each other, we make all sorts of presumptions; but in the field, in direct interaction, the reality is far more complicated and less one-sided.

Contrary to popular myths about the inherent racism of Christianity, the Bible paints a far-more egalitarian and inclusive picture of what it means to be a child of God (Pierce et al., 2004). The universality of humanity is proclaimed in Genesis 1:27 (New International Version), which states, "So God created man in his own image, in the image of God he created him; male and female he created them," in Galatians 3:28, which states, "There is neither Jew nor Greek, there is neither slave nor free, there is no male and female, for you are all one in Christ Jesus," and speaking of the community of believers, Paul says in Colossians 3:11, "Here there is not Greek and Jew, circumcised and uncircumcised, barbarian, Scythian, slave, free; but Christ is all, and in all."

As a 20-year old, these verses (and stories like Kipling's) helped me understand that all human beings, regardless of their geo-political status, are civilized and deserve respect (and possibly even admiration), but that pre-conceived notions (on all racial and ethnic sides) often create needless conflict and confusion (Audet & Pare, 2017).

INSIGHTS FROM THE EXPERTS

"Social Issues in Mansa Zambia: Part Two"

When my time as a volunteer in the *Peace Corps* (2020) was finished, I stayed behind and connected with a local pastor, and we started an *NGO* that works with widows and orphans (NGOsource.org). The name *Busalo* was chosen for the organization (Maslen, 2019). It is a local word which means, "to choose." We are choosing to love the people in our community, choosing to love the orphans, widows, and vulnerable. Those whom the community has rejected, we tell that they matter, and they are loved. Busalo has evolved over the years to meet the needs in the community.

Currently, we assist 50 students with whatever they need to attend school. Sometimes they need help paying the fees, a uniform, or sometimes even just an advocate to get them registered. We opened a preschool for the children in the community and also started a feeding program for orphaned babies under 1 year of age. We try to provide assistance, skills training, and sometimes housing for young, single mothers living on the street. We work on planting churches where people can receive love, support, and work together. And the list goes on, depending on what shows up on our doorstep (Mihai, 2015).

One thing that I have learned when dealing with social issues is that there are a lot of gray areas. There are no black-and-white easy answers to the local social problems of poverty, racism, child abuse, slavery, and prostitution. The other thing to consider is the fact that they are often rooted into their culture. It is a normal way of life to them; the people do not see these social problems as being issues.

My observations are based on what I have seen in the *Mansa District* in Zambia. Mansa is very underdeveloped compared to the rest of Zambia. It is difficult to reach and there is nothing to bring in people from outside the area. There is very little infrastructure and/or industries. The majority of the people live in poverty and grow hopefully enough food for the year.

Poverty is a very big issue that has many different sides to it. A majority of the people that I interact with every day live in poverty. It is not something I can permanently solve for them. For these people, it is a normal way of life. They do not realize that they technically live in poverty. I have seen that, even in their poverty, they are happy and content.

The biggest misconception that I fight is that those in poverty are suffering and miserable, which is not always true (Reeves et al., 2019). They grow or find just enough food for each day. They do not have any cash in hand, but if they need money, they might sell some fruits or vegetables. Neighbors help each other. The children do not have store-bought toys but are very resourceful and will make their own. They live simply. We do not hand out money because they will just spend it on escapism things. We only hand out food or clothing very carefully to those who truly need it. Often, these include those whose life has been thrown a curveball because of a death in the family, serious illness, flooding, drought, and any other unexpected problems.

For instance, we have a grandma who is taking care of her four young grandchildren. She recently had a stroke and cannot walk. Every month, we deliver food for them. We also help with schooling and other needs like clothing. That family is just an example of who we help.

Handing out money or other items to just anyone or everyone can do more harm than help. If we blanketly give out handouts, people become lazy and do not make any attempt on their own to take care of themselves; they just sit around waiting for more handouts. Occasionally, I pass through a neighborhood and the kids are horrible about asking for things. I found out later it was because some missionaries passed through and handed out a lot of stuff. It set up this expectation that all foreign people are going to give them things and the begging got out of control.

Child slavery is real in Zambia and falls under the abuse category. What happens is that someone from town will go to the bush and take children home with them to be a maid or gardener. Often, children as young as 6 years old become slaves. They promise the parents and the child that they will send them to school and take care of all of their needs.

Once the child is removed from the parents, though, they are often not allowed to leave the house and are abused by others in the household. They are required to be the first one up in the morning to make breakfast and the last one to bed after washing the dinner dishes. They are not allowed to go to school, they are not allowed to play with friends, and they are rarely allowed to eat. Eventually, many run away from this abusive environment.

This touches upon the issue of prostitution. We have helped girls as young as 11 years old out of prostitution. They have been abandoned, kicked out of their home, ran away from an abusive situation, want to go to school, sent to earn money by their parents—the list goes on as to why they sell their bodies for sex. Mostly, though, the girls who are doing it are often not doing it because they want to, but just because they are trying to survive, financially.

We have worked with girls in every category. Most want to leave but they do not know how. A few seem happy and so we let them be; if they do not want to leave, we cannot force them. It has to be their decision, but if they are serious about a different life, we will do everything we can to help them.

There are many other issues, but these are the ones that I deal with just about every single day. There is no easy way for dealing with most situations. Not all the answers are black-and-white. People do desperate things when they get into desperate situations. What works with one young, single mother may not work with another. Every time I think I have seen it all, there is always something that surprises me.

Please feel free to contact me for more information. I love answering any questions that you might have on Zambia and the Busalo ministry. Also, please check us out on Facebook for more information at www.facebook.com/busalo.zambia/.

Jessica Maslen
Busalo Director
Zambia

Contributed by Jessica Maslen. © Kendall Hunt Publishing Company

CASE STUDY #10

Coach Tuhoy threw his clipboard atop his desk in frustration. A girl cannot play soccer on a men's team. Lalani, a recent transfer from Samoa, wanted to play on the men's soccer team. Her parents were throwing a fuss and threatening to sue over the issue. Even though Lalani was taller than half of the men on the team, she would get crushed in games. The assistant coach, Teressa, was excited at the prospects of getting a girl on the team and pushed hard for Lalani to join their practice. This only compounded the coach's problems. In fairness, Lalani was superior to the coach's men in technical capability but lacked the endurance to make it through practice. Teressa continued to advocate for Lalani, but Coach Tuhoy worried that it might cost him the season.

During practice, some of the boys made fun of Lalani for looking like a man. They teased and mocked her relentlessly, telling her to go back to her island. As word spread around the school about the conflict on the soccer team, people started avoiding Lalani. One day, she found her locker filled with dollar store hula skirts and fake flower necklaces. When she showed up to practice that night, the boys taunted her with choreographed dance moves mocking ceremonial culture. By the end of the week, Lalani was friendless and was pleading with her parents to let her stay home from practice.

DISCUSSION QUESTIONS

1. Based on the readings, how would a sociologist diagnose this situation?

2. What specific sociological factors are involved?

3. If you were Lalani, how would this make you feel about your racial identity?

Check out the Chapter 10 video at this link:

https://www.khpcontent.com/

VOCABULARY

Affirmative Action
Amalgamation
Assimilation
Busalo
Chicanos
Child Slavery
Colonialism
Critical Race Theory
Discrimination
Ethnic Groups
Ethnocentrism
Expulsion
Genocide
Glass Ceiling
Hate Crimes
Imperialism Era

Institutional Discrimination
Invisible Minority
Majority Groups
Mansa District
Minority Groups
NGOs
Peace Corps
Pluralism
Positive Discrimination
Prejudice
Racial Bias
Racial Groups
Racial Profiling
Racism
Segregation
Stereotypes

References

Audet, C., & Pare, D. (2017). *Social justice and counseling: Discourse in practice*. Routledge.

Fredrickson, G. M., & Camarillo, A. (2015). *Racism: A short history*. Princeton University Press.

Garrett, M., Baldridge, D., Bension, W., Crowder, J., & Aldrich, N. (2105). Mental health disorders among an invisible minority: Depression and dementia among American Indian and Alaksa native elders. *The Gerontologist, 55*(2), 227–236.

Glenn, C. L. (2012). Stepping in and stepping out: Examining the way anticipatory career socialization impacts identity negotiation of African American women in academia. In Gutiérrez y Muhs, G., Niemann, Y., Gonzalez, C., & Harris, A. (Eds.). *Presumed incompetent: The intersections of race and class for women in academia* (pp. 133–141). Utah State University.

Goffman, E. (1959). *The presentation of self in everyday life*. Doubleday.

Gopalakrishnan, V. S. (2019). The strange history of Kafiristan. http://creative.sulekha.com/the-strange-history-of-kafiristan_459575_blog

Haugen, D. M., & Musser, S. (Eds.). (2014). *Discrimination*. Greenhaven.

Kipling, R. (1888). The man who would be king. In *The Phantom Rickshaw and Other Eerie Tales*. A. H. Wheeler.

Kipling, R. (2014). The man who would be king. In *The Project Gutenbook EBook*. http://www.gutenberg.org/files/8147/8147-h/8147-h.htm.

Maslen, J. (2020). Busalo. www.facebook.com/busalo.zambia/

Mihai, M., Titan, E., & Manea, D. (2015). Education and poverty. *Procedia Economics and Finance, 32,* 855–860.

NGOsource. (2020). FAQ: What is an NGO? NGOsource.org

Peace Corps. (2020). Work for the world. *Peacecorps.gov.* https://www.peacecorps.gov

Pedrick, K. W., & Scham, S. A. (2018). *Inside affirmative action: The executive order that transformed America's workforce*. Routledge.

Pierce, R. W., Groothuis, R. M., & Fee, G. D. (2012). *Discovering biblical equality: Complementary without hierarchy*. InterVarsity.

Reeves, L. S., Parsell, C., & Liu, S. (2019). Towards a phenomenology of poverty: Defining poverty through the lived experiences of the 'poor.' *Journal of Sociology*, 1–16.

Sethi, R., & O'Flaherty, B. (2019). *Shadows of doubt: Stereotypes, crime, and the pursuit of justice*. Harvard University Press.

Turku, H. (2016). *Isolationist states in an interdependent world*. Routledge.

U.S. Office of Management and Budget. (1997). https://obamawhitehouse.archives.gov/omb/fedreg_1997standards

Wagley, C., & Harris, M. (1958). *Minorities in the New World: Six case studies*. Columbia University Press.

Wax, A. L. (2009). *Race, wrongs, and remedies: Group justice in the 21st century*. Rowman & Littlefield.

Yetman, N. R., & Steele, C. H. (1971). *Majority and minority: The dynamics of racial and ethnic relations*. Allyn and Bacon.

Ch 11 Gender

One of the most important facets of socialization concerns gender, a common reality or experience for all human beings. One's gender is not the same thing as one's sex, although there is evidence of traits and behaviors tied to *natural biology*. *Sex* refers to the biological differences between males and females; *gender* refers to the social and cultural assumptions and significances attached to these sexual differences.

Biologically, the hormone *testosterone* is significant in social interactions and provides biological predispositions different than for women whose main hormone is *estrogen*—an equally important substance in the human body. Additionally, because of estrogen (and other important pregnancy hormones), women are the only ones who can become pregnant, with which comes enormous opportunities and limitations. Much to the chagrin of some feminists, the historical reality has been that infants and children need the biological and instinctive talents of their mothers more than their fathers to survive and thrive (although it is debatable to what age).

Traditionally, *gender-role socialization* is predominantly fashioned and formed from within the family, with other important influences coming from friends, schools, church, and mass media. Parents, however, are their children's main and most important teachers regarding social parameters and etiquette. They teach the children what it means to be a man or woman, a father or mother, a son or daughter, and what children can expect (or hope) to do in greater society. They provide both rewards and sanctions for following or deviating from traditional or religious norms, with greater or lesser objectivity, at times.

Of course, men and women can (and do) share many of the same activities in life. Men can cook, women can be pilots, men can be nurturers, and women can be protectors even though sexual traits such as physical strength and emotional awareness frequently lead to normative social assignments. One could argue that although men and women can do most of the same activities, they each have "go-to" areas where their sex and physiology make them better suited to perform the tasks associated with particular activities (Miller, 2017).

Since the colonization of the New World and the later founding of the United States of America, huge assumptions have existed regarding gender roles in American society—for both men and women. Expectations and parameters have been proffered by all generations regarding the proper activities, behavior, attitudes, wardrobe, and so on, of men and women to abide by in society; however, many gender roles are not static. Not surprisingly, it seems with every generation that there is a cultural redefining of what people should be doing (or not).

For instance, one rarely sees a female worker at a building site; most construction workers are men because physical prowess and endurance are needed for that job (according to the U.S. Bureau of Labor Statistics (2020), less than 10% of construction workers are women); alternatively, more women are involved in daycare and nursery programs because of the deep and inherent nurturing skills required to meet infant and children's emotional needs (according to the U.S. Bureau of Labor Statistics, 93.8% of daycare workers are women). Neither of these social realities is necessarily because of sexist laws and regulations, but cultural standards and biological expectations are still a factor in hiring decisions for many businesses across America.

These cultural norms can lead to stereotyping or restricting people according to preconceived notions of their sex limitations or abilities—rather than being meritoriously egalitarian at an individual level. Thus, *sex typing* is a common cultural reality for both men and women across the globe, with an association of some activities being "female" and others "male." Still, interculturally and internationally, sex typing for many activities is more fluid than static, although greater prestige is still given to "male activities" (Miller, 2017, online). This relates to *gender stratification*, which is the presumption that men and women have unequal access to power, prestige, and property on the basis of their sex.

A big item of contention is the *gender wage gap*, with men making more money in their jobs than women. This has been blamed on unfair pay practices and a conspiracy to oppress women for decades; however, according to Danielle Paquette (2016),

> Since 2003, when government researchers started collecting the data, men have reported devoting more life to paid labor than their female counterparts. In 2015, employed men recorded working an average 42 minutes per day longer than employed women. Women, meanwhile, said they spent more time on housework: 2.6 hours, compared to the men's 2.1 hours. (online)

Still, there are other vocational fields in America and across the globe where sex and gender are irrelevant to one's job performance, and personal resources and abilities are more important to vocational functionality and success. For instance, questions on whether men should be allowed to be nurses or preschool teachers, or if women should be allowed to be firefighters or fight alongside men in the military, have arisen in the past. The answers to the aforementioned matters rest mostly upon the natural resources that men and women possess (both intellectually and physically) and upon individual rights for equal opportunities in society.

There has been a huge sociological shift regarding the genders and work opportunities since the *Victorian Era* (1837–1901). Many women objected to the traditional two-dimensional summary of womanhood, and they became more involved in public politics (such as the Abolition Movement and the Suffrage Movement). Before and during the Civil War, women like Maria Stewart (1803–1879), Maria Chapman (1806–1885), and Prudence Crandall (1803–1890) circulated anti-slavery petitions and pamphlets, organized boycotts of slavery-made products, ran fundraisers, supported or taught in schools for Black children, and so on.

This activism in the public sphere led to many other freedoms and rights for women in America, including legally gaining personal control over their earnings and inheritances, the establishment of more equitable divorce laws, laxer clothing standards and city ordinances, legally being able to decide whom they marry or not, and deciding if they wanted to be a mother (before their pregnancy).

It also helped women win the right to vote in U.S. elections (also called Women's Suffrage, which was enacted in the 19th Amendment in 1920), due much to the sustained efforts of women such as Susan B. Anthony (1847-1919), Elizabeth Stanton (1815-1902), Lucretia Mott (1793-1880), Esther Morris (1814-1902), Anna Howard Shaw (1847-1919), and Sojourner Truth (1797-1883).

The reality of gender socialization for men and women is far more complex and more contextual than most people realize. In demonstration, one of my favorite activities and assignments in my residential Social Problems class (after several weeks of study) is to show them the blockbuster movie, *The Giver* (Silver & Bridges, 2014). We watch the entire movie, stopping occasionally for them to discuss its sociological significance. Finally, I then have them write an essay on the movie's sociological elements and their overall response to the movie. The students' views speak to both the sociological agenda of the movie and the students' own gender/sex socialization received up until college.

In *The Giver*, it is clear that *Social Identity* and *Social Roles* are major factors that the producers wish to explore throughout the movie. The setting of the movie presents a seemingly utopian yet communistic community that was established after an apocalyptical, devastating social event called "The Ruin." To preserve order and avoid the previous social problems, all emotion has been excised chemically from community members and all former social constructs, presumptions, and preferences have been replaced with an orchestrated, sexless, totalitarian/fascist society.

The script often touches upon questions regarding social equalities between men and women (including traits and behaviors tied to natural human biology), and they often push back against gender assumptions and the cultural presumptions attached to social identity and roles. For instance, civil roles for each person in the community are decided by an institutional commission—who have been observing them since birth—and not by personal preferences or gender abilities. Men are nursery workers; women are law enforcement agents, and so on.

Another major discussion in the movie concerns "The Release," a white-washed term for abortion and euthanasia, which is coldly implemented whenever people in the community (including babies) are no longer considered to be contributing members because of health and other issues. The system is efficient and aesthetically charming; yet, despite its outward appearance, the community is dead inside and operates more like a meat manufacturing plant than a robust, creative society. Ironically, in trying to solve all social problems, the founders of this community unknowingly created the biggest social problem of all time, eclipsing all others.

The historian of the community (played by Jeff Bridges) desperately wants his apprentice Jonah (played by Brenton Thwaites) to regain the very human qualities of love, passion, caprice, even deviance that have been stolen from all people in the community by the institution. Yet, the judge of the community (played by Meryl Streep) mechanically and maniacally strives to preserve the order and social rigidity of the community, lest they slip back into old social habits and customs that caused the ruin in the first place.

In the end, the movie shows the dangers of social engineering and the priceless value of human choice. While the historian represents the soul of humanity, the judge represents the neuroses and fears of humanity, Jonah represents the spirit of freedom that all human beings possess, and Jonah's love interest, Fiona, represents the hope and inspiration that all people need to live their lives to the fullest. Conflict theorists may dislike this ending because it affirms traditional ideas about family units, governmental over-reach, and social conventions, and then condemns cold-hearted social engineering that is done for pragmatic and political sake alone.

MAIN SOCIOLOGICAL APPROACHES

Truly, for men and for women, gender expectations are tricky to maneuver through—especially when personal agency gets challenged by social convention. Both men and women share a desire for personal empowerment, intellectual fulfillment, and captivating distractions; both men and women face regular and sustained institutional or cultural barriers that may or may not affirm their autonomy or personal gender; and both men and women have expectations of the other gender that may not seem fair or kind. This is evident in the *feminist movement*, which promotes female social empowerment, and in the *masculinist movement*, which promotes male social empowerment.

As mentioned earlier in the chapter, the *conflict theorist's perspective on gender* issues focuses on the eternal battle between the "haves" and the "have-nots," which could be reduced down to the social problems caused by a patriarchal culture. Typically, the presumption is social tyranny by men over women; however, in postmodernity, with many societies shifting from a patriarchal to matriarchal culture, social problems can be more about social choices, which often come with unwelcome consequences.

The *symbolic interactionist's perspective on gender* issues focuses on what it means to be a man or woman in Western society. According to Carter & Fuller (2016), "Symbolic interactionists shift their attention to the interpretation of subjective viewpoints and how individuals make sense of their world from their unique perspective" (p. 932). For instance, in the past, females have felt an obligation to be more passive and restrained in social settings and opinions. Many people (feminists and egalitarians, alike) have suggested a social conspiracy at work to oppress women, with women being portrayed on television, the movies, and books as being helpless, passive, incompetent, and always needful of the *ideal man* to rescue them.

The 19th century popular cult of true womanhood portrayed just this notion with the *ideal woman* being morally superior, pious, pure, domestic, and submissive. Since the first and second waves of the feminist movement, though, that rigid and artificial model has been transformed into one more authentic, honest, and aspirational. One also wonders if there will be a future first and second wave of a masculinist movement—or if one has already begun in postmodernity.

Finally, the *functionalist's perspective on gender* issues focuses on preserving the system that achieves the highest level of organic productivity and peace. Thus, although men in Western society are more engaged with their children's day-to-day rearing than any time before in history, women are still the primary child caretakers, with men focusing more on other social aspects such as protection, construction, and supply. Few people would argue that men are better with babies than women, in general; nor would people argue that women are better construction workers than men, in general—because of male/female natural abilities (Miller et al., 1993; Ogden et al., 2004).

Of course, the true functionalist still recognizes that *sexism* and cultural dysfunction are social problems that must be addressed for peaceful coexistence to occur. As Levitt (2019) notes, "On a cultural level, strong historically based expectations made clear to the participants that aspects of their selves were irreconcilable or unacceptable . . . and the power behind these messages was so overwhelming that it often silenced participants' internal sense of themselves" (p. 310). Dismissed dysfunction only leads to increased social hardships and expanded social distress—the exact opposite of the functionalist's goal for society.

DEALING WITH MATTERS OF THE DARK

The relationship of gender and religion has long been a controversial subject in Christianity and Judaism (and perhaps in most other faiths, too). The advent of feminism and postmodernism has offered many new and provocative interpretations, goals, and conclusions to this important topic, but the Bible has also provided its own suppositions and judgments on the value and role of women in humanity. Yet, perhaps no higher goals are promoted in the scriptures than those of truth, love, affirmation, and submission. Therefore, a careful examination and analysis of *women in the Hebrew scriptures* (and the Greek) must begin and end with these quintessential pillars of the faith.

Historically and globally, governmental and community powers have traditionally rested in the hands of men. There are exceptions in history, of course—Deborah the Judge, Queen Cleopatra of Egypt, Elizabeth I of England, Catherine the Great of Russia, and so on, are all famous examples of fine and proficient rulers in their times and regions. Generally speaking, in patriarchal societies, women have held secondary roles in governance and held gender-specific assigned duties. This is not just a Christian or Jewish reality; most cultures from Asia to Africa to the Americas embraced or promoted a male-dominated society, at least superficially. Tetlow (1980) remarks, "Judaism in the first century had emerged from the oriental patriarchal tradition in which women were considered the property of men with no rights, no role in society except childbearing, and no education."

Yet, in human existence, women have never been without important influence or power within their homes, their cultures, and their nations. Biblically, there is no Genesis story without Eve; there is no patriarch promise without Sarah; there is no defeat of Sisera without Deborah and Jael; there is no eternal throne of David without Bathsheba; and there is no virgin birth without Mary, to name a few. Women have held (and continue to hold) crucial, invaluable roles in the story of God and his people. Still, there are biological realities to consider when it comes to men and women.

Although very much alike in ability and value, our bodies have different strengths; parts of our minds are wired differently (so says science); often, our social bonding is based on different priorities, and so on—all leading to biological consequences and limitations for both men and women. Genesis 3:16 (New International Version) speaks of these truths when God explains to rebellious Eve, "I will make your pains in childbearing very severe; with painful labor, you will give birth to children, your desire will be for your husband, and he will rule over you."

Somewhat telling of the eternal connection between man and woman, God also says to Adam, "Cursed is the ground because of you; through painful toil you will eat food from it all the days of your life; it will produce thorns and thistles for you; and you will eat the plants of the field. By the sweat of your brow you will eat your food until you return to the ground; since from it you were taken; for dust you are and to dust you will return" (Genesis 3:17–19, New International Version).

Though egalitarian in human hardship and obligations, many from both sides of the subject point to both gender restrictions and gender failures. Some masculinists rigidly appeal to biblical traditions and specific scriptural verses to justify the limitation of women's roles in greater society and the church. Women are

© GoldenEyes71/Shutterstock.com

weaker (they say)—physically, mentally, and spiritually—which is why God created men to dominate them. Grenz and Kjesbo (1995) explain, "Proponents of this view believe that certain Scripture references clearly show that the female cannot bear the divine image to the same degree as the male (e.g., 1 Corinthians 11:7)."

John Piper (2017) adds,

> To the degree that a woman's influence over a man, guidance of a man, leadership of a man, is personal and a directive, it will generally offend a man's good, God-given sense of responsibility and leadership, and thus controvert God's created order.

Evangelist and teacher Paul Washer (2017) writes,

> One of the problems we have is the church is so busy doing the work of the mother and of the wife. If women were to dedicate themselves to the ministry of their husbands and dedicate themselves to raising up a godly heritage unto the Lord, it would free the church to do more work in evangelizing the lost and spreading revival.

Countering this, some feminists condemn the Bible as a solely flawed and biased product of masculine political domination. Scholz (2007) states, "The Bible as the sacred text of Christianity and Judaism provides central clues about the cultural, political, economic, social, and religious dynamics of past and present gender oppression." The Bible, written and translated by men, is unfair and inaccurate in its interpretations, judgments, and applications of/for women. Radical philosopher Mary Daly (1973) writes, "If God is male, then male is god," and Bible scholar Phyllis Trible (1992) states,

> The Bible was born and bred in a land of patriarchy; it abounds in male imagery and language. For centuries, interpreters have exploited this androcentrism to articulate theology, to define the church . . . and to instruct human beings, female and male, in who they are, what roles they should play and how they should behave. (p. 23)

Despite any motivation for doctrinal reverence or social justice, the extreme nature of such inflexible masculinism and feminism, the lack of conclusive scriptural evidence, and advocates' unwillingness to consider the holistic context of the Bible and its stories reveal the dangers of both positions. Genesis begins with Adam and Eve being partners in human existence. "So, God created mankind in his own image, in the image of God he created them; male and female he created them" (Genesis 1:27, New International Version).

This simple verse and later Genesis 2:18, where God reflects, "It is not good for the man to be alone. I will make a suitable helper for him," contains much significance, relationally. They speak of the first couple's unity in each other, of their closeness and their oneness, of their complementary natures and abilities, and of their equality of human frailty and failings. Adam and Eve, like all men and women in loving relationships, are made for each other in that they are both imperfect beings who need each other, perfectly.

Women have had pivotal roles in the Hebrew and Greek scriptures. They are instigators for both positive and negative events and actions; they demonstrate heroic personal qualities and at other times are the villain; they have definite and critical roles in the great plans of God; they have the capacity to follow and to lead or instigate—but regardless, the biblical stories often and regularly revolve around the lives and needs of women of whom God cares about, eternally.

What then should be the goal for God's children? Simply, Christians are to reflect God's kind and truthful standards in the treatment of every individual in the community. Rather than striving for a system that pushes down one gender in order to step up to a higher position, the scriptures suggest a humble partnership of men and women, willing to "submit to one another out of reverence for Christ" (Ephesians 5:21, New International Version), understanding that peace and love are central to the fulfillment of God's design for human relationships. Real power, real nobility, real righteousness comes from self-restraint, not from visceral domination or exploitation by either sex or gender.

As Jesus says in Luke 22 (New International Version),

> The kings of the Gentiles lord it over them; and those who exercise authority over them call themselves Benefactors. But you are not to be like that. Instead, the greatest among you should be like the youngest, and the one who rules like the one who serves. (vs. 25–26).

Thus, based on biblical precedent, *gender empowerment* should not be the ultimate goal; *servanthood* should be the main objective for all men and women who call themselves followers of Jesus Christ.

Despite His overwhelming cosmic power, Jesus gently and respectfully waited on and helped those in need. Despite His overwhelming colossal intellect and understanding, He patiently and devotedly spent time helping others understand the roots of their social problems. Despite His overwhelming sinless nature, He loved people fully despite their sinfulness and imperfect flaws. Despite His overwhelming sense of purpose, He endured the ignorance and mockery of those who surely did not know what they were doing. Succinctly, the love of Jesus transcended any and all social barriers.

© shinphoto/Shutterstock.com

INSIGHTS FROM THE EXPERTS

"Puff. Puff. Pass."

Let's talk about the obvious thing in the room—you know . . . the cheetah. Yes, I am aware that most people use "elephant" as the adjective describing a socially vulgar construct, but considering the topic at hand, I figured to keep with the cannabis theme and modernize the phrase to a faster, higher variety.

Drug *addiction* and alcoholism are not social constructs close to me. I have had friends and even family members struggle with these issues, and yet, I have been blessed to be free of these struggles. I hope to continue this trend until returning to the dust from which I came. Still, I can speak on the roots of these problems, as they all fall under the same umbrella of sin.

"Sin" is a vulgar word within itself, often used by the most judging of society to control people, like public hangings employed by old-miner towns in the West to deter crime. Alternatively, some have also used religion to keep children from engaging in actions that could result in sorrow, them wishing for death, or a having a baby before fully grown themselves. Addiction is rooted on a need not met, internally, and thus is medicated, externally. *Self-pleasure* is a prime example of this. Sexual curiosities, mixed with chemicals raging at speeds faster than a politician can craft a lie, manufacture opportunities for personal stress, loneliness, or boredom that seeds behavioral immorality.

Other addictions may not be so lustful but are rooted in lacking the same foundational components in life. These might be the need to purchase items to relieve stress or by having the need to exaggerate situations so that attention is drawn to oneself. Shopping is a need of ownership, and hyperbole is a need for attention and control (due to self-doubt). These may not be the easiest to identify, but they are all remedied by the same thing.

Although the Baptist in the room may cringe, there is a very real, very present battle at "foot." That battle is not between flesh and blood, but of the spiritual variety (Ephesians 6:12). Despite the devil being truly defeated by the redemption of Christ, we each must understand the present struggle, the choice to give reverence to the Son as the only path to the Father, and to be in constant construction to further adumbrate (dimly resemble) Jesus as best we can. This does not mean one needs to find the nearest snake-holding "church," but you do need to take control over the enemy and say, "This far you have come Lucifer, but no further!"

In His ministry, Jesus does this often, such as in Matthew 8:28–33:

> And when He came to the other side, to the country of the Gadarenes, two demon-possessed men met him, coming out of the tombs, so fierce that no one could pass that way. And behold, they cried out, 'What have you to do with us, O son of God? Have you come here to torment us before the time?' Now a herd of many pigs was feeding at some distance from them. And the demons begged Him stating, 'If you cast us out, send us away into the herd of pigs.' And He said to them, 'Go.' So, they came out and went into the pigs, and behold, the whole herd rushed down the steep bank into the sea and drowned in the waters. (ESV)

This continues onward into Paul's ministry (Acts 16:16–18) after Jesus gives permission to all His disciples (including ones of today's age—You!) to cast out demons and heal the sick. Luke 9:1 states, "One day Jesus called together His twelve disciples and gave them power and authority to cast out all demons and to heal all diseases" (NLT). As stated previously, Paul does this in the book of Acts, after the death and resurrection of Jesus. Thus, the authority continues well beyond one event and time, a time that still stretches into today.

Many works of the enemy are sweet. "Satan disguises himself as an angel of light. So, it is no surprise if his servants, also, disguise themselves as servants of righteousness" (2 Corinthians 11:14–15, ESV). My mother, just the other day, spoke to me regarding Eve and she said,

> I can understand why Eve ate from the tree. In our present age, we have so much information about the enemy and how to defeat the works of the evil one, but Eve did not. She was just told by Adam, not even God himself to avoid the sin.

The works of the enemy are very real and manifest in every imaginable way, from masturbation, to self-harm, to prostitution, to homosexuality, to drinking and drug use. Moreover, these often are generational. A dad will be abusive and have children who replicate those tendencies;

alcoholic mothers will often have alcoholic daughters; suicide will usually re-emerge throughout a family tree, unless the cycle is broken.

My mother is a neuro-coach getting her PhD in Christian Counseling. She has also been a praying healing minister for many years, and she said that only about 5% of secular counseling actually works, but true *deliverance ministries* have over a 95% success rate. My great grandparents are a wonderful example; for years, my family has had a history of being a part of the cult of the Freemasons, and likewise, we have really struggled with many health and self-doubts, for the Masons depend on a cycle of dependence and curses to keep their operation running.

Derek Prince (2013), a prominent deliverance evangelist has written,

> The problem with most religious people is they try and earn *grace,* but you can't earn it. And if you are trying to earn it by works, you do not receive it. At some point, you just have to stop trying to earn it and just receive it. (p. 15)

The short of it is, we can try to be a part of belonging, and medicate ourselves with culture, or clans, tribes, high clubs, and so on; but nothing takes the place of Jesus. We cannot strive for completion but must receive it in Christ.

Addiction, no matter what form, is serious and often a journey taken by yourself with people on all sides holding you up; but even more so, you depend upon God, for He is the only path to healing, and likewise salvation from struggle. See, many believe that He is just here to get you into heaven. Truly, He is not just a ticket, but the path is the abundance of spiritual inheritance.

Skylar Collins
Senior, Biomedical Sciences
Liberty University

CASE STUDY #11

Tyrone yelled and charged at his opponent; after all, a game of tag is a serious competition. His target, a classmate, named Tessa, darted away, shrieking in laugher. When Tyrone caught her, as he always did, he pulled her braids and retreated fearing retaliation. At 7 years old, Tyrone was the largest and fastest boy in his class, and he used it to his advantage. The couple ran through the school playground tugging and hitting each other, laughing the entire time. Their teacher, an older lady named Darly, would supervise them with a watchful eye to make sure nothing got too out of hand. Rarely, if ever, did Tyron require correction for playing too roughly.

One day, Principal Lacy came outside to talk to Darly and saw the scene on the playground. Immediately, she stopped all play and dragged Tyrone off to her office. An hour later, both parents were at the school as Principal Lacy explained the situation. At first, Tyrone's father and mother resisted the notion that their son had done anything wrong. Tyrone's actions weren't violent or intentional. Nobody was hurt or complaining. Tyrone was just a boy. Principal Lacy was appalled that they failed to see the issue and reprimanded them on how they were raising their son, even going so far as to suggest putting Tyrone on Adderall. After 45 minutes of arguing, the parents finally relented because Principal Lacy was, after all, the expert. Tyrone was not allowed to run on the playground again and was instead confined to his teacher's side during recess.

DISCUSSION QUESTIONS

1. Based on the readings, how would a sociologist diagnose this situation?

2. What specific sociological factors are involved?

3. What does the principal's assessment of Tyrone tell readers about her view of boys?

Check out the Chapter 11 video at this link:

https://www.khpcontent.com/

VOCABULARY

Addiction

Deliverance Ministries

Estrogen

Feminist Movement

Gender

Gender Empowerment

Gender Role Socialization

Gender Stratification

Gender Wage Gap

Grace

Ideal Man

Ideal Woman

Masculinist Movement

Natural Biology

Self-Pleasure

Servanthood

Sex

Sex Typing

Sexism

Social Identity

Social Roles

Testosterone

Victorian Era

Women in Scripture

References

Carter, M. J., & Fuller, C. (2016). Symbols, meaning, and action: The past, present, and future of symbolic interactionism. *Current Sociology Review, 64*(6), 931–961.

Daly, M. (1973). *Beyond God the father: Toward a philosophy in women's liberation.* Beacon.

Grenz, S., & Kjesbo, D. (1995). *Women in the church: A biblical theology of women in ministry.* InterVarsity.

Levitt, H. M. (2019). Applications of a functionalist theory of gender: A response to reflections and a research agenda. *Psychology of Women Quarterly, 43*(3), 309–316.

Miller, A. E., MacDougall, J. D., Tarnopolsky, M. A., & Sale, D. G. (1993). Gender differences in strength and muscle fiber characteristics. *European Journal of Applied Physiology and Occupational Physiology, 66*(3), 254–262. doi:10.1007/BF00235103

Miller, C. (2017). Why men don't want the jobs done mostly by women. The *New York Times.* https://www.nytimes.com/2017/01/04/upshot/why-men-dont-want-the-jobs-done-mostly-by-women.html

Ogden, C. L., Fryar, C. D., Carroll, M. D., & Flegal, K. M. (2004). Mean body weight, height, and body mass index, United States: 1960–2002. *Advance Data From Vital and Health Statistics, 347.* National Center for Health Statistics.

Paquette, D. (2016). Men say they work more than women: Here's the truth. *The Washington Post.* https://www.washingtonpost.com/news/wonk/wp/2016/06/29/men-say-they-work-more-than-women-heres-the-truth/?noredirect=on&utm_term=.381fd66d016e

Piper, J. (2017). Ask Pastor John. *Desiring God.* http://www.desiringgod.org/ask-pastor-john

Prince, D. (2013). *By grace alone: Finding freedom and purging legalism from your life.* Chosen Books.

Scholz, S. (2007). *Introducing the women's Hebrew Bible.* Bloomsbury T & T Clark.

Silver, N., & Bridges, J. (2014). *The giver*. Walden Media.

Tetlow, E. (1980). The status of women in Greek, Roman and Jewish society. In *Women and Ministry in the New Testament*. Paulist.

Trible, P. (1992). If the Bible's so patriarchal, how come I love It? *Bible Review, 8*(5), 44–47, 55.

U.S. Bureau of Labor Statistics. (2020). https://www.bls.gov

Washer, P. (2017). What role should women . . . http://www.sermonindex.net/modules/newbb/viewtopic.php?topic_id=25798&forum=35.

Ch 12 Homosexuality

Regarding the LGBTQ movement, *homosexuality* (or being *gay*) refers to people who are sexually attracted to members of their own sex. According to the 2018 Gallup.com poll, around 4.5% of people within the United States embrace the homosexual lifestyle, with more women identifying as lesbian than homosexual men (Gallup.com). Although the current social trend in America is more approving and permissive of the gay lifestyle, most other non-Western cultures consider the practice to be an anomaly and one to be avoided.

This is based on several conclusions: (a) it threatens the *biological function* of the traditional family structure, (b) it violates many *religious dogmas* and *scriptural prohibitions*, (c) it is associated with other socially unsanctioned activities long considered taboo, and (d) gay identification often originates in physical or sexual abuse and emotional neglect or abandonment (Roberts et al., 2013). Since the removal of homosexuality as a mental illness from the Diagnostic and Statistical Manual of Mental Disorders (*DSM*) in 1973 (Drescher, 2012), attitudes began to change about the LGBTQ lifestyle in many U.S. institutions and public forums. As of 1987, all references to homosexuality were completely removed from the DSM.

According to Finnerty et al. (2017), "Today, the standard of psychotherapy in the U.S. and Europe is gay affirmative psychotherapy, which encourages gay people to accept their sexual orientation" (online). Not everyone agrees with the progressive facilitation of the LGBTQ lifestyle, though, as nothing has changed medically about homosexuality.

As Sorba (2007) notes, "Dishonesty and intimidation had won the day for the same-gender sex movement, and when activists publicly claim that this [1973] vote was a scientific decision, they hide three years of [self-admitted] deceit and intimidation" (online). Only about 35% of *American Psychological Association* (n.d.) members voted, "Yes," to remove homosexuality as a mental illness. Thus, the decision to change the *LGBTQ classification* was mostly a political one, stemming from intense LGBTQ activism, lobbying, and some say intimidation. Adding to this, the AIDs epidemic of the 1980s and 1990s brought into question the validity of assumptions that same-sex coupling was natural, healthy, and a safe social relationship.

Currently in America, the LGBTQ movement has made huge political bounds; however, it still finds great resistance from middle America and conservative churches, who point to biblical texts that clearly outlaw the practice as being immoral and unhealthy (Genesis 19:1–11, Leviticus 18:22, Leviticus 20:13, Judges 19:16–24, 1 Kings 14:24, 1 Kings 15:12, 2 Kings 23:7, Romans 1:18–32, 1 Corinthians 6:9–11, 1 Timothy 1:8–10, Jude 7). Although more *liberal churches* are trying to find middle ground (or promotional) on the issue, "Considering the effect and seriousness of the early church's witness regarding sexuality, it is hard to imagine any scenario in which the nature of mar-

riage and sexuality would be considered an 'agree to disagree' issue for the earliest Christians" (Wax, 2019, online).

As with other social issues, homosexuality shows no signs of ceasing to be a divisive issue in an era of fractured, egocentric, dysfunctional social environments. Its deviant existence (less than 5% of the population) and historical propensity of participants to have suffered or to continue to suffer physiological, psychological, or emotional trauma (Roberts et al., 2013) still needs to be addressed—despite prohibitory laws against anti-gay counseling in the more progressive states. Moreover, *psychotherapy techniques* that mainly facilitate neuroses instead of treating them are not psychotherapeutic, in truth; they are just political appeasements that inevitably end with the logical negative consequences of ignoring the mental and emotional suffering of the vulnerable in society.

DEALING WITH MATTERS OF THE DARK

With the culturally proclaimed period of postmodernism, a very negative practice is observable in *progressive Christian apologetics*—the embrace of fallacies in order to explain and promote divergent religious principles running contrary to traditional biblical thought. Thus, it is easy to find the utilization of illogic in the writings and argumentations of theologians and pastors like Rob Bell, Brian McLaren, and Matthew Vine, to name a few.

No doubt, most readers and listeners are unaware of the frequency of these fallacies, but they occur often and with set purpose, unfortunately. Thus, it is important to investigate several different key cultural speakers and thinkers in progressive Christianity and examine the sophistic tools they use to sway readers and listeners in regard to key doctrinal ideas.

The "Transcript" of Matthew Vines's video on *gay Christianity* (see matthewvines.com) is a very clear example of this embrace of illogic in progressive Christianity. Mr. Vines makes an eloquent, emotional, personal argument defending homosexual activity for the gay Christian, meandering through biblical passages that one-sidedly condemn the activity, utilizing specific Christian ethics and verses to affirm gay relationships, but unfortunately implementing multiple misconstructions and inaccuracies throughout his testimony to justify his position.

Vines's discourse begins with a *strawman fallacy*, setting up a universal dichotomy that is not proven in order to promote his agenda. Vines states,

> The most common themes voiced by those who support changing traditional church teaching on homosexuality are those of acceptance, inclusion, and love, while on the other hand, those who oppose these changes express concerns about sexual purity, holiness, and most fundamentally, the place of Scripture in our communities.

So, only pro-gay Christians are loving, inclusive, and accepting; anti-gay Christians are legalists and literalists who have an exclusive vision of individualism in the Christian community? Such a conclusion comes across as diluted and cursory (and ironic), considering the artificial parameters presented by Vines.

Second, Vines points to evidence throughout his defense that only supports his pro-gay position while casually dismissing other truths that refute his assertion; this is known as a *confirmation bias fallacy*. For example, he points to six passages that condemn homosexuality but then immediately points out that they are six verses out of 31,000; however, there are over a dozen verses that specifically condemn the practice and a case could be made for over a dozen more that indirectly refute Vines's position. A more important question is how many biblical verses directly and specifically affirm the gay lifestyle for the Christian and the non-Christian? (answer: none). Moreover, I suspect if one biblical verse stated, "Don't bully homosexuals," that would be a sufficient proof for Progressives.

Another one of Vines's illogical habits is the *confusion of correlation and causation fallacy*. One of his clearer inconsistencies is evident when he states, "But everyone has a sexual orientation—and it isn't just about sex," which is like saying everyone has elbows, but they're not connected to their arms. Additionally, he writes, "Family is not about sex, but for so many of us, it still depends upon having a companion, a spouse," and yet, he is arguing for gay Christians to be able to express themselves sexually in a relationship with same-sex partners. Friendship is an integral part of Christianity, and no traditionalist is demanding that gay Christians not have friends or family in their lives.

Additionally, condemning traditional *Christian sexuality and morality*, Vines claims, "Gay people are told to avoid romantic relationships entirely," which is false. Gay people are told to avoid romantic relationships with members of the same sex alone. All Christians are told to avoid all unhealthy, lustful, romantic relationships, regardless of their gender orientation, and same-sex relationships are completely acceptable provided that they are based on agape love and not sexual eros alone. The relationship of David and Jonathon versus David and Bathsheba are fantastic examples of this notion (Rowe, 2013). Vines's assertion is that gay Christians just want what heterosexual Christians want; but a more accurate comparison would be gay Christians want what adulterous Christians want, which are relationships forbidden in the Bible as destructive and unhealthy.

One of Vines's biggest false assertions is that because of his gay orientation, "According to the traditional interpretation of Scripture, as a Christian, I am uniquely excluded from that possibility for love, for companionship, and for family." Ultimately, Vines is saying that gay Christianity is not about sex; however, he also says that gay Christians are unhappy because they cannot have sexual relationships with same-sex lovers. They are deprived of *human dignity* because they cannot have culturally affirmed same-sex lovers, which is in their embraced lifestyle.

Again, using this reasoning, a heterosexual person with a natural lust problem would be prevented from experiencing love, companionship, and family if he or she was unable to express him or herself in an adulterous relationship outside of marriage, which would be absurdly unhealthy. Love and companionship are easily and regularly found outside of sexual activity; in fact, platonic relationships are more of the norm in society than sexual relationships.

Vines continues,

> By holding to the traditional interpretation, we are now contradicting the Bible's own teachings: The Bible teaches that it is not good for the man to be forced to be alone, and yet now, we are teaching that it is.

Of course, most theologians and biblical scholars would point out that Adam was lonely before he and Eve were aware of their sexuality. Thus, God gave Adam a friend to tend to his emotional/intellectual—but not sexual—needs. Sexuality was not an issue until the first couple went against the word of God and brought destruction upon themselves for another natural, innocuous activity, but one rightly prohibited by God (Gellman, 2006). Ironically, like Adam and Eve, Vines wants his listeners to think that gay Christianity is "good fruit," acceptable to God despite it being prohibited clearly and unequivocally in both the Hebrew and Greek scriptures.

The sorrow of this situation (and what Vines misses overall in his discourse) is that intimacy is defined by God in the Bible and is not defined by sexuality alone, culturally, but that is what Vines is trying to do (and not do) at the same time—dismissing the Word of God and proclaiming sexual needs to be quintessential for fulfillment in life. Vines utilizes other fallacies to win his argument (appeal to ignorance, argument from authority, begging the questions, composition fallacy, and so on), and although his intentions are sincere and his goals may be noble, in the end his illogical, self-serving arguments negate the authority of his efforts. One cannot build a true bridge on false beams; it will collapse, unavoidably, with the weight of reality.

In our modern world of sacro-egoism (Knox, 2016), self-serving fallacies are commonly used by progressives to promote their radical religious agenda, illogically appealing to the personal, emotional wants and needs of people, while ignoring the biblical, evidential facts established by God in the Holy Scriptures long ago. And while gay Christians' wants, needs, and human dignity should definitely be important to all Christians (if we are to love one another as Jesus commanded), using fallacies to appease their suffering is just a placebo, at best. Being human, homosexuals deserve truth, in as gentle a delivery as possible (Galatians 6:1).

What every human being needs, regardless of sexual orientation, is a right relationship with God that transcends our humanity. Finding that right path to emotional well-being and healing begins and ends in truth alone—something that C. S. Lewis wrote about in his book, *The Four Loves* (1960), a personal essay on love, based on Lewis's experiences of love.

The Four Loves is written from a 1st-person point of view, without a plot, character, or story. Lewis did not write it as an absolute authoritative tome; it was simply his reflections on the kind of loves that people experience in their lives (Edwards, 2007). Although Lewis touches upon the differences between affection and pleasure, he narrows it down to four expressions of love for humanity: storge, philia, eros, and agape.

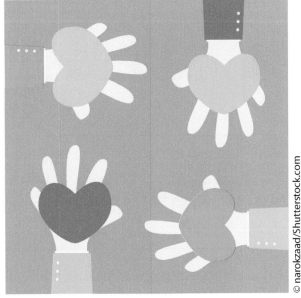

Storge is the affectionate type of love that a mother and child might share between each other. It is perhaps most similar to the love found in animals, who act upon a bond that is found in nature. It is the least discriminating of all loves, it is the humblest of all loves, and it is the silliest of all loves.

As such, it ignores all sorts of barriers that typically come between people. It transcends education, age, gender, and social class. Typically, people are unaware of when storge begins, but realize when they are in it. It is a love that does not need to be earned, and it is one better done in private than in public.

Lewis's second type of love is called *philia*, meaning friendship. It is an others-focused sort of love, that seeks common truth, vision, and unity with a person. Some people think that philia is the least of the loves, but it is the most beneficial (especially for same-sex friendships). It is a love that one man might feel for another man as his best friend (think King David and King Saul's son Jonathan). It does not expect anything in return; the friendship itself is the treasure in the person's heart.

The third type of love is *eros*, which is more than just being sexually aroused. It is the sensation or feeling that one has when he or she is "falling in love" or "being in love." Eros seeks emotional connections between people; it is passionate; it is romantic. It wants to have a beloved person as the center of its focus.

Due to the intensity of this love, the possibility of idolatry is present; however, like a flash fire that dies out soon after starting, Eros claims to be eternal but normally is not, with both sides blaming each other for its failure. While commitment is shown at the beginning of the relationship, excitement wanes after the honeymoon period and dwindles on the way out.

Lewis's final form of love is called *agape*. It is the highest form of all love; it is self-sufficient, a Christian virtue (Lorio, 2015). It is unconditional, not based on any characteristic of the person in particular. Some might consider it to be a deontological form of love in that it focuses on the principle more than the person. In many ways, agape love is God's type of love. It is a divine gift, which is a love for all. The person expressing agape love does so not out of neediness but out of charity and with admiration in the heart for others.

Ultimately, for Lewis, all loves point to God and Jesus in heaven. Still, some forms of love have deeper roots than others and reach higher into the sky. As Malanga (2007) states, "Even so, some will still mistake similarity for sameness. And they will give to human loves the unconditional allegiance that Lewis says we owe only to God" (p. 55). The natural form of love, according to the Bible, is just for between specific people on earth.

Agape love, however, is the divine form of love that meets the eternal love needs of all people and is sustained for all eternity. It is relational, unconditional, and always available—regardless of one's failures. Other loves may get distorted or perverted or confusing, but agape love is a clear, sweet spring that never ceases to flow. It satisfies the cravings of the flesh with a spiritual feast for the soul. It is the essence of God's love for humanity.

INSIGHTS FROM THE EXPERTS

"Gender Dysphoria"

Check out a video for more on this topic here:

https://www.khpcontent.com/

Doesn't it seem odd that in Genesis 3:7, after Adam and Eve have sinned, it says, "Then the eyes of both of them were opened, and they realized they were naked . . ." "Naked"—why didn't they say, "I feel guilty" or "I'm afraid God will find out," or something similar? But no, the first thing that sin did was cause people to realize their nakedness, and thereby harm sexuality from the very beginning. Ever since then, shame and confusion about sexuality are common experiences, and that manifests itself in numerous ways.

The third edition of the *Diagnostic and Statistical Manual* (DSM-III)—the official list of psychological diagnoses published in 1980—introduced the idea of diagnoses for *Gender Identity Disorder*, the very similar precursor of *gender dysphoria*. The American Psychiatric Association (APA, n.d.) defines gender dysphoria as "a conflict between a person's physical or assigned gender and the gender with which he/she/they identify." Essentially, the person, for whatever reason, identifies as the opposite sex from the original genitalia at birth.

Physicians can identify some sex differences, acknowledging that males on average weigh about 15% more than females and are 6 inches taller (Ogden et al., 2004). Also, women are approximately 50 to 60% as strong as men in the upper body, and 60 to 70% as strong in the lower body (A. E. Miller et al., 1993). They may also tell you that males have 56% greater lung volume per body mass, and that a man's heart is 15 to 30% larger than a female heart (Prabhavathi et al., 2014). The undeniable differences in male and female anatomy comprise a huge list and these items mentioned above are but a sampling.

With all these differences, that no sex change operations can alter, one would think that the mental health professions would diagnose gender-confused persons as disturbed in their perception of themselves. Sadly, many large mental health organizations say that if a man thinks he's a woman, then he is. Ironically, if that same man said he thought he was a chimpanzee, he would likely be given a diagnosis such as *Brief Psychotic Disorder*—298.8 (F23), even though human males are significantly different from both females and chimpanzees. When a psychological problem involves sexuality, basic logic sometimes gets ignored.

Having worked with many people over the years who thought they were born into the wrong-sexed body, I have observed that they have high rates of emotional and sexual abuse in their backgrounds. Often, emotionally abused victims who were never accepted as their birth sex (or were molested) internalize the abuse message that their birth sex is unacceptable, and then they try to adjust to that message.

All of these psychological debates are also occurring in a Western culture that is sinking ever deeper into a postmodern perspective. Postmodernism posits that there is no objective reality, there is no scientific or historical truth (objective truth), and that people create their own reality (Dulgnan, 2019). People sometimes suggest postmodernism when they rhetorically ask, "If a tree falls in the woods and no one hears it, does it make any noise?" They want you to believe that if you didn't hear it, then it didn't make any sound. In essence, your hearing is presumed to be the judge of the existence of all sound in the universe. Postmodernists also say, "There is no such thing as Truth," which is absurd, as it is a self-contradictory statement, but they usually don't let simple logic like that dissuade them.

Ironically, developmental psychologist Jean Piaget studied what he termed, *Object Permanence*, in infants. Piaget said that infants achieved this developmental stage when they realized, "Objects exist even if out of sensory experience" (Wong et al., 2015). Piaget would take a ball and hide it under a blanket or put it behind his back, and infants who did not have this understanding would act as if it had disappeared, whereas those who had achieved this developmental milestone would look under the blanket or behind his back for the ball. Piaget found this to be true not just with balls, but with parents, as infants whose parents left for a short period were calmer in the understanding that they were still alive even if they could not see them.

Tragically, many infants understand that things continue to exist when they cannot discern them with their own senses but grown adults in Western countries buy into the emotionally stunted idea that if they don't believe it, then it does not exist (both postmodernism and ego-centrism). To make matters worse, the large mental health organizations are telling people struggling with gender dysphoria that if they feel like they were born into the wrong body, then they are right, contrary to all cardiac, respiratory, skeletal, neurological evidence. The consequences of applying an agenda-driven philosophy into the lives of mental health clients has been catastrophic.

James et al. (2016) reported that the suicide rate for transsexuals (those who pursue altering their body to match their sex perception) is nearly nine times higher than for most in the U.S. population. Zucker (2017) stated regarding the prevalence of gender dysphoria, "It has increased in the past couple of decades, perhaps reflected in the large increase in referral rates to specialised gender identity clinics" (p. 405). Bear in mind that these clinics encourage clients to adopt their gender dysphoric view of their sex (they parse words like "sex," "gender," "identity" in highly creative ways) . . . and then these clinics profit financially from the services to address that desire.

Although many mental health organizations believe that "therapies that aim to change a child or adolescent's gender identity are considered unethical" (Society of Clinical Child and Adolescent Psychology, n.d.), this leaves the person with gender dysphoria only one direction to pursue some form of gender transition in most therapy settings, and that direction may not be in the client's best interest or desire. I suggest that the more ethical approach is to work with a client, if willing, to examine how his or her upbringing or possible abuse history has shaped desirability toward one's own biological sex. I suggest empathetically examining the implicit and explicit messages regarding sex in any abuse or neglect based on life experiences. I also suggest that the therapist help the client think through the often-irreversible consequences of either following or not following through with various forms and levels of sex transition.

I further suggest that the therapist inform the client on the highly undesirable mental health statistics that describe transsexual people, which are not all explained away by blaming lack of societal acceptance. Is it possible that obtaining a transsexual body is inherently unsatisfying, hence all of the psychological problems correlated with it? As there are so many psychological problems connected with transsexualism, is it a violation of the *Beneficence Principle* for mental health organizations to promote it?

These suggestions, which could be achieved through numerous theoretical approaches, could help the client put gender dysphoria feelings in the context of life history and thereby make more sense. Offering these options to the client is ethical in that they respect client autonomy with therapy direction, rather than imposing the ideology of some mental health organizations on the client. The current trend to automatically endorse any gender dysphoria feelings as accurate smacks of bias.

Postmodernism says there is no such thing as Truth, but Jesus said, "I am the way, the truth, and the life" in John 14:6 (NIV). Postmodernism says that we create our own reality, but Genesis 1:1 (NIV) says, "In the beginning God created . . . " Man only has perceptions of reality and can be creative with things like music and art. It is a classic example of "delusions of grandeur" for humans to think they can create reality like God, and that includes their gender. However, some clients will refuse to examine how their history shaped their current gender dysphoria feelings, and they will choose to pursue some level of transition. Once they make some transition and come to realize (often after a "honeymoon period") that it does not satisfy or complete them as they were told, they will need a caring, gracious therapist all the more, and I hope you are that type of therapist at that point.

Dr. Kenyon Knapp, PhD
Dean, School of Behavioral Sciences
Liberty University

Contributed by Kenyon Knapp. © Kendall Hunt Publishing Company

CASE STUDY #12

Brody had been at the small Christian university for a few weeks and he was still unsure what he thought about it. When his parents let him know that they would pay for his education if he came there, he was agreeable but had no idea how super-serious these guys were in their Christian beliefs. All the other students seemed so clean-cut and boringly traditional, like the guy who sat next to him in class each day with a bow tie on. Seriously, what 18-year-old wears a bow tie? Even more annoying was the constant diatribe from the chapel pulpit about proper sexual behavior. Young people want to have fun; who were they to tell them what to do with their own bodies? None of their business, really, he vehemently (but silently) concluded.

He wasn't a virgin; he'd had sex multiple times before with both men and women. In fact, the first sex he'd ever had was with his "favorite" uncle (at the time). After that experience, he felt bad about himself for a while, but when a friend of a friend at a party approached him for a special party "favor," he thought it might make him feel better, maybe normal again. He even had a girlfriend right now at school. They were juniors, and she kept bugging him about a more serious commitment, and he probably would try to do the right thing and marry her. But at night, in his dorm room alone, he found himself surfing the web and chatrooms, talking with older men that reminded him of his uncle.

DISCUSSION QUESTIONS

1. Based on the readings, how would a sociologist diagnose this situation?

2. What specific sociological factors are involved?

3. What do Brody's relationships tell you about his search for intimacy?

Check out the Chapter 12 video at this link:

https://www.khpcontent.com/

VOCABULARY

Agape
American Psychological Association
Beneficence Principle
Biological Function
Brief Psychotic Disorder
Christian Sexuality and Morality
Confirmation Bias Fallacy
Confusion of Correlation and Causation Fallacy
DSM
Eros
The Four Loves
Gay
Gay Christianity

Gender Dysphoria
Gender Identity Disorder
Homosexuality
Human Dignity
LGBTQ Classification
Object Permanence
Philia
Progressive Christian Apologetics
Psychotherapy Techniques
Religious Dogmas
Scriptural Prohibitions
Storge
Strawman Fallacy

References

American Psychiatric Association. (n.d.). What is Gender Dysphoria? https://www.psychiatry.org/patients-families/gender-dysphoria/what-is-gender-dysphoria

Drescher, J. (2012) The removal of homosexuality from the DSM: Its impact on today's marriage equality debate. *Journal of Gay & Lesbian Mental Health, 16*(2), 124–135, https://doi.org/10.1080/19359705.2012.653255

Dulgnan, B. (Ed.). (2019). Postmodernism. *Encyclopedia Britannica*.

Edwards, B. L. (2007). *C. S. Lewis: Life, works, and legacy, 4 vols.* Nestport.

Finnerty, P., Kocet, M. M., Lutes, J., & Yates, C. (2017). *Affirmative, strengths-based counseling with LGBTQI+ people.* In M. M. Ginicola, C. Smith, & J. M. Filmore (Eds.), *Affirmative counseling with LGBTQI+ people* (p. 109–125). American Counseling Association. https://doi.org/10.1002/9781119375517.ch10

Gallup.com. (2018). In U.S., estimate of LGBT population rises to 4.5%. https://news.gallup.com/poll/234863/estimate-lgbt-population-rises.aspx

Gellman, J. (2006). Gender and sexuality in the Garden of Eden, *Theology & Sexuality, 12*(3), 319–335, https://doi.org/10.1177/1355835806065391

James, S. E., Herman, J. L., Rankin, S., Keisling, M., Mottet, L., & Anafi, M. (2016). *The report of the 2015 U.S. Transgender Survey.* National Center for Transgender Equality.

Knox, J. (2016). *Sacro-egoism: The rise of religious individualism in the West.* Wipf & Stock.

Lewis, C. S. (1960). *The Four Loves.* Harcourt.

Lorio, G. (2015). *Sociology of love: The agape dimension of societal life.* Vernon.

Malanga, M. (2007). The four loves: C. S. Lewis's theology of love. In *C. S. Lewis: Life, Works, and Legacy.* Praeger.

Miller, A. E., MacDougall, J. D., Tarnopolsky, M. A., & Sale, D. G. (1993). Gender differences in strength and muscle fiber characteristics. *European Journal of Applied Physiology and Occupational Physiology, 66*(3), 254–262. doi:10.1007/BF00235103

Ogden, C. L., Fryar, C. D., Carroll, M. D., & Flegal, K. M. (2004). Mean body weight, height, and body mass index, United States: 1960–2002. *Advance Data From Vital and Health Statistics, 347*. National Center for Health Statistics.

Prabhavathi, K., Selvi, K. T., Poornima, K. N., & Sarvanan, A. (2014). Role of biological sex in normal cardiac function and in its disease outcome: A review. *Journal of Clinical and Diagnostic Research, 8*(8), BE01–BE4. https://doi.org/10.7860/JCDR/2014/9635.4771

Roberts, A. L., Glymour, M. M., & Koenen, K. C. (2013). Does maltreatment in childhood affect sexual orientation in adulthood? *Archives of sexual behavior, 42*(2), 161–171. https://doi.org/10.1007/s10508-012-0021-9

Rowe, J. Y. (2013). *Sons or lovers: An interpretation of David and Jonathan's friendship.* Bloomsbury T & T Clark.

Society of Clinical Child and Adolescent Psychology. (n.d.). Gender Dysphoria. https://effectivechildtherapy.org/concerns-symptoms-disorders/disorders/gender-dysphoria/

Sorba, R. (2007). The "born gay" hoax. http://parentsofgaychildren.com/uploads/The_Born_Gay_Hoax__-_Ryan_Sorba.pdf

Vines, M. (2014). *God and the gay Christian: The biblical case in support of same-sex relationships* (1st ed.). Convergent Books.

Wax, T. (2019). Is there really an 'orthodox' view on sexuality? https://www.thegospelcoalition.org/blogs/trevin-wax/really-orthodox-view-sexuality/

Wong, D. W., Hall, K. R., Justice, C. A., & Wong Hernandez, L. (2015). *Counseling individuals through the lifespan.* Sage.

Zucker, K. J. (2017). Epidemiology of gender dysphoria and transgender identity. *Sexual Health, 14*, 404–411. https://doi.org/10.1071/SH17067

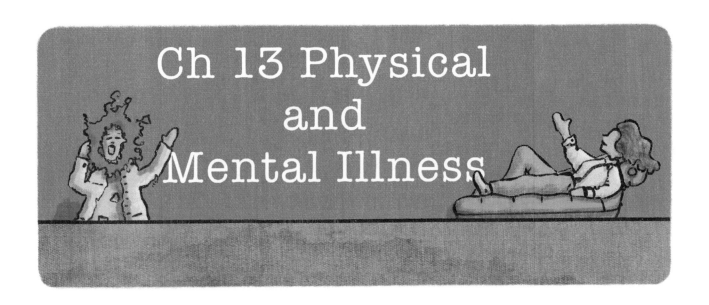

Ch 13 Physical and Mental Illness

Physical illness and *mental illness* have more than just a biological impact upon the people within society. There is a context in meaning of being ill, of being disabled, that is relative to culture. For some, being sick or having a disability brings public disdain or shame in some regions of the world; for others; it brings a sense of pride and/or personal identity. For instance, in many deaf communities, the members resist being thought of as disabled, insisting that nothing is wrong with them—"Don't fix us!" they demand.

In postmodernity, however, becoming ill or disabled is far easier than before in American society. With more leisure time on their hands and with more modern conveniences, people fall prey to maladies such as alcoholism, drug abuse, sexually transmitted diseases, heart disease, diabetes, and so on. Obesity is at an all-time high and is often blamed on poor diets and an inadequate exercise regimen.

Others find themselves in a disabled capacity due to no fault of their own. A *disability* is a physical or mental impairment that substantially limits one or more "normal" major life activities. Disabilities can involve walking, seeing, hearing, speaking, breathing, learning, working, and autonomous living. *People with disabilities (PWDs)* experience *impairment*, which is the disruption at a system level of bodily organ or physical/mental function; and/or *handicaps*, which are physical or social environmental obstacles that disadvantage the disabled person.

Besides their physical challenges, PWDs also face unfair cultural stumbling blocks. Several myths are promulgated regarding PWDs that have no basis in reality. First, everyone with severe autism is a bizarre genius. Second, the disabled are merely takers and not givers, being only "useless eaters" in society. Third, disabled people are always powerless and perpetual victims. Fourth, most disabled people should only be pitied and placated. Finally, most disabled people are bitter and argumentative warriors with emotional hang-ups regarding life.

All of these *myths* are absurd reductionisms and steal away the humanity and social value of PWDs. According to most rehabilitation counselors, all PWDs deserve respect and encouragement, the severity of a person's disability can be increased or reduced by adjusting environmental conditions, coping or adjusting to disability is dependent upon understanding environmental problems, each PWD has their own set of personal resources (to a lesser or greater degree), and the social significance of a disability is influenced by individual feelings about the person's self and social situation (Wright, 1983).

With a growing frequency, there is a mislabeling of normal human functions. In many schools, children are diagnosed as being *hyperactive* or *ADHD* and given prescription drugs to "calm them down," but boisterous behavior is not necessarily deviant or socially dangerous. Having testosterone or having estrogen is a normal state of physiology, not a disease. Drugs are supposed to be utilized for pain management, disease treatment, or for curative purposes, and not predominantly for behavioral control or suppression.

CHRISTIANITY AND SOCIAL PSYCHOLOGY

To be human is to have the capacity to think and to feel emotions through the various stages and passages of life. While no approach is perfect, both logic and emotion can bear witness to truth, although an imbalance from a lack of information or a distortion of perspective can also lead to dysfunction and suffering. This is where both Christianity and psychology can provide steps toward greater mental health for those willing to personally embrace their axioms. Yet, a greater question arises regarding each ministration's origins and presumptions.

Christian truth comes from God, who is the absolute Knowledgeable One. Not only did He design the human mind ages ago, He can presently and perfectly discern our inner psychological and moral states through His innate supernatural powers. *Psychology*, on the other hand, is a human innovation that relies mostly (or totally) upon outer observations or personal interactive analyses. *Psychologists* attempt to uncover the mental/emotional forces at work in a person's life to either understand or help him or her in society; ministers attempt to uncover the moral/spiritual forces at work in a person's life to both understand or help him or her (Entwistle, 2015).

So, both deal in truth although the latter (Christianity) uses scriptural truths to get to the heart of the matter while the former (psychology) uses cognitive and behavioral truths to get to the heart of the matter. Both are personal, both can be effective in comprehending and treating mental ailments leading to personal dysfunction, and both are somewhat limited by the agency and cooperation of the treated and treater.

Some people consider Christianity to solely concern questions of eternity and psychology to focus solely on questions of immediacy. No doubt, the reality is far more complex and intertwined. I personally like what the great second-century apologist, Justin Martyr, said in his *First Apology* (155–157 CE):

> First, Christ is the first-born of God and . . . he is the Reason (Logos) of which the whole human race partakes from the beginning. So then, all who live according to Reason are Christians, even though some may mistake them for atheists. (46:1–4)

In other words, all good things come from God, including psychological theory, if morally sound and mentally efficacious.

From what I have discerned over the years, many churches are hesitant to embrace or endorse any social science, including psychology. I do not think their concern is unmerited; since its inception, psychology has often introduced numerous questionable conclusions and treatments (many of which rested upon an anti-Christian supposition) toward bolstering good mental health. Yet, the danger is to "toss out the baby with the bath water."

Christian psychology has definitely also shown itself to be a beneficial value to humanity (McMinn, 2011). The danger truly only occurs when man-made psychological theory supplants God-made personal injunctions. Current transgender treatment options come to mind backing up my aforementioned assertion. Still, that is just one slice of the overall field of psychology.

Succinctly, I would say that, as in all things, the foundation of any endeavor determines its effectiveness and outreach. Christianity rests upon the truths of God in Jesus Christ, who shared with His first-century Disciples (and His successive disciples throughout the centuries) how to find and maintain good spiritual health, leading to good mental health, with love of God and love of one's neighbor as the bedrock of personal wellness. Thus, *psychological pursuits* that do not rest upon biblical truths or that challenge/contradict biblical truths, are destined for failure. There might be a short-term abatement of suffering, but without deep and eternal treatment, any improvement is simply a temporary, stop-gap effort (Coe & Hall, 2010). A balm for the mind must include (and begin with) a balm for the soul.

Although the Bible is replete with biblical proofs of God's role as our great Psychologist, Psalm 42:2–5 is one of the best examples of perfect, proper *Counseling from Above*. King David writes,

My soul thirsts for God, for the living God.
When can I go and meet with God?
My tears have been my food day and night,
While people say to me all day long,
"Where is your God?"
These things I remember
As I pour out my soul:
. . .
Why, my soul, are you downcast?
Why so disturbed within me?
Put your hope in God,
For I will yet praise him,
My Savior and my God.

Psychology and Christianity need not be adversaries or counteragents to good mental health, if understanding and treatment begins, continues, and ends in God. As the Apostle James wrote in his epistle, "Every good and perfect gift is from above, coming down from the Father of the heavenly lights, who does not change like shifting shadows" (James 1:17, New International Version). With this in mind, true psychological enlightenment—and true healing—can be shared with those in the darkness.

THE HEALTH CARE BUSINESS

Even the medical community can contribute to social problems, though. Many deaths are caused from the *medical errors* of doctors, nurses, and labs. Both with and without the medical community, however, bad philosophies are often offered on what constitutes good, healthy standards, leading to arbitrary or dangerous practices—an example of this being the anti-vaxxers or the pro-marijuana faction.

Other social problems come from how people think about practitioners in the medical field, in general. Ostensibly, doctors and nurses are not gods, but many, if not most, health-care providers are more than efficient at their jobs and deserve commendation for their skills and their services rendered, faithfully. There are many doctors in the United States, with some regions having greater resources than others. For example, Idaho has 171 doctors per 100,000 people; Massachusetts has the most with 474 per 100,000 people; and Virginia has 278 doctors per 100,000 residents.

Sometimes, though, physicians and nurses misdiagnose patients. Sometimes, they prescribe the wrong medication or in the wrong dosage. Sometimes, they get promoted despite their personal incompetence. This creates problems in a social institution whose main purpose in existing is to do the opposite—to solve problems.

There are multiple reasons for the problems dogging health care, overall. No one factor is to blame. Health care has transformed from a *health service institution* into a big, moneymaking business built upon diagnoses, complicated treatment plans, expensive medical procedures, assorted fees, high insurance costs, and so on. So, it is no wonder that the health care field has added to the social problems facing people in America and across the globe. Take into account that in 1962 the *annual health care cost* in America was $28 billion. By 2012, the annual health care cost had

risen to $3 trillion. A good part of this is due to the resumption of excess of health care spending and increased middle-class taxation in the past decade.

One of the ways that the American government tried to deal with the rising costs and obligations of medicine under President Obama was through the *Affordable Care Act of 2010* (ACA), also called *Obamacare*. The President and Democratic majority controlling congress promised to slow down or reverse rising health care costs through the ACA. It covered 10 essential health benefits (including OB/GYN service for men and prostate services for women, contrary to scientific facts or need). It permitted (or mandated) insurance coverage for preexisting medical conditions. Children were allowed to stay on their parents' insurance policies until they were 26 years old. It was supposed to lower out-of-pocket costs by $2,500 per year and guarantee that no one would lose their existing insurance coverage (as President Obama promised on television, officially). Although ACA did help some people in the lower classes, for most people in the middle class, if they did not have employer-provided insurance, it was a costly and frustrating law.

Some of the problems included the presumption that younger people would voluntarily shoulder the costs of elderly patients; they did not, choosing to take the IRS penalty for not purchasing personal medical insurance. Second, there were innumerable managerial failures in the ACA exchanges, unanticipated economic consequences, and massive exchange closures. Third, many Americans resented the *individual mandate* of the ACA, being forced out of better, former policies and into worse, new policies that crippled them, financially.

Many middle-class families discovered that their reasonable $400 per month policy (for a family of four) with a $1,000 deductible was no longer available, that they were ineligible for any federal subsidy to assist with costs and would be forced to pay $1,300 a month for a policy with a $9,500 deductible (which was my family's experience in 2014). Instead of saving $2,500, it more than quadrupled medical costs for many people. Not surprisingly, since 2010, every single one of the exchanges lost money, and very few exchanges, if any, remain open, currently.

Unfortunately, there is a growing number of elderly people in America who still need medical assistance. Plus, the burden of illegal immigrants who seek medical treatment in America has substantially increased in the past 5 years. Medical technologies and research are experiencing great financial challenges to fund and to develop. Medical care has turned into an industry with treatment turning into yet another commodity to sell to willing or able buyers in the public (if they can get access to care). The social problems surrounding medical care still exist and abound, needing to be carefully and wisely solved by future legislative ranks—and the sooner, the better.

DEALING WITH MATTERS OF THE DARK

More than three million people currently suffer from traumatic brain injuries in the United States, including both children and adults (NCIPC, 2020). *Traumatic brain injury* is a very serious debilitating disorder, affecting the memory processes in many ways—including both short-term (temporary storage) and long-term memory (permanent storage). More than that, it affects the learning processes that rely upon memory acquisition, planning, and management.

Studies have shown that most people's brains gradually mature regarding their cerebral cortex and other higher central executive functioning by the age of 25 years old (Starr, 2017). Although this process begins at birth, it actually extends and continues far beyond youth, with all people accumulating vast amounts of information stored in their brains for future retrieval and utilization at the various crucial junctions and necessities in life.

Regarding human existence and behavior, the brain is a marvelous machine. Different parts of the brain control different processes

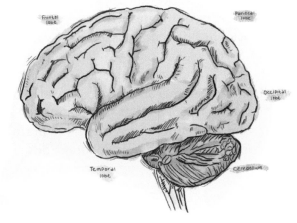

Frontal lobe
Parietal lobe
Occipital lobe
Temporal lobe
Cerebellum

© RJ Amado/Shutterstock.com

(with some blended influence) that are key to normal cognitive function. The frontal lobe controls the working memory, the occipital region controls vision and special understandings, the prefrontal cortex controls both verbal and auditory function, and the parietal region deals with touch and sensation (Farrell, 2011).

Beyond this are numerable neuronal and brain region crossovers for memory storage and retrieval that researchers and doctors continue to discover year after year. Not surprisingly, brain damage has a huge impact (no pun intended) on the *cognitive function* of most people (Farrell, 2011). Injury in any one of the aforementioned critical areas hampers or prevents the key cognitions, which interrupts the learning processes that rely upon memory and higher central executive functions (Klingberg, 2012).

Much research has been undertaken to investigate traumatic brain injuries and how they impact both memory and learning processes. Specifically, researchers have sought to determine how, when, and where memory is affected by traumatic brain injury—whether people post-traumatic brain injury can learn again, and whether one's age is a factor in cognitive recovery (Mandalis et al., 2007).

Most researchers, scientists, and doctors concur that traumatic brain injury hampers or prohibits key cognitive functions, but the debate is still ongoing as to probable or possible levels of recovery or if age is a factor in cognitive recovery. The main areas of the brain—the frontal, parietal, temporal, and occipital—each control quintessential parts of cognitive function. Thus, a brain injury can hamper or prevent one's comprehension, reflection, and reasoning; one's focusing and remembering; or create problems in decision-making (and other higher brain functions). This occurs with a variety of brain injuries including concussions, skull fractures, diffuse axonal injury, hematomas, hemorrhages, and edema. Together or separately, these injuries affect victims' physical, cognitive, and social and behavioral functionality.

Treatment and recovery of traumatic brain injury centers on three different areas: the medical, psychological, and occupational. The medical approach utilizes surgical interventions, physical therapy, and pharmaceutical treatment. The psychological approach utilizes cognitive behavioral theory (CBT) as well as other *psychotherapeutic methods* of memory restoration, recall, and retrieval. The occupational approach is more of a pragmatic, vocational, functional skills training matter. All the aforementioned can take months (if not years) to complete (or even never), with success rates based upon the severity or location of the traumatic brain injury.

With the aforementioned in mind, several key aspects can be highlighted. First, the general scientific notion is that certain brain areas control learning and memory. Not surprising, traumatic brain injury affects these areas; however, the effects of the traumatic brain injury can be typical or atypical depending upon the injury to the person, the person's individual brain structure (and potential deviance), or the treatment.

The second important aspect to consider is the overall problem surrounding traumatic brain injury and learning/memory recovery, which is the complexity of both the human brain functionality and individual differences based on a variety of aspects such as age, gender, or type of injury. The third important aspect to consider is the ongoing past and present research of traumatic brain injury and its effects upon brain functionality, anatomically.

Despite the numerous sources available for consideration (and their contributions to knowledge on the subject), much is left to be discussed and studied. Specialists in the field need to know more about why, how, and where traumatic brain injury affects people's brain function and cognitions. The aforementioned complexity only adds to the mystery of how people's brains respond to traumatic brain injury.

An analysis of these numerous articles on traumatic brain injury shows that although established theories of brain functionality and cognitive recovery are reliable, the plethora of personal responses to traumatic brain injury defy established theories, sometimes. For instance, in 2006, my stepfather fell down a flight of stairs carrying a heavy wooden door, landing—headfirst—on a concrete basement floor. He suffered terrific brain damage to his prefrontal cortex, which negatively impacted his short-term memory abilities and some central executive function, including his working memory.

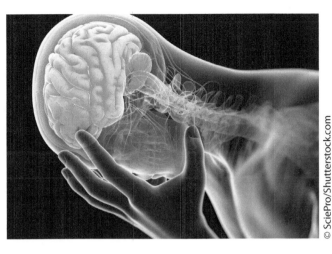

My stepfather's doctors told my mother that he would most likely not survive the night, but he stabilized and eventually was released from the hospital several weeks later to return home—albeit in a much-debilitated state. He still had his old personality, but he could not remember many of the basic activities of life. I remember helping him figure out which side of the knife to use to cut his steak and taking him out golfing, showing him how to drive the ball and putt.

At moments like that, one might have presumed his prospects were pretty grim; however, day by day, month by month, and year by year, my stepfather continued to improve and slowly regain some parts of his memory (and central executive function). Five years later, I doubt anyone would have known that he had suffered a traumatic brain injury or had undergone brain surgery to remove dead tissue.

Even more astounding was that he made so much improvement at such an advanced age (perhaps a testimony to eating oatmeal every morning and golfing two to three times a week for decades), defying commonly presumed mortality factors. For your information, my stepfather lived for another 11 years, dying at age 93 when he (sadly) fell down another flight of stairs, suffering serious, life-ending injuries.

Still, more research done to investigate and to understand how brain function is lost or hampered through traumatic brain injury only adds to the scholarly world's understanding of the affliction. Considering the importance of this matter, it is quintessential that scholars, scientists, and doctors find new ways to test the depth and width of the neuropsychological schema regarding traumatic brain injuries and brain functionality. Of course, as always, social testing carries with it the great burden of *scientific responsibilities*.

Fortunately, we live in an age of ever-increasing technology and ever-improving techniques to analyze, diagnose, and treat traumatic brain injuries. Of course, this does not mean that old concerns regarding ethical treatment and studies of patients is no longer a factor to consider. In fact, one can see that it might be all too easy to lose the humanity of patients with traumatic brain injury or multiple sclerosis or hypertension or diabetes (and so on) amidst the sea of scientific studies, titillating technology, and sophisticated surveillance.

Yet, future investigation is still needed to increase scientists' understanding of these monumental topics. Scholars and researchers need to begin more meta-analytical studies and also longitudinal studies to investigate how mental and physical health problems affect people differently in infancy, childhood, adolescence, early adulthood, middle adulthood, older adulthood, and so on.

INSIGHTS FROM THE EXPERTS

"The Pervasive Subtle Effects of Internet/Smartphone/Facebook Addiction"

One of my favorite classes to teach is Behavior Modification, in which LU students choose to change a problematic behavior that they have personally experienced. Many of the students choose cell phone, social media, Facebook, and so forth, addictions—and then we work throughout a semester to treat them. Others choose sleep issues, procrastination, and anxious negative thought patterns (among others) that are largely affected by overuse of the internet. I have worked with many secondary and university students who are struggling with and gaining victory over addictions to technology. Thus, from the education that I have earned and the experiences I have gained, I want to share about internet addictions to help readers to assess their life and activities and to make decisions to be the person that they want to be.

A primary need of people is to be in relationships (Sahin & Kumcagiz, 2017). We were created to belong. From Genesis to Revelation, God displays His yearning for us to have a relationship with Him and with other people.

College students today have grown up never knowing a world without constant access to the internet and social media. Their grandparents began life without computers and with a phone attached to a wall. In every generation, people have developed addictions—often to nicotine, caffeine, alcohol, and/or drugs. This new generation, however, has the physical and biochemical draw toward the addictive nature of technology. Psychologically, they yearn for self-esteem and a sense of well-being; sociologically, they are modeled, and peer-pressured to be on their phones and computers; and spiritually, they yearn to fill the God-shaped void in their lives. As Weinstein et al. assert (2014), "Problematic Internet use (PIU) or *Internet Addiction Disorder* (IAD) is characterized by excessive or poorly controlled preoccupations, urges, or behaviors regarding Internet use that lead to impairment or distress" (p. 99).

Effects—Physical, Psychological/Social/Spiritual

Physically, internet addiction leads to sleep deprivation, and scientists have found neurological effects for people who spend hours a day on technology. Hart and Frejd (2013) remark,

> There is a part of the brain called the hippocampus that manufactures more than a million new brain cells every day. Neurologists have now embraced the concept that the brain is plastic and can even repair itself. This phenomenon is called neuroplasticity and refers to the brain's susceptibility to change under certain conditions, such as changes in behavior, in our environment, or after the loss of certain parts of the brain. (p. 59)

What researchers do not know is the long-term effects that will occur to human brains when people overuse technology; will these brains be able to recover functionality of neurons that have been pruned due to underuse?

Psychologically, internet addicts experience emotional depression and anxiety, often removing themselves from face-to-face contact to escape the internet (Young, 2007). Internet addiction is currently not classified in the DSM-V (Hafner, 2010). Scott et al. (2017) described the discussion that occurred as the DSM-V was being written. The authors only included, "*Internet Gaming Disorder* as a condition for further study. Gambling disorder remains the only non-substance related disorder included as an addictive disorder in the DSM-5" (p. 613).

In the debate, some stressed the fact that many people have to use technology long hours for work, so they focused on the comorbidity of technology use with other psychological conditions such as obsessive-compulsive disorder or ADHD. Thus, there was caution about placing an internet addiction diagnosis that may, in fact, be the comorbid disorder seen in the natural setting of the use of technology.

A number of researchers have been studying the significance of comorbidity. Among these, "A review of 20 studies correlating *problematic Internet use* (PIU) and mental disorders found that 75% reported significant correlations of PIU with depression, 57% with anxiety, 100% with symptoms of ADHD, 60% with obsessive-compulsive symptoms, and 66% with hostility/aggression" (Carli et al., 2013—as cited in Weinstein et al., 2014, p. 102). Sindermann et al. (2018) and Sahin and Kumcagiz (2017) all conducted studies on associations between Machiavellianism, psychopathy, narcissism, and internet-use disorder.

Sociologically, problems often develop with inabilities to interact with others face-to-face, lower grades in school, and difficulties at work. "The Facebook world, even if it is employed to stay connected with offline friends and family members . . . may contribute to the aggravation of existing problems or result in the emergence of new problems" (Brailovskaia et al., 2018, p. 9).

Yuchang et al. (2017) studied the correlation of smartphone addiction with dysfunctional attitudes and self-esteem. They found that "anxious attachment style positively predicted smartphone addiction . . . negative core beliefs about themselves and others and greater anxiety in relationships" (p. 1131). With the focusing of one's attention on others' seemingly "perfect" lives, viewers often develop depression, anxiety, and loneliness. It often causes problems in relationships in marriages, and families.

As they prioritize online friends, face-to-face friendships are neglected. "There are researchers who also believe that life in the digital world is causing us to lose our 'depth'—our depth of thinking, contemplation, feeling, and emotions, as well as depth in our relationships and work" (Hart & Frejd, 2013, p. 43).

Spiritually, people are both internally motivated and shaped by the environment (Powlison, 1995). When "something or someone besides Jesus the Christ takes title to your heart's trust, preoccupation, loyalty, service, fear and delight" (Powlison, 1995, p. 35), that is called idolatry. "Idolatry is a problem both rooted deeply in the human heart and powerfully impinging on us from our social environment" (Powlison, 1995, p. 38).

Treatment

Behavioral treatment: Many educators and those involved in the technology industry use preventive and interventionist actions in choosing to send their children to schools that do not have computers, but "focuses on physical activity, interpersonal engagement, and learning through creative, hands-on tasks" (Hart & Frejd, 2013, p. 52).

Cognitive behavioral therapy is often the treatment of choice for internet addicts. Some treat it pharmacologically and even use "electro-acupuncture with psychological intervention on cognitive function and event-related potentials" (Weinstein et al., 2014, p. 108).

Biblical counseling: Biblical counselors approach internet addiction with a biblical world-view. "No psychology has conceptual resources adequate to make sense of the interface between responsible behavior, a shaping social milieu, and a heart which is both self-deceived and life-determining" (Powlison, 1995, p. 38).

The deep question of motivation is not *"What* is motivating me?" The final question is, *"Who* is the master of this pattern of thought, feeling, or behavior?" In the biblical view, people are religious, inevitably bound to one god or another. People do not have needs. We have masters, lords, gods, be they oneself, other people, valued objects, Satan (Powlison, 1995, p. 39).

Conclusion

A full biblical analysis of social problems would be a "psycho-social-spiritual-somatic-volitional-experiential" analysis. To understand the exact weight of each variable is, obviously, to quest after something which is—from a human point of view, the intentions of social scientists not withstanding!—ultimately elusive. But the Bible's answer is always powerfully applicable: turning from idols to the living God, renewal of mind and heart in the truth, activities captured in shorthand by the phrase, "repentance and faith" (Powlison, 1995, p. 47).

Finally, something to consider—as mentioned earlier, I have taught Behavior Modification for years and have had many groups of students do an ABAB experiment focusing on their smartphone or social media addiction. They are often shocked at the time they have wasted on devices when they do their baseline observation. They choose various treatment methods that work for them. Inevitably, as their time online has decreased, they report being happier, having better relationships with friends and family, with higher GPAs, getting more sleep, and spending more time with the Lord. They report being more at peace and wanting to tell their still addicted friends that getting off of the devices is a wonderful event in their physical, emotional, relational, and spiritual lives.

Dr. Beth Sites, PhD
Professor of Psychology
Liberty University

Contributed by Elizabeth Sites. © Kendall Hunt Publishing Company

CASE STUDY #13

Starting at a typical age (mid-20s), Brenda and John had experienced seven miscarriages due to a translocation of Brenda's first and fifth chromosomes. So, when she managed to get and stay pregnant, they were even more thrilled when their son Jacob was born healthy, albeit 2 weeks late. He grew up healthy and strong and in 5 years they tried to have another child but suffered another miscarriage and then John's dad died from liver cancer the next year. Needless to say, it was a difficult time, but life was still good. One night, they heard their 6-year-old son praying, "Dear Jesus, I would like my front teeth and a baby brother, please." So, Brenda and John prayed about it and tried one last time to get and stay pregnant. She was 37 and John was 42, so it was a high-risk pregnancy.

The baby made it past the first trimester and all the way to term, but when delivery-day came, they had to dilate (by hand) and baby Joe popped out IUGR (intrauterine growth restricted), weighing about 3 pounds. He also had a heart defect involving his aorta, which required surgery at 4 days. Additionally, Brenda had undiagnosed preeclampsia, so she almost died during delivery and had to be hospitalized for a week. Baby Joe was in the hospital for a month but survived and is healthy despite racking up a $150,000 out-of-pocket medical bill. Their family and friends rallied around them to help, and John managed to work 60 hours a week for 3 years until he paid off the entire bill (with Brenda's help). Joe is now 10, Jacob is now 17, John is now 52, but Brenda somehow is still 37.

DISCUSSION QUESTIONS

1. Based on the readings, how would a sociologist diagnose this situation?

2. What specific sociological factors are involved?

3. How could the physical and economic problems experienced in this family affect them, socially?

Check out the Chapter 13 video at this link:

https://www.khpcontent.com/

VOCABULARY

ADHD
Affordable Care Act of 2010
Annual Health Care Cost
Behavioral Treatment
Biblical Counseling
Christian Truth
Cognitive Behavioral Therapy
Cognitive Function
Disability
Handicaps
Health Care Business
Health Service Institution
Hyperactivity
Individual Mandate
Internet Addiction Disorder
Internet Gaming Disorder

Impairment
Medical Errors
Mental Illness
Myths
Obamacare
People with Disabilities
People with Disability Myths
Physical Illness
Problematic Internet Use
Psychological Pursuits
Psychologist
Psychology
Psychotherapeutic Methods
PWDs
Scientific Responsibilities
Traumatic Brain Injury

References

Brailovskaia, J., Rohmann, E., Bierhoff, H.-W., & Margraf, J. (2018). The brave blue world: Facebook flow and Facebook Addiction Disorder (FAD). *PLoS ONE, 13*(7), e0201484.

Chiaravalloti, N., Sandry, J., & Moore, N. (2015). An RCT to treat learning impairment in traumatic brain injury: The TBI-MEM trial. *Neurorehabilitation and Neural Repair, 30*(6), 539–550.

Coe, J., & Hall, T. (2010). A transformational psychology view. In *Psychology & Christianity: Five views* (pp. 199–226). InterVarsity.

Entwistle, D. (2015). *Integrative approaches to psychology and Christianity: An introduction to worldview issues, philosophical foundations, and models of integration* (3rd ed.). Wipf and Stock.

Farrell, M. (2011). *The effective teacher's guide to sensory and physical impairments sensory, orthopaedic, motor and health impairments, and traumatic brain injury*. Taylor & Francis.

Hafner, K. (2010, March 15). 'Defriending' Facebook: When social networking starts to get in the way of real life, some teens are deciding to log off. *The New York Times Upfront*. Upfrontmagazine.com.

Hart, A. D., & Frejd, S. H. (2013). *The digital invasion: How technology is shaping you and your relationships*. Grand Rapids, MI: Baker Books.

Klingberg, T. (2012). *Learning brain: Memory and brain development in children*. Oxford University Press.

Mandalis, A., Kinsella, G., Ong, B., & Anderson, V. (2007). Working memory and new learning following pediatric traumatic brain injury. *Developmental Neuropsychology, 32*(2), 683–701.

Martyr, J. (155–157 CE). *New Advent*. http://www.newadvent.org/fathers/0126.htm

McMinn, M. R. (2011). *Psychology, theology, and spirituality in Christian counseling* (Rev. ed.). Tyndale House.

NCIPC. (2020). https://www.cdc.gov/injury/index.html

Powlison, D. (1995). Idols of the heart and "vanity fair." *The Journal of Biblical Counseling, 13*(2), 35–50.

Sahin, C., & Kumcagiz, H. (2017). The predictive role of narcissism and self-esteem on social media addiction. *Ijoess, 8*(30).

Scott, D. A., Valley, B., & Simecka, B. A. (2017). Mental health concerns in the digital age. *International Journal of Mental Health Addiction, 15*, 604–613. https://doi.org/10.1007/s11469-016-9684-0.

Starr, C. (2017). *To root & to rise: Accepting brain injury.* Spiritual Path.

Weinstein, A., Feder, L. C., Rosenberg, K. P., & Dannon, P. (2014). Internet addiction disorder: Overview and controversies, 99–117. In K. P. Rosenberg & L. C. Feder (Eds.). *Behavioral addictions: Criteria, evidence, and treatment* (pp. 99–117). Academic Press. https://doi.org/10.1016/C2012-0-02731-7

Wright, B. A. (1983). *Physical disability: A psychosocial approach* (2nd ed.). HarperCollins.

Young, K. S. (2007). Cognitive behavior therapy with internet addicts: Treatment outcomes and implications. *CyberPsychology and Behavior, 10*(5), 671–679. https://doi.org/10.1089/cpb.2007.9971

Yuchang, J., Cuicui, S., Junxiu, A., & Junyi, L. (2017). Attachment styles and smartphone addiction in Chinese college students: The mediating roles of dysfunctional attitudes and self-esteem. *International Journal of Mental Health Addiction, 15*, 1122–1134. https://doi.org/10.1007/s11469-017-9772-9

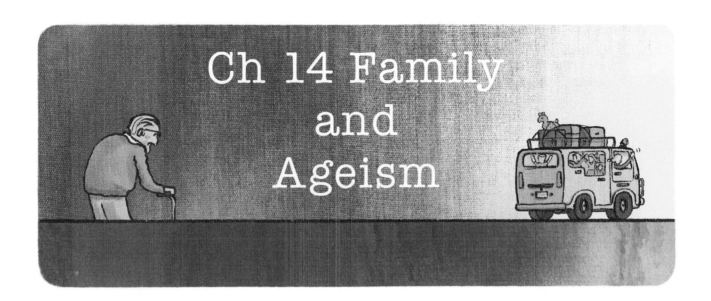

Ch 14 Family and Ageism

Few social institutions have more influence and power over the lives of individuals and groups than that of the family unit. *Family* is traditionally defined as a social unit of people related through marriage, birth, and/or adoption. They reside together in sanctioned relationships, they engage in economic cooperation, and engage in proper sexual relationships between members. They are committed, they have love attachments, reproduction or procreation is part of their relationship, and they engage in child-rearing together.

White et al. (2015, p. 13) provide four theories on family theory that seem to suggest a universality of the social group named, "a family." These four theories are relatively general, so there are no absolute parameters—such as specific duration, number of intergenerations or biological/romantic relationships between members, or linkage to a bigger kinship system. For example, a *patrilocal kinship* has the wife residing with the husband and his social group; a *matrilocal kinship* has the husband moving with the wife to live with her family of origin. No doubt, there are pros and cons for each approach, and surely personality types and psychological factors are key parts of any decision on marital residence.

This is not just an American phenomenon, though. There seem to be examples of these four theories found in other non-Western cultures. For instance, in China, people are married and take care of children until they reach adulthood; some households include children, parents, as well as grandparents (or great grandparents); cultural rules and taboos exist for the health of members within this social group; and innumerable manifestations of the Chinese family unit are found in all cities and villages in all regions across China. This would suggest a universality to the four theories offered by White et al.

Generally, sociologists look at the family structure's place in society and categorize family social circles in two ways: there is the *nuclear family*, which is one married couple residing together with any children they might have together, or there might be an *extended family*, with a network of parents, children, and relatives that they come into contact with, occasionally (Knox, 2017). Within this family network, various kinship agreements exist (or are adhered to) in deciding who can marry whom, when, where, and so on. *Kinship systems* decide how property is passed on for older generations to younger generations, they decide where the family should reside, they decide how social power inside the family will be distributed, they decide the appropriate number of marriage partners, and often they even decide who is permitted to marry whom.

MAIN SOCIOLOGICAL APPROACHES

With the *functionalist perspective*, the family unit is likened to an organism (Witt, 2009, p. 13). As such, one could expect deviations to naturally occur as parents and children grow older and experience different complications, consequences, and social contexts to emerge. Some might consider the functionalist perspective to be the sole lens for family life; however, family mechanics are far less monolithic but still allow for adjustments and adaptation to occur to regain/maintain/retain harmony and unity within the group.

For example, a middle-aged parent may suddenly find their teenager pregnant, which would set about a chain of events and interactions previously unneeded and unwanted. Similarly, a 30-year-old child could lose both aged parents, leading to an unexpected and unprepared future. Thus, certain ages bring with them certain risks, realities, and *dysfunction,* which automatically elicit change and/or deviant behaviors (Hiedemann et al., 1998, p. 229). Ultimately, any deviation is integrated into family norms when the deviation has a positive effect for all members of the family unit—or rejected if the family unit cohesion is dissolving.

Within family relationships (especially with the inclusion of *stepfamilies*), a variety of expectations can be found; some

stepfamilies are merely considered "close relatives" while others make no distinctions between children from a bloodline or remarriage; some families employ a hierarchical governance—others are more laissez-faire. In America, some people honor and promote their *family system of lineage* (like the Mormons or some Asians); others could not tell you much about their family line or history beyond their grandparents. A simple Google Scholar search proves that there are many additional and/or specific family theories in Eastern cultures.

Ultimately, how much or how little these theories are in play in a particular non-Western culture could be determined by utilizing the empirical fit, testability, contextualization, and practical utility for each family structure. Whatever the case, for family stability to continue (in the functionalist perspective), any deviance needs to be addressed and then adopted or abandoned based on its value, which may relate to symbolic interactionism (Ziyanak & Williams, 2014). If allowed, the deviance is integrated into the family system and into any nonfamily institutional activities too (White et al., 2015, p. 117). Thus, although deviance may have individualist origins, its value and place within the family social system is determined by its benefit or harmfulness to both the individual and the collective, which sounds a bit like rational choice theory (Thompson & Gibbs, 2016).

For the symbolic interactionist, it is clear that the understanding of the family has changed. With all the legal and cultural transformation in the past decade, perhaps the easiest definition of family in America (for better or worse) is to call it a primary group of people who form a cooperative economic unit. Of course, this is an embrace of reductionism that overlooks the complex overarching needs and functions of members that are typically found within all families. An abdication or skewing of familial roles may seem revolutionary or noble, but the reality is that men, women, and children have needed certain permanent social components to thrive or even to survive in society. In the healthiest of families, husbands and wives take care of each other—physically, emotionally, and economically; and parents love, raise, and protect their children.

That being said (and as mentioned earlier), the boundaries of what constitutes the life of a family is somewhat murky. In some regions of America, children stay with the parents well into their late 20s or early 30s; in other parts of the world, children leave as soon as they reach legal adulthood. Furthermore, in America, the proximity or frequency of *intergenerational contact* varies greatly. Some adult children see their parents daily or weekly; other situations stretch into the months or years; having grandparents living with their adult children seems more the exception than the norm in America, presently (Huo et al., 2018).

In regard to that, one of the biggest familial parameters or taboos is that of *incest*, which comes with a huge stigma and shame for both parties in the unhealthy coupling. Historically and universally, there has been a prohibition of sexual relationships and marriage between close kinsmen. This is done or enforced for various reasons. First, it is not biologically healthy for family members to marry other family members. Many blood disorders and genetic abnormalities occur when the bloodlines are too closely tied. Second, besides any physical harm, though, the emotional or psychological damage done in incest cannot be understated. So, although one can marry a second cousin with a reasonable degree of confidence that no health issues will occur for any offspring, marrying or having deviant sexual liaisons with first cousins, half siblings, or one's parents are not allowed, wisely.

For the conflict theorist, it is assumed that all social groups, especially the family, include *hierarchies of power*. In the United States, there is much variance regarding social power and access to resources and decision-making for the family. If the family embraces *patriarchy*, men hold the most social power; if it is a *matriarchy*, women hold the most social power; but in many families in America and all over the world, *egalitarianism*, where husbands and wives share the power, is embraced. One could also make the case that in some millennial families (especially), children hold the power, which amounts to *anarchy*, where no one holds any power (Lehman, 2019).

Speaking of children, currently in America, a quarter of all children live with only one parent at some point in their lives (Kramer, 2019). The reasons behind this figure are quite complex and can involve such factors as teen pregnancy, a high divorce rate, economic stresses, and a lack of cultural support systems. Regarding teenage mothers in the United States, the South has the highest percentage of teenage pregnancies while the Northeast (including Pennsylvania, New York, Vermont, Connecticut, Massachusetts, and Rhode Island) has the least. Additionally, the West Coast has fewer teenage pregnancies than the central United States, possibly due to higher abortion rates.

Many marriage and family issues stem from the 3 As of dysfunctional parenting: *authoritarianism*, *abdication*, and *absenteeism*. Regarding authoritarianism parents, Maisel (2018) admits,

> I think that the following are among the consequences of growing up with an authoritarian dad [or mom]. One is an overwhelming sense of guilt when I put my own needs first. A second is my inability to relate to my siblings without casting on them the same judgment my [parent] leveled on them. (p. 48)

The effects of parents who "lead from behind" is overwhelming. As Barton and Hirsch (2016) note, "Permissive parents tend to avoid limit-setting with their children, allowing children to control their own behaviors with few maturity demands" (p. 1). The end result is children who become adults with stunted personal and emotional growth, leading to social strife and frustration (Wischerth et al., 2016).

Perhaps the worst situation is one where the parent just "checks out" and ignores the needs of their family. Regarding absentee parents (fathers, in particular), Balthazar (2007) remarks,

> The men whom we have to call fathers are often men who leave their homes and go about their business without living up to their responsibilities. Ignoring our mothers and leaving them to suffer and struggle while these men are enjoying themselves with friends and women. (p. 545)

MARRIAGE AND DIVORCE

For millennia, in the countless cultures across the globe, marriage has been the central foundation of family life. Ostensibly, people enter into marriage commitments for emotional fulfillment, social stability, and personal security; and contrary to current shallow postmodern myopia, monogamy has been the standard form, with marriage restricted to an exclusive relationship between husband and wife.

Marriage and family seem to go hand-in-hand in society. Parents marry, have children, and then those children go on to marry other people. Historically, there have been numerous marriage parameters placed upon people regarding whom they can marry or be coupled with, in society. Common factors permitting or prohibiting marital unions include age, gender, religion, race, ethnicity, economics, and so on.

That being said, in some countries and cultures, one can find other marriage agreements in place. Marriages are typically made with exogamy or endogamy in mind. *Exogamy* is the selection of a permanent life partner outside one's social group; *endogamy* is the selection of a permanent life partner inside one's social group. The final judgment is undecided as to which one is more common (just ask Romeo and Juliet).

Polygamy has been allowed (even in the Bible), which is multiple marriage partners. Additionally, *polygamy* is the marriage of one husband to multiple wives, and *polyandry* is the marriage of one wife to multiple husbands. Very few cultures or communities allow for *polyamory*, which is a romantically open relationship between all the members of a social group or clique of people (Klesse, 2006, p. 566). These are exceptions, of course, but an exception is not the norm or always socially accepted.

Regarding marital statistics, the age of marriage has risen sharply in the past 50 years. In 1977, the average age of marriage was 21 for women and 23 for men. In 2010, the average age of marriage for women was 27 and the average age for men was 29. This is dramatically different than in 1955, when the average age of a female to get married was 20 and the average age of a man to get married was 22.

The shift in age of marriage also corresponds to a shift in parenting age. Although the term has been around for a couple of decades, many millennial couples are referred to as *DINKs*, which means "Double-Income-No-Kids" (Pew Research, 2015). Currently, American families are smaller than their parents or grandparents' families, having fewer children and children more closely spaced in age. Married couples make up a smaller proportion of households in America, with single parent, post-childbearing couples, and LGBTQ couples on the increase. Finally, there are more female-headed households than any time before in American history.

Various reasons can be seen to contribute to this phenomenon. The most likely factor for changes in female marital age would be the empowerment that women have gained since the civil rights movement in the sexual revolution of the 1960s (a very definite conflict theory assertion). Before the 1960s, women were expected to stay at home and do more of the domestic chores and duties while the men worked outside the home. For both sexes, social roles were far more rigid and gender typed.

In postmodernity, compared to their grandmothers, more women work in the paid labor force than ever before in American history, they enjoy far more independence and autonomy in society, and have wider access to personal resources. For men (besides fewer women being open or inviting of exclusive, closed marriages), there are fewer social stigmas for men in remaining bachelors and focusing more on their careers and recreational lives than in previous decades. Still, some men are mocked for being in their 30s and still living in their parents' basement, which seems indicative of stunted social development (Bentley & McCallum, 2019).

Living together is also very common now among single people in American and European society. This *cohabitation* occurs when two people live together in a sustained, committed relationship, but without any legal or binding vows or agreements. In fact, three times as many unmarried couples live together now than in the 1970s. Unfortunately, cohabitation is only a short-term fix for many/most people. Plus, the divorce statistics for people who cohabitate is rather high (Rosenfeld & Roesler, 2019, p. 43).

Speaking of divorce, the United States leads the world in divorce rate. Although death used to be the typical major cause of early family disruption, as of late, divorce has now taken over that spot, statistically. Currently, nearly 20,000,000 people have divorced but not remarried. The American divorce rate used to be higher in the 1970s and 1980s, but it has recently declined. Still, since 1960, the divorce rate has doubled. The marriage rate is 8.4 per thousand people; the divorce rate is 4.0 per thousand people.

© zimmytws/Shutterstock.com

For people claiming to be "Christian," another factor of divorce is church attendance and gender (to a small degree). Half of all divorces occur to people who do not attend weekly church services; however, if people do attend, men only have a 32% chance of getting a divorce while women have a 41% chance of getting a divorce. Nondenominational churches members have the highest divorce rate at 34%, Baptists come in second at 29%, Episcopalians are third at 28%, Pentecostals are fourth at 28%, Methodists are at 26%, Presbyterians are at 23%, and, perhaps because of their liturgical sacramental understanding of marriage, Catholics and Lutherans have only a 21% chance of getting divorced.

DEALING WITH MATTERS OF THE DARK

The Bible is replete with stories focused on marriage partners and their families, near and far. It starts with Adam, Eve, Cain, and Abel. It also includes marriage and family stories with Abraham, Sarah, Ishmael, and Isaac; Ruth and Boaz; King Saul, King David, Michel and Bathsheba; Ahab, Jezebel;

Hosea, Gomer; Joseph, Mary, Herod, Anaias, Sapphira, and so on. These family stories are probably one of the most relevant and relatable parts of the biblical texts because of the sheer amount of social conventions and deviances that follow God's people (also known as human beings) on Earth. They, like us, interact with each other, for better or worse, creating social problems and finding social solutions.

For instance, escaping his brother's wrath for "stealing" the first-born birthright from their blind father, Isaac, the Patriarch Jacob traveled all the way to Haran to find sanctuary. He connected with his Uncle Laban, and while living there, he fell in love with Laban's daughter, Rachel (his first cousin). He asked Laban if he could take her to be his wife (arranged marriages were the norm in ancient times), and Laban agreed if Jacob first served him for 7 years. Keep in mind that Jacob was not a spring chicken to begin with, but his love for Rachel gave him the motivation and strength to persevere for the prize. Genesis records that because of Jacob's love for Rachel, time "seemed but a few days." Ahhhh . . . wuv.

This would be a sweet love story destined for the Harlequin Romance aisle, but it soon turned into a Shakespearean tragedy, when Jacob learned the following morning (after an apparent wild night of partying and drinking) that he was tricked into marrying Leah, Rachel's older sister and Laban's eldest daughter. Not surprisingly, Jacob was angry and confused about what had transpired—how he had become the victim of (someone else's) trickery. Laban's justification was that he had an obligation to first marry off his eldest daughter, Leah, but Jacob could still have Rachel if he honeymooned with Leah for a week (presumably to get her pregnant) and worked for Laban for another 7 years.

Jacob complied with Laban's demands, but it put a terrific strain upon the relationship between Jacob and Leah, not surprisingly. One's honeymoon is supposed to be a time of joy, ecstasy, and pleasure between the husband and wife (emotionally, spiritually, and sexually), but poor Leah woke up to a husband who despised her presence and who never learned to fully love her. They eventually had four sons together and with each child she hoped that "at last my husband will become attached to me," but he never does, sadly. It must have been sheer torment to know that Jacob "loved Rachel more than Leah" (Genesis 29:30).

Laban's actions were a quick fix to an immediate problem; however, in the long run, his deceit created greater misery and insecurity than he could ever imagine. Jacob's household became a miserable mess of frustrated emotions and jealousy between the wives and their children. Living alongside the family and children of Laban only made it worse when Jacob's flock greatly increased, and the blessings of God grew evident to all around him.

Compounding the situation was that like Sarah and like Rebekah, Rachel was barren too, and in desperation, she asked Jacob to impregnate her maidservant, Bilhah, so that Rachel could have their baby as her own. Eventually, though, God remembered Rachel's situation, and she became pregnant with Joseph, who immediately became Jacob's favorite son, much to the irritation and sorrow of his other older children by Leah.

With so much jealousy and anger about him (both within his own tents and from Laban's immediate family), the danger of warfare began to rise, and so God told Jacob to return to his homeland, finally. Understandably, Jacob quickly grabbed his wives, children, herds, and property and fled from Laban's camp. He must have been terribly conflicted in his journey. On the one hand, he wanted to see his parents again before they (or he) died; on the other hand, he remembered that Esau had threatened to kill him for his earlier "deceit."

Jacob must have felt like he was being squeezed between two great scalding irons with Esau on one side and Laban on the other. When Laban discovered that Jacob had fled the country to return to his former home, he became very angry and chased after Jacob. As Birch et al. state, "Deceit is really a hallmark of these episodes and even occurs in the very last one—'Jacob deceived Laban the Aramean in that he did not tell him that he intended to flee' (31:20)."

Laban was clearly a very narcissistic man who had rationalized his misbehavior and refused to admit his sins against Jacob a decade earlier. Furthermore, unbeknownst to Jacob, his wives had stolen property from their father and made the situation even worse for Jacob. Laban is filled with self-righteous rage, but God warned him in a dream to be careful what he said and did to Jacob.

When the two finally meet, Laban showed much self-restraint, but Laban's strong personality shows up anyway. Laban informed Jacob of God's message in his dream and then asked why Jacob left him in such a hurry, without giving Laban time to say goodbye to his daughters and his grand-children. Laban's sense of ownership and dominance is evident, but he does come to realize that Jacob has the blessing of God and is on his way to make a great and powerful nation. With much wisdom (finally), Laban makes a covenant with Jacob not to harm each other before he peacefully retreated home.

For biblical readers, the dramatic scene involving Jacob, Leah, Rachel, and Laban may seem reminiscent of their own life story. The intersection, intertwining, and internal politics of most families demonstrates a soap opera of sorts for most people. For Christians, the goal of family life (and marriage) is to reflect the love of God for His Son and His earthly children—in our kindness, our selflessness, and our socialization for those under our charge or at our side. So many social problems could be avoided with the understanding that we are not here on Earth to exploit or drain resources from those around us; quite the opposite, we are here to give of ourselves and our blessings from God to those needing care, protection, and affirmation—starting with our spouses and our children first.

INSIGHTS FROM THE EXPERTS

"Growing Old"

If you are or about to turn 65, you are entering the aging process as defined by many disciplines. However, according to those who have studied aging for many years (in some cases decades), aging defies any easy definition and to date, we have no reliable measurement to determine the biological age of humans, and most other animals for that matter.

Having just turned 74, I now spend a great deal of my time thinking about how many years I might have left to live and in what condition I will spend those years. Since my background involves a number of different branches of psychiatric and mental health nursing, I am naturally drawn to how I will psychologically endure the aging process. This paper addresses my concerns as well as my hopes for this new chapter of my life.

There are several theories regarding *psychosocial development* but the one that stands out in my mind is the one evolved by Erik Erikson, a famous psychoanalyst. His theory states that at certain stages of life (starting at infancy), a person is forced to deal with a conflict that serves as a turning point for further development. These stages do not necessarily follow in sequential order however, nor do they fit into tightly sealed compartments. There is much overlap between stages, making each personality a complex human being. The final psychosocial stage is known as *integrity versus despair*, which normally begins at about age 65. In this stage, the person looks back on his life with the major question, "Did I live a meaningful life?"

In his newly released book, *Successful Aging* (2020), neuroscientist Daniel Levitin states that the most solid finding (among masses of research that he has consolidated) is that the personality of the individual that has developed over the life span is the most powerful predictor of successful aging—both in terms of health and happiness. To me, that says that the individual has somehow successfully integrated the stages of psychosocial development outlined by Erikson decades ago.

Since these stages do not always follow chronologically, nor do they resolve fully (I have met people over 65 who are still working on stage one—*trust versus mistrust*—the first stage of life, birth to 18 months), how do any of us wind up in our elder years with personalities that will hold us in good stead to the end? Maher Baba, the holy master of India, has said, "All growth is gradual, and it is only through slow and gradual stages that man truly begins to grow up and discover his true self, and to relinquish the childish playthings of hate, greed, and anger" (1974, p. 46).

"Letting go" has become a popular phrase in our culture today, but it has profound implications. Twyla Tharp (2019), in her book, *Keep It Moving*, says it best: "Practice growth. What you do today is an investment in tomorrow" (p. 9). She also says (with love), "Shut up and dance"—further stating that this was the advice she gave herself for her 65th birthday. By the way, Ms. Tharp is now 78, began her career in 1965 as the creator of more than 130 devices for her own company and the Goffrey Ballet, the New York City Ballet, the Paris Opera Ballet, London's Royal Ballet, and the list goes on.

Of course, she is talking about physical movement primarily, but nowhere in my studies have I seen such a masterful blend of mind and body as in her writing. She further states, "You can take the mystery out of letting go by thinking ahead. Imaging yourself in a future makes leaving the past more appealing." Her whole philosophy is grounded in moving forward, embracing the aging process, and "dancing."

As a choreographer, she defines "dancing" as moving through time and space both physically and psychologically, but always with a "pledge," something she says is revealed over time. A pledge, she says, comes into clearer focus over the course of our lives. We determine our pledge through our choices, she concludes.

We have all heard that we are the product of our choices. At age 74, I now see that my health and my finances are the products of choices that I have made over a very long period of time. As we age, these two areas of our lives assume the greatest importance and it becomes necessary to develop a new mindset (and a more precise attitude) about both. There is a smaller margin of error regarding one's medication routine and one's bank account than ever before. While I have developed an increasing number of health problems since turning 65 (including cancer of the breast, which has been successfully treated to the point that I am now considered a survivor), my main focus and concern has turned to my heart. And while I have enjoyed a nice place to live and nice things (including international travel), I must watch my checkbook like a hawk.

If you don't mind, I would like to talk about my health. I have high blood pressure, pre-diabetes, and kidney disease. My blood pressure has gone into "crisis" range in recent months and has necessitated my being put on blood pressure medications (I take two different meds). When I was a young nurse, I learned that it was necessary to have the right medicine, at the right time, in the right dose in order to have a meaningful outcome. But with my advanced training and degrees in psychiatric nursing, I began to look deeper into physical disease that was thought to have a strong underlying psychological component. High blood pressure was first on the list.

Shortly after my graduation from OHSU (with my new master's degree and certification as a psychiatric mental health nurse practitioner), I discovered a book by Robert S. Eliot, MD, *Is It Worth Dying For?* (This book would make Dr. Eliot renowned as a cardiologist.) I recognized immediately that my fluctuating blood pressure and family history of seriously high blood pressure would make my ongoing life difficult if I didn't address this issue. To date, everything he said in his book has come to pass with my heart, especially the link between the high blood pressure and stress. Now, I can actually feel my blood pressure rise when I get angry or I am hurried.

More than blood pressure itself, however, was the whole idea of how I have treated my heart over the last 40 years. Eliot quotes a 17th-century physician (William Harvey, 1578–1657) in the very beginning of his book: "Every affection of the mind that is attended with either pain or pleasure, hope or fear, is the cause of an agitation whose influence extends to the heart" (Harvey, 1993, p. 75).

In other words, all roads lead to the heart. The *heart*, the innermost depth of one's being, is to be guarded and treated with the utmost respect. Why else is the "heart" so often equated with love? And the opposite, having "no heart" is often equated with the very things that Meher Baba (1987) said we should relinquish—hate, greed, and anger. Coupled with how poorly I have watched over my heart is (ironically) how poorly I have watched over my finances—buying more than I need, spending more than I have (with credit cards, of course), and so on.

Robert Morris (2019), senior pastor of Gateway Church in Dallas, Texas, says in his book, *Beyond Blessed*, that many people (Christians included) do not trust God to provide for their needs, that He is good, faithful, and trustworthy. We don't trust Him to bless us, so we take it into our own hands to bless ourselves. This is why I have two (at least!) of everything I own. "Buy one, get one free" is my favorite grocery sign. As a senior, I appreciate this, but two of everything else—in case one wears out? Nothing that I own "wears out."

So, here I am back at stage one of Erikson's psychosocial model of "trust vs. mistrust" (Erikson, 2015). I am one of the many still working on this level of development. Aging, I have discovered, is a matter of *trust*. Somehow, it all comes together as we get through it, and there is more to come that we will get through also.

Still, Billy Graham (2013), the renowned evangelist, says in his book, *Nearing Home*, that we should have hope for *this* life and hope for the *life to come*. *Hope and trust* are strongly linked. Perhaps they are even the same thing.

Faith Jane Knox
Psychiatric Mental Health
Nurse Practitioner (Retired)

CASE STUDY #14

Over the last 14 weeks, your knowledge and skills in the field of sociology have increased (hopefully) through your study of each chapter's material and each case study's discussion. Knowledge gained in college is not just for knowledge's sake; you are going to classes to learn and grow and become socialized, in a sense. With that in mind, carefully reflect upon your Case Study #1 essay, and answer the following discussion questions.

DISCUSSION QUESTIONS

1. Revisiting your answers to the case study discussion questions in Chapter 1, has your perspective of your life changed at all with your newfound sociological knowledge? Where?

2. Has your understanding of your parents and siblings changed with what you know now about sociological theory and thought? Explain.

3. What sociological concepts could you use right now to explain some of the events currently happening in American society?

Check out the Chapter 14 video at this link:

https://www.khpcontent.com/

VOCABULARY

Abdication	Hope and Trust
Absenteeism	Incest
Anarchy	Integrity Versus Despair
Authoritarianism	Intergenerational Contact
Cohabitation	Kinship Systems
DINKs	Matriarchy
Dysfunction	Matrilocal Kinship
Egalitarianism	Nuclear Family
Endogamy	Patriarchy
Exogamy	Patrilocal Kinship
Extended Family	Polyamory
Family	Polyandry
Functionalist Perspective	Polygamy
Family System of Lineage	Psychosocial Development
Heart	Stepfamily
Hierarchies of Power	Trust Versus Mistrust

References

Baba, M. (1987). *Discourses* (7th ed.). Sheriar Foundation.

Baba, M. (1974). *Life at its best* (4th ed.). Sifism Reoriented.

Balthazar, P. (2007). How anger toward absentee fathers may make it difficult to call God "Father." *Pastoral Psychology, 55,* 543–549.

Barton, A. L., & Hirsch, J. K. (2016). Permissive parenting and mental health in college students: Mediating effects of academic entitlement. *Journal of American College Health, 64*(1), 1–8.

Bentley, D., & McCallum, A. (2019). Rise and fall: The shift in household growth rates since the 1990s. *CIVITAS.* http://www.civitas.org.uk/content/files/riseandfalltheshiftinhouseholdgrowthratessincethe1990s.pdf

Birch, B., Brueggemann, W., Fretheim, T., & Petersen, D. (1999). *A Theological Introduction to the Old Testament.* Abingdon.

Eliot, R., & Breo, D. L. (1989). *Is it worth dying for? How to make stress work for you—not against you.* Random House.

Erikson, E. H. (2015). *Identity and the life cycle.* W. W. Norton.

Graham, B. (2013). *Nearing home: Life, faith, and finishing well.* HarperCollins.

Harvey, W. (1993). *On the motion of the heart and blood in animals* (Great Mind Series). Prometheus.

Hiedemann, B., Suhomlinova, O., & O'Rand, A. M. (1998). Economic independence, economic status, and empty nest in midlife marital disruption. *Journal of Marriage and Family, 60,* 219–231.

Huo, M., Kim, K., Zarit, S., & Fingerman, K. (2018). Support grandparents give to their adult grandchildren. *Journals of Gerontology, 73*(6), 1006–1015. https://doi.org/10.1093/geronb/gbw208

Klesse, C. (2006). Polyamory and its 'others': Contesting the terms of non-monogamy. *Sexualities, 9*(5), 565–583. https://doi.org/10.1177/1363460706069986

Knox, J. (2019). *Sociology is rude! A conversation on sociological theory and thought.* Kendall Hunt.

Kramer, S. (2019). U.S. has world's highest rate of children living in single-parent households. *Pew Research Center.* www.pewresearch.org/fact-tank/2019/12/12/u-s-children-more-likely-than-children-in-other-countries-to-live-with-just-one-parent/

Lehman, J. (2019). *Your child is not your equal: Why you have to be the boss.* https://www.empoweringparents.com/article/your-child-is-not-your-equal-why-you-have-to-be-the-boss/

Levitin, D. J. (2020). *Successful aging: A neuroscientist explores the power and potential of our lives.* Penguin.

Maisel, E. (2018). Whole scarred families. In *Helping Survivors of Authoritarian Parents, Siblings, and Partners.* Routledge.

Morris, R. (2019). *Beyond blessed: God's perfect plan to overcome all financial stress.* FaithWords.

Pew Research Center. (2015). The rise in dual income households. www.pewresearch.org/ft_dual-income-households-1960-2012-2/

Rosenfeld, M. J., & Roesler, K. (2019). Cohabitation experience and cohabitation association with marital dissolution. *Journal of Marriage and Family, 81*(1), 42–58.

Tharp, T. (2019). *Keep it moving: Lessons for the rest of your life.* Simon & Schuster.

Thompson, W. E., & Gibbs, J. C. (2016). *Deviance and deviants: A sociological approach.* John Wiley & Sons.

White, J., Klein, D., & Martin, T. (2015). *Family theories: An introduction.* Sage.

Witt, J. (2009). *SOC.* McGraw-Hill.

Ziyanak, S., & Williams, J. (2014). Functionalist perspective on deviance. *Journal of Human Sciences, 11*(2). https://www.j-humansciences.com/ojs/index.php/IJHS/article/view/2791

Ch 15 Warfare

People love warfare. At least, they seemed to love war before most wars actually begin. Here are some examples of early wartime slogans (Archives West, 2007):

"Avenge Pearl Harbor! Join the Navy Now!"
"Do Your Duty. Join the Marines."
"Help Them Defend America on Land or Sea."
"Do Your Part. Join the WAAC."
"Americans Will Always Fight for Liberty."
"For Liberty's Sake, Enlist in the Navy."
"Even a Dog Enlists. Why Not You? (Army)"
"Step Into Your Place."

Poster slogans such as these were rather inspirational and stirred the patriotism and courage of many men and women in America and the U.K. Once the battles actually began, though, and loved ones died with former playgrounds being reduced to rubble, and a war that was supposed to be over in a year took 5 years or longer, then people saw it less favorably.

The reality of war is that it, like all the other social problems, is complicated and contextual, but has been part of human existence since time immemorial. War is supremely serious. War is violent. War destroys societies. War protects societies. War takes a huge toll on human lives. War saves innumerable people.

As one can see, warfare is a confusing topic to consider. Sometimes, the justification for war is blatant; sometimes, it is more indirect. Sometimes, a war is not justified; sometimes, not going to war is a crime against humanity. Warfare defies reductionism but demands definition and delineation, lest an act to solve a social problem becomes far worse that the social problem itself (Antony, 2013).

Generally, two main opinions persist regarding warfare: war is bad, or war is good. If one takes the former position, then war should be avoided at all costs. Sometimes, though, not going to war is the lesser evil of other bad choices. If one takes the latter position, that war is good, the initiation of it will hopefully end up righting a serious wrong or punishing the wicked. Yet, as President Teddy Roosevelt admitted, "Wars are, of course, as a rule to be avoided; but they are far better than certain kinds of peace" (Roosevelt, 1897).

Choices, judgments whether to go to war or not are not so simple to determine. Emperor Napoleon once lamented, "What my enemies call a general peace is my destruction. What I call peace is merely the disarmament of my enemies. Am I not more moderate than they?" (Herold, 1955). This is why it is important to have a general agreement between battling social groups on the ethics of warfare to help protect the goals and mission of any war.

These *war ethics* help leaders decide what is right or wrong, they help contribute to debates over public policy, they help direct government and individual action, they can lead to the creation of formal codes of war, they can regulate the drafting of soldiers and limit what they do as soldiers, and they can help determine appropriate punishment for war crimes (Sorabji & Rodin, 2006). War ethics start with three questions:

- ▶ Is it ever right to go to war?
- ▶ When is it appropriate to wage war?
- ▶ What is the moral way to conduct a war?

As mentioned earlier, not everyone thinks war is good. In fact, some people think war is so bad that they refuse to ever sanction or participate in one. This mindset is called *pacifism*, and it rests on the notion that war and violence are never justifiable. Succinctly, all conflicts need to be peacefully settled. Pacifists might base this upon religious convictions, an appreciation for the sanctity of life, or an awareness of the tragic loss of soldiers (who tend to generally be young men in their teens and 20s).

There are several different expressions of pacifism (Cady, 2010). *Absolute pacifists* believe there should be no war, even in self-defense. In times of warfare, these people are often labeled as *conscientious objectors*. *Conditional pacifists* believe that war is bad in principle, but in some circumstances, it is a necessity. *Selective pacifists* believe that some wars are OK while others are taboo (based on individual or arbitrary standards). *Active pacifists* will participate in some war activities (such as driving an ambulance or being a medic or doctor), but they refuse to fight.

Some people are advocates for the *doctrine of double effect*, which states that the act of war must be good in itself (or at least indifferent) and the direct effect of the war must be morally acceptable (Woodward, 2001). Wars should not be begun for petty personal gain, or as a means to selfish ends. The good effect of the war must be sufficient to compensate for the evil consequences of the warfare. Moreover, the agent of war seeks to minimize the evil effect, accepting the cost to himself.

One of the greatest warfare commentaries of the early Middle Ages was written by a bishop named *Saint Augustine*. He is credited for setting up most of the theological categories that are still used in today's Christian seminaries. Known by his contemporaries as "The Knowledgeable One," this great theologian came up with some warfare advice for the Roman rulers of his day (Schulzke, 2017).

For Augustine, a *just war* had to follow certain requirements. First, the war must be for a just cause. The war must be officially declared by a lawful authority. The intention behind the war must be goodness. All other reasonable ways of resolving the problem should have been tried first. There must be a reasonable chance of success. Finally, there must be proportionality in response to any military attacks. Ultimately, in a just war, only appropriate force should be used, innocent people and noncombatants need to be protected and unharmed, and internationally agreed-upon war regulations ought to be obeyed.

As Pope John Paul II (1982) wrote,

> Peace, as taught by Sacred Scripture and the experience of men itself, is more than just the absence of war. And the Christian is aware that on earth, a human society that is completely and always peaceful is unfortunately a utopia, and that the ideologies which present it as easily attainable only nourish vain hopes. The cause of peace will not go forward by denying the possibility and the obligation to defend it. (online)

Wartime conduct is a tricky affair. Just because a war is just in its cause does not automatically guarantee that it has been fought in a just manner (or vice versa). Thus, soldiers were/are taught *jus in bello* (Just Conduct in War Standards) through various methods. This answers difficult questions for them like, who can you fight in a war? How much force is ethical to use? What is a proportionate response to a military attack? Is the use of certain weapons always wrong? What about chemical, biological, or nuclear weapons, or the size of them? What is the role and authority of international conventions in wartime? What is an appropriate punishment for genocide, mass rape, or torture?

In modernity, the international communities came together (in times of peace) to create diplomatic bodies and agreements to settle such questions. One of the first ones was the *Hague Convention of 1907*, which discussed an attempt at disarmament, the creation of laws of war and war crimes, the banning of poisonous weapons, banning the killing or wounding treacherously, banning the killing of surrendering soldiers, banning the declaration of "no mercy" for defeated opponents, and banning using arms, projectiles, or material calculated to cause unnecessary suffering by the enemy (Donohue, 1994).

With many of those agreements in place, 40 years later, the *Genocide Convention of 1948* dealt with how each side would treat the wounded and the sick, the shipwrecked, prisoners of war, and civilians. It also addressed treaties: how they were to be established (by signature and ratification), who they were binding upon and on what terms, and it wrestled with customary law and its implications upon warfare (Smith, 2010).

Despite these meetings and measures, some nefarious war crimes still occurred. Specifically, the Japanese pushed the ethical limits of warfare with the *Bataan Death March* in 1942. During this military transfer, 76,000 American and Filipino POWs suffered brutal treatment as they were forced to march through the jungle with no food or water (Murphy, 2014).

Though some people try to deny its occurrence, Hitler's genocide of the Jews (also known as the *Holocaust*) in WWII was, to that date, one of the worst atrocities against humanity in the history of mankind. Also, although the final figures are impossible to know, in the German concentration camps, it can be assumed that up to 11 million people could have died— including the Jews, Poles, Gypsies, and other ". . . undesirables like the mentally ill, political dissidents, and homosexuals" (Friedman, 1990).

© Elzbieta Sekowska/Shutterstock.com

After Germany and Japan lost in WWII, the Nuremburg Trials were held in Switzerland, with multiple Nazi leaders being convicted and executed for *war crimes*. Although many tried to defend or rationalize their actions, saying that they were only "obeying orders," they were still held responsible for their monstrous warfare actions and punished.

Interestingly (and sadly), WWII also led to the creation of *Japanese Internment camps* in America after the bombing of Pearl Harbor in Hawaii. Roosevelt and his war panel decided it was best to take a precautionary action just in case Japanese spies had already made it to the continental United States and were about to aid the enemy with similar ambushes as in Hawaii. However, this really only amounted to innocent and loyal Japanese Americans being imprisoned for crimes that they never committed, and increased racism and prejudice against the Japanese on the West coast of America for years to follow.

Since WWII, most American governments have presumed that most democracies, even those far away, overseas, do not want to go to war against other democracies. This is called the *democratic peace theory*. This has led to the creation of various coalitions in warfare, with mutual oaths of defense and protection in warfare, and mutual support of similar goals and principles in times of peace (Goldsmith, 2007). Thus, since the 1960s, America, France, England, and Germany have not directly fought against each other in military combat. Support from this is not only at an institutional level; due to globalism, most citizens of the countries of the world do not want to go to war unless attacked, because of the terrible consequences that inevitably follow warfare.

DEALING WITH MATTERS OF THE DARK

The book of *Joshua* is a narrative-like tome in the Pentateuch. It describes the Israelite preparations for advancement into the *Promised Land*, details their military campaigns to take territory across the region from north to south, and explains the division of land between the Israelites once they had won their offensive. It provides readers with a clear sociological depiction of Middle Eastern life 4,000 years ago.

The book was written by Joshua, Moses's successor, who ruled Israel around 1400–1380 B.C.E. Described as the son of Nun, he emerged as an early military leader during the Exodus; it is possible that he might formerly have been an officer in the Egyptian army based upon his campaign strategies and battlefield tactics. Due to his noble character, sincere commitment to God, and his capable skills, Joshua was one of only two adults in the Exodus who made it to the Promised Land (the other being Caleb); the rest of that generation passed away in the desert. As Geisler points out, "Moses led Israel out of bondage, but it was Joshua who took them into blessing" (Geisler, 1977).

Joshua wrote the book after his conquest of Canaan and addressed it to his Israelite co-conquerors. It was written to affirm and validate the promise given to Abraham in Genesis 15:18–19:

> On that day the Lord made a covenant with Abram and said, "To your descendants, I give this land, from the Wadi of Egypt to the great river, the Euphrates—the land of the Kenites, Kenizzites, Kadmonites, Hittites, Perizzites, Rephaites, Amorites, *Canaanites*, Girgashites and Jebusites."

Some secularist scholars dispute both the Exodus and the Conquest, asserting,

> The conflict over the land in Joshua (and Judges) is a deep conflict within the population already in the land. That is, there was no invasion, or perhaps only at the most a 'revolutionary' cadre of those who brought news of Yahweh from the Exodus. (Birch et al., 1999)

The first part of Joshua could be considered an ancient form of a "pep talk" from their "coach," Joshua, to the Israelite conquest team. In Joshua 1:5-6, Joshua states,

> No one will be able to stand against you all the days of your life. As I was with Moses, so I will be with you; I will never leave you nor forsake you. Be strong and courageous, because you will lead these people to inherit the land I swore to their ancestors to give them.

Not only does Joshua recognize that the people need to be physically ready, but they also must be mentally strong too and have realistic expectations of what is to come in the upcoming battles.

Joshua also made sure to always bring along their "mascot" or, more appropriately, their "star first-string player"—the Ark of the Covenant—when-

ever they marched into battle. Additionally, they made sure that they knew their enemy before they met on the field, which is why Joshua sent over two men to scout out the lay of the land and the resources of their opponents. Though these men ended up needing some protection from Rahab, the prostitute of Jericho, they returned to camp with crucial news for the campaign. The next section of the book of Joshua, Chapters 6-12, focuses on their attacks and battles to conquer the land, but always with God at their back as the head coach of their head coach. Joshua 6:2-5 states as follows:

Then, the Lord said to Joshua,

> See, I have delivered Jericho into your hands, along with its king and its fighting men. March around the city once with all the armed men. Do this for six days. Have seven priests carry trumpets of rams' horns in front of the ark. On the seventh day, march around the city seven times, with the priests blowing the trumpets. When you hear them sound a long blast on the trumpets, have the whole army give a loud shout; then the wall of the city will collapse and the army will go up, everyone straight in.

In the scriptures, God even manipulates the rotation of the planets to assist Israel in victory over the five kings of the Amorites (Joshua 10:13). Secularist scholars and scientists will cry that stopping the rotation of the planets or the stars would destroy everything, and if this was a natural phenomenon, that would be true, but logically, if God can manipulate nature and physics, then he can protect life, too—if he is that powerful. Regardless, Joshua 10:14 states, "There has never been a day like it before or since, a day when the Lord listened to a human being. Surely the Lord was fighting for Israel!"

Regardless, Joshua and Israel ended up defeating the northern and southern kingdoms and the remainder of the chapters, Joshua 13–21, focus on the distribution of the lands among the tribes of Israel. Chapter 22 discusses a territorial dispute involving an altar, and Chapters 23–24 end with Joshua's final speeches and his death.

Joshua states the following:

> Now fear the Lord and serve him with all faithfulness. Throw away the gods your ancestors worshiped beyond the Euphrates River and in Egypt and serve the Lord. But if serving the Lord seems undesirable to you, then choose for yourselves this day whom you will serve, whether the gods your ancestors served beyond the Euphrates, or the gods of the Amorites, in whose land you are living. But as for me and my household, we will serve the Lord. (vv. 24:14–15)

After hundreds of years of traveling and planning and waiting to officially have a homeland, Israel, the nation, had finally settled and controlled the Promised Land. As Geisler (1977) concludes, "[Joshua] is a book of triumph for faithful obedience to God" (p. 96)—but a sociologist might see it a tad different depending upon his or her approach.

Certainly, Geisler's aforementioned appraisal shows a functionalist mentality, with the people of Israel's peace and prosperity being intertwined with their obedience, unity, and faith. In fact, the Bible is fairly consistent in this approach. When Israel falls (or leaps) into deviance, they suffer; when they conform to God's holy ways, they thrive. Moses even mentions this reality to the Israelites before they go into Canaan, addressing their potential and probable future dysfunction (Deuteronomy 31:20, New International Version).

For the conflict theorist, Joshua's (and Israel's) campaign into Canaan was based on a battle for resources (McKenzie & Haynes, 1999), which has some biblical support in its descriptions of the land and Israel's use for it. After all, the Prophet records in Ezekiel 20:6 (New International Version),

> On that day I swore to them that I would bring them out of the land of Egypt into a land that I had searched out for them, a land flowing with milk and honey, the most glorious of all lands.

Others think that Israel was simply acting as God's agent of righteousness (Walton, 2017) more than just sweeping in to take over the region's resources (ref).

Equally intriguing would be the symbolic interactionist's perspective of the region that Israel conquered in Canaan. The Bible refers to the land as "the Promised Land" (implying hope), a "land flowing with milk and honey" (rich, natural resources), a land of "Rest" (peace), and a gift to their "offspring" (future social security).

Of course, for the Canaanites, Israel and Yahweh symbolized something far more sinister and destructive, although current scholarship and archaeological finds suggest that the Canaanites were far from innocent. Rather, they behaved in wicked, detestable ways (Deuteronomy 9, 18; Leviticus 18) that God condemned, which brought harsh punishment upon them. Thus, Joshua's conquering Canaan is a tale rich with sociological relevance.

INSIGHTS FROM THE EXPERTS

Check out a video for more on this topic here:

https://www.khpcontent.com/

"Military Education Hurdles"

"On the battlefield, the military pledges to leave no soldier behind. As a nation, let it be our pledge that when they return home, we leave no veteran behind."
—Dan Lipinski

Military-Connected Students in Higher Education

The number of *military-connected students* in higher education in the United States has increased from 350,000 in 2000 to an estimated 3.7 million in 2020 (Dudley-Miller & Radel, 2020). A military-connected student is "any student who is active duty personnel, a reservist, veteran or member of the National Guard" (Molina & Morse, 2017, p. 2). Military-connected students are a diverse group demographically and socioeconomically. They also bring a diverse set of skills, experiences, and perspectives to the classroom; they possess maturity, significant life experience, and a cross-cultural awareness that many traditional-age college students lack (Kelley et al., 2013; Wilson Cox, 2019). Institutions of higher education (*IHEs*) have a tremendous opportunity to effectively support military-connected students' academic success by leveraging the value they bring to the academic community and gaining a deeper understanding of their needs (Andrewartha & Harvey, 2019; Williams-Klotz & Gansemer-Topf, 2017).

Educational Challenges

Military-connected students enter college with unique challenges and strengths. *Combat veteran students*, a subset of military-connected students who were deployed and served in a combat zone, face some of the most formidable challenges on their educational journey. The rate of disability and injury is significantly higher in the current generation of combat veterans (Williams-Klotz & Gansemer-Topf, 2017). Risk factors such as post-traumatic stress disorder (PTSD), traumatic brain injury (TBI), depression, or a combination of these and other physical injuries and mental health issues may contribute to academic difficulty (Ness et al., 2014; Wilson Cox, 2019).

Military-connected students often encounter transition difficulties as they embark on their educational journey (Aikins et al., 2015; DiRamio et al., 2008; Wisner et al., 2015). In making the transition from military to civilian life, they miss the camaraderie that they experienced serving beside fellow soldiers (DiRamio et al., 2008; Ness et al., 2014; Wisner et al., 2015). In the educational setting, the stark contrast between the regimented military culture and the fluid nature of university life intensifies the challenging transition (Vacchi, 2012).

Applying for and securing educational benefits is an institutional hurdle that contributes to the difficult transition from combat zone to college campus. Many are not aware of the full scope of benefits that are available, have difficulty accessing the benefits, and find that it takes too long for the benefits to be applied. Unfortunately, some colleges and universities lack adequate support services to meet the unique needs of military-connected students on campus (Griffin & Gilbert, 2012).

Ignorance and a negative attitude toward war from professors and other students inhibit the development of positive relationships in the academic environment. Without supportive relationships with professors and peers, military-connected students may become isolated, jeopardizing their educational dreams. One relational component that can make the transition very challenging is the perceived immaturity of younger traditional students (Parks & Walker, 2014). The disparity between military-connected students and traditional students is a leading source of frustration.

Non-disclosure is concerning for military-connected students suffering from any combat-related injuries as many believe there is a stigma attached to the disclosure of limitations (Church, 2009; Hammond, 2016). Unfortunately, this perpetuates the problem; military-connected students do not receive the support they need if they do not disclose their limitations. Furthermore, when student veterans choose not to secure proper accommodations, there is an increased risk of academic failure (Hammond, 2016).

Balancing the demands of school, work, and family responsibilities is a challenge that many military-connected students face throughout their educational journey. In contrast to traditional-age college students, military-connected students are generally older, have families, and live off-campus (Dudley-Miller & Radel, 2020; Wilson Cox, 2019). Yet, in spite of the challenges they face, many find a way to overcome and achieve their academic goals.

Strategies for Success

Fostering supportive relationships between faculty and students may be the single most important factor in students' academic achievement but even more so for military-connected students who face a unique set of challenges in higher education which include combat-related injuries, transition difficulties, securing benefits, feelings of isolation, and work and family responsibilities. Military-connected students prefer to request help from faculty with whom they feel a sense of connection and may feel more comfortable reaching out to them for mental health support rather than a complete stranger (Dudley-Miller & Radel, 2020). Hence, IHE's should require training for faculty and staff that focuses on understanding the unique needs and experiences of military-connected students in order to provide them with the support they deserve. Faculty and staff should be prepared to help military-connected students access the educational benefits that are available to them.

In addition to faculty and staff training, IHE's should develop and/or strengthen academic and support service offerings for military-connected students such as first-year transition programs for student veterans, peer-group interactions, and Student Veterans of America chapters (Andrewartha & Harvey, 2019). Social support from peers who have shared experiences or injuries can be especially helpful in protecting military-connected students' mental health and easing the transition to the college environment (Stalides, 2008; Whiteman et al., 2013).

Another strategy for success is to enlist family support. Spouse and family support are crucial to military-connected students' academic success. While family responsibilities can be a source of stress, the support that families provide for their military-connected student has been reported as the greatest influence on the student's persistence (Williams-Klotz & Gansemer-Topf, 2017). Furthermore, 8 out of 10 participants in my dissertation study cited spouse support as one of the most important factors that contributed to their degree attainment.

An awareness and appreciation of the strengths they possess is critical to the academic success of military-connected students. Military-connected students arrive on campus already having developed a specific set of skills and abilities that can be helpful in the classroom; they have a sense of global awareness and cultural intelligence, self-discipline, leadership and teamwork abilities, and time-management skills as a result of their military service (Ford & Vignare, 2015; Olsen et al., 2014). Furthermore, military-connected students are more academically focused compared to their civilian counterparts which they attribute to their military service (Durdella & Kim, 2012; Wheeler, 2012). The intense military training and life-changing combat experiences undoubtedly created soldiers who had to be mission-focused as a matter of life or death. This mission focus can serve military-connected students very well in the academic setting and help them to overcome potential difficulties (Ford & Vignare, 2015).

As the number of military-connected students enrolled in higher education continues to grow, institutes of higher education are confronted with the opportunity to establish and strengthen much-needed resources to support the academic achievement of military-connected students. Gaining a deeper understanding of the challenges that military-connected students face and the value they bring to the academic community is an important first step in effectively addressing the academic needs of a very special student population.

Dr. Ester Warren
Dean, General Studies
Liberty University

CASE STUDY #15

The President slumped in his chair and contemplated his options. Four nations had already mobilized their military forces and were moving troops toward the South Pacific, taking over international waters. The United States' Navy, now bisecting the region with a blockade, would not hold up against the whole of forces from Russia, China, Iran, and North Korea. Diplomatic negotiations have failed, and the United Nations had disbanded under the threat of violence. The media relentlessly promoted an anti-war message and incited their viewers toward civil disobedience. He would need more troops, but recruitment was at an all-time low. Economic advisers warned him that a revamped military industry would reap destruction on the economy. Out of time and options, he had already declared a national emergency, further compounding cultural strain.

Fortunately, an expert consultant to the President (you!) has been called into the oval office to answer the President's questions and provide possible solutions. The President will utilize the suggestions and implement a strategy, which either starts or prevents WWIII. The stakes are high, and billions of lives are on the line. The potential conflict might impact food supplies, water purity, access to infrastructure, and destabilize the economy for billions of people. What the President needs is an erudite, pragmatic, and coherent plan of action from his adviser (you!).

DISCUSSION QUESTIONS

1. Based on the readings, how would a sociologist diagnose this situation?

2. What specific sociological factors are involved?

3. What might be the fastest route(s) to peace and stability?

Check out the Chapter 15 video at this link:

https://www.khpcontent.com/

VOCABULARY

Absolute Pacifist

Active Pacifist

Bataan Death March

Canaanites

Combat Veteran Students

Conditional Pacifist

Conscientious Objector

Democratic Peace Theory

Doctrine of Double Effect

Genocide Convention of 1948

Hague Convention of 1907

Holocaust

IHE

Japanese Internment Camps

Joshua

Jus in Bello

Just War

Military-Connected Students

Pacifism

Poster Slogans

Promised Land

Saint Augustine

Selective Pacifist

War Crimes

War Ethics

References

Aikins, R. D., Golub, A., & Bennett, A. S. (2015). Readjustment of urban veterans: A mental health and substance use profile of Iraq and Afghanistan veterans in higher education. *Journal of American College Health, 63*(7), 482–494.

Andrewartha, L., & Harvey, A. (2019). Supporting military veterans in Australian higher education. *Journal of Veterans Studies, 4*(1), 94–109.

Antony, L. (2013). *Ethics and the laws of war: The moral justification of legal norms*. Routledge.

Archives West. (2007). Wartime posters collection, 1914–1953. http://archiveswest.orbiscascade. org/ark:/80444/xv35211

Birch, B., Brueggemann, W., Terence Fretheim, T., & Petersen, D. (1999). *A Theological introduction to the Old Testament*. Abingdon.

Cady, D. L. (2010). *From warism to pacifism: A moral continuum*. Temple University Press.

Church, T. E. (2009). Returning veterans on campus with war related injuries and the long road back home. *Journal of Postsecondary Education and Disability, 22*(1), 224–232.

DiRamio, D., Ackerman, R., & Mitchell, R. L. (2008). From combat to campus: Voices of student-veterans. *Journal of Student Affairs Research and Practice, 45*(1), 73–102.

Donohue, J. P. (1994). Treaties—Hague Convention—Private parties barred from asserting rights under Hague Convention of 1907. *Suffolk Transnational Law Review, 17*(1), 298.

Dudley-Miller, V., & Radel, J. (2020). Experiences and challenges of students with a military background at an academic medical center. *Journal of Veterans Studies, 6*(1), 112–121. https:// doi.org/10.21061/jvs.v6i1.114

Durdella, N., & Kim, Y. K. (2012). Understanding patterns of college outcomes among student veterans. *Journal of Studies in Education, 2*(2), 109–129. http://doi.org/10.5296/jse.v2i2.1469

Ford, K., & Vignare, K. (2015). The evolving military learner population: A review of the literature. *Online Learning, 19*(1), 1–2.

Friedman, T. L. (1990). *From Beirut to Jerusalem*. Farrar, Straus, Giroux.

Geisler, N. (1977). *A popular study of the Old Testament*. Baker.

Goldsmith, B. E. (2007). Defense effort and institutional theories of democratic peace and victory: Why try harder? *Security Studies, 16*(2), 189–222.

Griffin, K., & Gilbert, C. (2012). *Easing the transition from combat to classroom: Preserving America's investment in higher education for military veterans through institutional assessment*. Center for American Progress. https://www.americanprogress.org/issues/higher-education/report/2012/04/25/11473/easing-the-transition-from-combat-to-classroom/content/uploads/issues/2012/pdf/student_veterans.pdf

Hammond, S. P. (2016). Complex perceptions of identity: The experiences of student combat veterans in community college. *Community College Journal of Research and Practice, 40*(2), 146–159. http://doi.org/10.1080/10668926.2015.1017891

Herold, C. (1955). *The mind of Napoleon: A selection of his written and spoken words*. Columbia University Press.

Kelley, B. C., Smith, J. M., Fox, E. L., & Wheeler, H. (2013). *Preparing your campus for veterans' success: An integrated approach to facilitating the transition and persistence of our military students*. Stylus Publishing.

McKenzie, S. L., & Haynes, S. R. (Eds.). (1999). *To each its own meaning: An introduction to biblical criticisms and their applications*. Westminster John Knox Press.

Molina, D., & Morse, A. (2017). Differences between military-connected undergraduates: Implications for institutional research. *New Directions for Institutional Research, 171*, 59–70. https://doi.org/10.1002/ir.20194

Murphy, K. C. (2014). *Inside the Bataan Death March: Defeat, Travail and Memory*. McFarland & Company.

Ness, B. M., Rocke, M. R., Harrist, C. J., & Vroman, K. G. (2014). College and combat trauma: An insider's perspective of the post-secondary education experience shared by service members managing neurobehavioral symptoms. *Neuro Rehabilitation, 35*, 147–158.

Olsen, T., Badger, K., & McCuddy, M. D. (2014). Understanding the student veterans' college experience: An exploratory study. *U.S. Army Medical Department Journal, 2014*, 101–110.

Parks, R., & Walker, E. (2014). Understanding student veteran disabilities. *College and University, 90*(1), 53–60, 62–74.

Paul II, J. (1982). Message of his holiness Pope John Paul II for the celebration of the Day of Peace. *The Vatican*. http://www.vatican.va/content/john-paul-ii/en/messages/peace/documents/hf_jp-ii_mes_19811208_xv-world-day-for-peace.html

Roosevelt, T. (1897). *Life of Thomas Hart Benton*. Houghton, Mifflin and Company.

Schulzke, M. (2017). *Just War Theory and civilian casualties: Protecting the victims of war*. Cambridge University Press.

Smith, K. E. (2010). *Genocide and the Europeans*. Cambridge University Press.

Sorabji, R., & Rodin, D. (2006). *The ethics of war shared problems in different traditions*. Ashgate.

Stalides, D. (2008). *College veteran transition stories: The use of weblogs to explore military-to-college transition narratives* (Doctoral dissertation). Retrieved from Proquest (Publication No. 1456880).

Vacchi, D. T. (2012). Considering student veterans on the twenty-first-century college campus. *About Campus, 17*(2), 15–21.

Walton, J. (2017). *The lost world of the Israelite conquest: Covenant, retribution, and the fate of the Canaanites*. IVP.

Wheeler, H. A. (2012). Veterans' transitions to community college: A case study. *Community College Journal of Research and Practice, 36*, 775–779.

Whiteman, S. D., Barry, A. E., Mroczek, D. K., & Wadsworth, S. M. (2013). The development and implications of peer emotional support for student service members/veterans and civilian college students. *Journal of Counseling Psychology, 60*(2), 265–278. https://doi.org/10.1037/a003165

Williams-Klotz, D. N., & Gansemer-Topf, A. M. (2017). Military-connected student academic success at 4-year institutions: A multi-institution study. *Journal of College Student Development, 58*(7), 967–982.

Wilson Cox, A. (2019). Military students' strengths and challenges based on their military experiences: An integrative review. *Journal of Nursing Education, 58*(7), 392–400. https://doi.org/10.3928/01484834-20190614-03

Wisner, B. L., Krugh, M. E., Ausbrooks, A., Russell, A., Chavkin, N. F., & Selber, K. (2015). An exploratory study of the benefits of a mindfulness skills group for student veterans. *Social Work in Mental Health, 13*(2), 128–144.

Woodward, P. A. (2001). *The doctrine of double effect: Philosophers debate a controversial moral principle*. University of Notre Dame Press.

CONTRIBUTORS

CHAPTER ONE: "THEOLOGY OF SOCIAL PROBLEMS"

Dr. Rob Van Engen is currently residential and online faculty at Liberty University in Lynchburg, Virginia. Married to his wife, Tuesday, they have two married children. Van Engen was born and raised in Michigan and moved to Virginia to attend Liberty. He has served local churches in Virginia and Michigan in various capacities. Van Engen has a PhD in Organizational Leadership (Regent University), a MA in Ministry Leadership (Grand Rapids Theological Seminary of Cornerstone University), and a BS in Pastoral Leadership (Liberty University). He has created worldview and leadership courses for the university. He has presented at multiple conferences on higher education pedagogy, human resource development, faith and integration, teaching large classes and worldview.

CHAPTER TWO: "RESILIENCE IN TROUBLED TIMES"

Major General Bob Dees, U.S. Army, Retired, served in the Army for 31 years, followed by careers in business, ministry, higher education, politics, and humanitarian causes on behalf of our nation's veterans. He has authored six books on resilience, the latest being *Resilience God Style* with accompanying video series and training guide. Bob speaks in numerous venues, was featured as one of "30 Master Leaders in America" by noted author George Barna, and was awarded the Council for National Policy George Washington Military Leadership Award in 2018.

CHAPTER THREE: "AN ETHIC FOR CHRISTIAN DEVIANCE AND SOCIAL DISOBEDIENCE"

Rev. David R. Leonard is a chaplain and minister endorsed by the International Church of the Foursquare Gospel. He holds graduate degrees from Portland Seminary and Air University. He has earned six units of clinical pastoral education through Walter Reed Army Medical Center and San Antonio Military Health System. His other publications include "Peacemakers: Chaplains as Vital Links in the Peace Chain," in *JFQ*, 96; "Afterword," in *John Wesley's 52 standard sermons: An annotated summary*; "Christianity," in *Conflict in the Holy Land: An encyclopedic history from ancient times to the Arab-Israeli conflicts*; "Bahai," "Iraq," and "Syria" in *Conflict in the Modern Middle East: An encyclopedia of civil war, revolutions, and regime change*.

CHAPTER FOUR: "THE GREATEST THREAT TO CHILDREN AND YOUTH"

Dr. Janet Brown is Professor of Psychology with the School of Behavioral Sciences. She is a faculty advisor to Alpha Lambda Delta Honors Society and serves on several honors thesis committees. She is on the Board of Directors of the Safe Surfin' Foundation, a national non-profit organization dedicated to teaching parents, grandparents, educators, and young people on the dangers of the cyber world. She and her husband travel throughout the country in their efforts to promote awareness of this issue. Dr. Brown was a presenter at the National White Collar Crime Center Technology Conference in San Diego, California, in March of 2018. Her research interests include internet safety, cyberbullying, and social media behaviors.

CHAPTER FIVE: "PROBABLE EFFECTS OF CANNABIS UPON LIFE COURSE AND QUALITY"

Brooke Bragg was born in South Dakota and raised near Athens, Georgia. She earned a BA in Social Work from Liberty University, graduating Summa Cum Laude, a member of the Phi Alpha Honor Society, Dean's List, and with a minor in Psychology. Brooke has worked with the Foster Care system, several group homes, individuals with disabilities, facilitating groups, and in case management. Brooke lives in Joplin, Missouri.

CHAPTER SIX: "CRIMINOLOGY AND SOCIOLOGY"

Quinn Weinzapfel is a recent graduate from Liberty University and currently the resident graduate student assistant and research assistant to Dr. John S. Knox. He has a BS in Criminal Justice and is currently working on his Master's in Business Leadership at LU. At Liberty University, Quinn served as a community group leader for 2 years and has been a resident shepherd for 3 years, concurrently. Quinn is an amateur musician, avid exercise enthusiast, and an adoring fiancé to his future bride.

CHAPTER SEVEN: "WEALTH: GOOD OR EVIL"

Craig Brigman works as a financial adviser (but has also been an assistant professor of IT teaching technology), he was involved in telecommunication at AT&T, and he worked as a revenue agent for the IRS. Having served in the 82nd Airborne Division, Craig went on to multiple successful careers and is married to a wonderful woman. Together, they have four children. Craig has degrees in business, accounting, education, and currently spends his extra time mentoring and advising small businesses. Craig has helped launch more than 20 successful businesses and helped many to recover from financial distress and be successful.

CHAPTER EIGHT: "FAMILY DYSFUNCTION"

Dr. Margaret Gopaul is a clinical psychologist who specializes in neurodevelopment and neurocognitive disorders. She holds a Post-Doctorate in Clinical Psychopharmacology from Alliant University with training from Yale Child Study Center, Yale Parenting Center and Child Conduct Clinic, and Centra Autism and Developmental Center. She is certified by Weill Cornell Medicine–The Center for Autism and the Developing Brain to administer the Clinical Toddler Autism Diagnostic Observation Schedule (ADOS-2) and Modules 1–4 of the ADOS-2. She received training as a researcher at the Yale Neuroscience Lab while processing and analyzing data from a NIMH-funded study utilizing neuroimaging to assess associative memory deficits in patients with schizophrenia. She has published book chapters in the clinical application for ADHD in the *Principle-Based Stepped Care and Brief Psychotherapy for Integrated Care Settings* and Social Skills in the *Handbook of Intellectual Disabilities*. She serves as an Institute Review Board (IRB) member as well as a reviewer for the *International Journal of Online Graduate Education*.

CHAPTER NINE: "DIVINE SOCIAL DISTANCING"

John Knaus is a secondary education government and economics teacher in Lynchburg, Virginia. He has his MRE from Liberty Baptist Seminary and has spent most of his life as an entrepreneur in Central Virginia. In addition to teaching and working in business, he leads a high school drama program, in which he has directed 12 plays to date. John is intrigued by the many connections within sociology, economics, and government; and he is missioned to awakening reasoned pathways between these subjects.

CHAPTER TEN: "SOCIAL ISSUES IN MANSA ZAMBIA: PART TWO"

Jessica Maslen moved to Zambia in 2009. Her passion for people led her to become the Founder and Director of the Busalo School. She recently became involved building churches and is an ordained pastor in the Free Methodist Church. She shares her home with a dog, two cats, and several chickens.

CHAPTER ELEVEN: "PUFF. PUFF. PASS."

Skylar Collins is a senior at Liberty University and pursuing a degree in the biomedical sciences. He was chairman of the Florida Federation of Teenage Republicans, he has written a book on politics and activism, and he is currently researching and developing a new type of immunotherapy called, "The Yahweh Technique." Additionally, Skylar works as a medical and research consultant, providing advice to patients and groups in need of solutions and direction; he is launching a new health care system in Florida; and prototyping a new surgery platform to take tumors off the brain without a single incision on the body.

CHAPTER TWELVE: "GENDER DYSPHORIA"

Dr. Kenyon Knapp has a PhD in Counselor Education and Supervision from the University of Mississippi, a Master's in Community Counseling from Georgia State University, and a MA in Christian Psychological Studies from Richmont Graduate University. He has been a Counseling professor for over 20 years and is currently the Dean for the School of Behavioral Sciences at Liberty University. He is a Licensed Professional counselor in Georgia, has been previously licensed in two other states, and has over 20 years of experience in private practice counseling settings.

CHAPTER THIRTEEN: "THE PERVASIVE SUBTLE EFFECTS OF INTERNET/ SMARTPHONE/FACEBOOK ADDICTION"

Dr. Beth Sites was born and raised in the small town of Hershey, Pennsylvania. She earned her BA in Community Work at Simmons College in Boston, Massachusetts, and began working as a school social worker for Hershey schools for 1 year. Sometime later, she married and began a 20-year "maternity leave" program when she stayed home as a wife and a mother of four. Eventually, she worked as a school social worker in Perry County, Pennsylvania, earned a MA and a PhD in Professional Counseling from Liberty University, and has taught at LU in the Department of Psychology since 2002. One of her favorite classes to teach is Behavior Modification, which is the environment where she has worked with many students on internet and smartphone addictions.

CHAPTER FOURTEEN: "GROWING OLD"

Faith Jane Knox received her basic nurses training (ADN) at Clark College in Vancouver, Washington, in 1973, followed by a BA in Psychology from Oregon State University in 1980. She returned for her MN in Psychiatric/Mental Health Nursing at the Oregon Health Sciences University in 1983 during which time she was awarded the Sigma Theta Ian Nursing Award for outstanding research in the field of Psychiatric/Mental Health Nursing. She resides in Myrtle Beach, South Carolina, with her husband and dog, Maxwell.

CHAPTER FIFTEEN: "MILITARY EDUCATION HURDLES"

Dr. Ester Warren serves as the Dean of General Education for Liberty University in Lynchburg, Virginia, and teaches online doctoral courses for Liberty University's School of Education. For her doctoral dissertation, she examined the experiences of combat veterans' degree attainment in online higher education. Her research interests are educational leadership, educational resilience, and academic success. She lives in Virginia with her husband, Kenneth, and their two children, Bailey and Molly.

GENERAL INDEX

Felony, 69
Feminist Movement, 133
Firstfruits, 72
Folkways, 27
The Four Loves, 147
Four Main Principles of Social
    Stratification, 81
Fraud, 70
Functionalist Perspective, 5, 170

G

Gay Christianity, 145
Gay, 143
Gender Dysphoria, 149
Gender Empowerment, 136
Gender Identity Disorder, 149
Gender Stratification, 130
Gender Wage Gap, 131
Gender-Role Socialization, 129
Gender, 129
Genocide Convention of 1948, 186
Genocide, 119
Gigolos, 39
Glass Ceiling, 120
Global Community, 105
Global Inequality, 109
Global Slavery Index, 81
Globalization Movement, 105
Grace, 138
Groupthink, 107

H

Hague Convention of 1907, 185
Halfway Houses, 71
Handicaps, 155
Hate Crimes, 119
Have-Nots, 96
Having, 97
Health Care Business, 158
Health Service Institution, 158
Heart, 178
Heavy Drinkers, 54
Heroin, 53
Hierarchies of Power, 172
Holocaust, 186
Homosexuality, 143

Hook, 39
Hope and Trust, 172
Human Dignity, 146
Hyperactivity, 156

I

Ideal Man, 133
Ideal Woman, 133
IHE, 190
Illicit Drugs, 55
Impairment, 155
Imperialism, 105
Imperialism Era, 122
Incest, 172
Individual Mandate, 159
Innovation, 28
Institutional Discrimination, 119
Instrumental Leader, 106
Integrity Versus Despair, 176
Intergenerational Contact, 172
Internet Addiction Disorder, 162
Internet Gaming Disorder, 163
Internet, 107
Invisible Minority, 120
Involuntary Manslaughter, 70

J

Japanese Internment Camps, 186
Johns, 39
Joshua, 187
Judeo-Christian Values, 76
Jus in Bello, 185
Just War, 185

K

Kinship Systems, 169

L

Labelers, 28
Labeling Theory, 28
Laissez-Faire Leader, 107
Larceny, 70
Latent Function, 14
Law Code of Hammurabi, 75
Laws, 27